# A TEAM OF
# THEIR OWN

# A TEAM OF THEIR OWN

## How an International Sisterhood
## Made Olympic History

## SETH BERKMAN

HANOVER
SQUARE
PRESS

HANOVER
SQUARE
PRESS

ISBN-13: 978-1-335-00553-3

A Team of Their Own: How an International Sisterhood Made Olympic History

Copyright © 2019 by Seth Berkman

Library of Congress Cataloging-in-Publication Data has been applied for.

HanoverSqPress.com
BookClubbish.com

**Printed in U.S.A.**

To Emma and Monica. May you follow in the brave footsteps of Korea's first Olympic women's hockey team.

# A TEAM OF
# THEIR OWN

# TABLE OF CONTENTS

A Note on Style . . . . . . . . . . . . . . . . . . . . . . . . . . . . . . .11
Prologue . . . . . . . . . . . . . . . . . . . . . . . . . . . . . .13

**PART ONE** . . . . . . . . . . . . . . . . . . . . . . . . . . . . .17
Chapter One: Atlas Shrugs . . . . . . . . . . . . . . . . . . . . . .19
Chapter Two: Not Like Hannah . . . . . . . . . . . . . . .28
Chapter Three: Phishing for Talent . . . . . . . . . . . . . .39
Chapter Four: Seoul Sisters . . . . . . . . . . . . . . . . . .51
Chapter Five: The Junger . . . . . . . . . . . . . . . . . . . . .60
Chapter Six: The Hen Crows . . . . . . . . . . . . . . . . . .71
Chapter Seven: The Coach with the Blue Eyes . . . . . . . .84
Chapter Eight: Babos . . . . . . . . . . . . . . . . . . . . .100
Chapter Nine: The Boy Crying Wolf . . . . . . . . . . . . . 111
Chapter Ten: Boss-Ass Bitches . . . . . . . . . . . . . . .127
Chapter Eleven: Be Who You Are . . . . . . . . . . . . . 141
Chapter Twelve: Under Pressure . . . . . . . . . . . . . .156
Chapter Thirteen: Lost and Found . . . . . . . . . . . . . 167

**PART TWO** . . . . . . . . . . . . . . . . . . . . . . . . . . . . . . . . . . . . 183
Chapter Fourteen: The Slap Shot Heard
  Round the World . . . . . . . . . . . . . . . . . . . . . . . . . 185
Chapter Fifteen: Suffering or in Joy,
  to the Love of Country . . . . . . . . . . . . . . . . . . . . . 198
Chapter Sixteen: Family . . . . . . . . . . . . . . . . . . . . . . 212
Chapter Seventeen: Comrades . . . . . . . . . . . . . . . . . . 230
Chapter Eighteen: One Step at a Time . . . . . . . . . . . . 238
Chapter Nineteen: A Spotlight Stolen . . . . . . . . . . . . 251
Chapter Twenty: Unified No More . . . . . . . . . . . . . . 260
Chapter Twenty-One: Make Korea Proud . . . . . . . . . . 267
Chapter Twenty-Two: Becca . . . . . . . . . . . . . . . . . . . 281
Chapter Twenty-Three: The Miracle Off Ice . . . . . . . . 291
Chapter Twenty-Four: A Foggy Road . . . . . . . . . . . . . 304
Chapter Twenty-Five: Evolution . . . . . . . . . . . . . . . . 314
Chapter Twenty-Six: One Body . . . . . . . . . . . . . . . . . 324
Chapter Twenty-Seven: Nothing Else Matters . . . . . . . 335

Acknowledgments . . . . . . . . . . . . . . . . . . . . . . . . . . 351
Notes . . . . . . . . . . . . . . . . . . . . . . . . . . . . . . . . . 355
Index . . . . . . . . . . . . . . . . . . . . . . . . . . . . . . 367

# A NOTE ON STYLE

Following cultural convention, South Korean players are introduced in each chapter with their surname first (ex. Shin Sojung). Subsequent mentions use only their first name (Sojung) in an effort to help the reader differentiate between players with the same last name. (Almost 50 percent of Koreans have the surname Kim, Lee, Park or Choi.) The one exception to this format is Susie Jo, who uses the Western styling of her Korean name.

In chapters where multiple Korean figures have the same last name (Kim Jong-un, Kim Jong-il, Kim Yu-na), the full name is used on second reference.

Like Susie, some additional characters prefer their name used while living in North America, with their Korean name in the middle (ex. Mia SeungEun Lee). Also, when abbreviated, the Korea Ice Hockey Association is always referred to as "KIHA" not "the KIHA."

A majority of quotes from South Korean players were translated through Seoul-based interpreter Kathy Yun.

# PROLOGUE

Duluth, Minnesota, is a port city on Lake Superior, known for textiles and its claim to serving the first pie à la mode. Locals often hold birthday or graduation dinners on the sixteenth floor of the downtown Radisson Hotel. There, a revolving room restaurant offers panoramic views of the ship canal, where 1,000-foot-long "lakers" and smaller, 740-foot "salties" enter under the Aerial Lift Bridge, the city's iconic landmark that resembles a gigantic mechanical mouth made of steel and cable.

Duluth can rightly be summed up as blue-collar, even vanilla. It is also the place where I felt the closest to Korea I've ever been.

During a frigid weekend in January 2017, I was on assignment for the *New York Times*, to report on South Korea's women's national hockey team, who were in town training for their Olympic debut, which would come on their home soil a year later at the 2018 PyeongChang Games.

In preparation, South Korea had boosted their ranks by adding players like Marissa Brandt; like me, Marissa was adopted from South Korea and raised in America. Almost immediately I related to Marissa. I learned that, like me, she never really identified with her birth country while growing up in the United States. Marissa, born Park Yoon-jung, was one of six "imports" on the roster—North Americans with Korean heritage—a moniker coined by the South Koreans to describe the new players, mostly due to its relatively simple context in translation, and since it sounded better than saying "foreigners."

Imports like Marissa worked alongside a motley collective of players with varied life stories. They were inventors, convenience store workers and rambunctious high school kids. As I watched these young women, in their matching navy tracksuits adorned with South Korean flags, walk with their arms linked through Duluth's snow-covered streets, I began to feel a sensation replace the chill of the below-zero temperatures of the cruel Minnesota winter. Observing their camaraderie, a sudden swell of patriotism came out of hibernation.

South Korea earned an automatic berth in the 2018 Olympic women's hockey tournament because they were the host country. No one expected them to come near the medal stand or even win a game. They would enter PyeongChang as one of the biggest underdogs in Olympic history. But that weekend, I began to realize that this team of women from two continents were embarking on a journey of self-discovery as much as hockey glory.

I began to track their journey, following players such as twenty-nine-year-old forward Han Soo-jin, a concert pianist who had mesmerized audiences performing in South Korea's grandest halls. She quit that career to play hockey, a forbidden passion that she had to hide from her mother. Her objective wasn't to make the Olympics. When she joined the national team a decade earlier, that wasn't even in the realm of possibility. Hockey consumed Soojin in ways that piano could not, and like many of the girls on the roster, she saw herself as an outcast who found something redeeming about the game. Their helmets and face masks shielded them from the outside world, which scorned them for being different—as women, as Asians, as loners—and transported them into an alternative universe where they felt like mythical warriors. Under this armor, even in a country where gender roles can feel as cemented in the culture as eating kimchi, the impossible seemed attainable. This euphoria is what made so many of them willing to make hockey the center of their lives. Like so many of us, that feeling of belonging was all they ever wanted.

How South Korea's women's national hockey team was even able to operate as a cohesive unit was fascinating in itself. The players' ages ranged from the midteens to early thirties. There were rich girls and poor girls. Nerds and tomboys and divas. But through a pure love of hockey and each other, they built bonds that would last far beyond the Olympics.

Before being invited to try out for the national team in 2015, Marissa never really felt she had the right to claim Korean heritage, nor did she necessarily want to. But her teammates provided a window into what her life could have been like in South Korea. They taught her about Korea's rich culture, and in return, she gave them insight about how relationships formed in America and opened them up to discuss their most hidden feelings, emotions that were taboo by Korean standards.

In each of the imports I saw traces of my own personality. The most indelible player I met that weekend was Randi Griffin, who had just joined the team full-time after almost a year of wavering. On the team's first afternoon in Duluth, they attended an exhibition hockey game at AMSOIL Arena, home of the five-time National Collegiate Athletic Association (NCAA) champion Minnesota-Duluth Bulldogs. During a playing of "The Star-Spangled Banner," Randi, a North Carolina native born to a white father and Korean mother, stood and put her hand to her heart, sliding her fingers barely over the word *Korea* emblazoned on the left chest of her team apparel. Later, Randi shared hours of introspective conversation on how she never felt comfortable claiming either nation. She described herself as a banana, a term I was quite familiar with, meaning "yellow on the outside, white on the inside," and talked to me about how this sense of a split identity affected her feelings living in both countries.

Randi spoke gently and with passion. You could see her mind constantly processing and often doubting situations, but hardly ever thinking about herself. That night as she ate with her Korean colleagues at a cantina, explaining to them Tex-Mex dishes they had trouble pronouncing in English, it became clear that Randi was one of them. Watching this connection, I began to think maybe, just maybe, South Korea could pull off a miracle at the Olympics.

South Korea's women's national hockey team.

Almost exactly one year later, I followed the team back to Duluth for their final pre-Olympic training camp. With one month to go before the opening ceremony, the team was stronger than ever, thanks to a full year of integrating the imports into their systems. They were confident that they were in prime position to pull off an upset and shock the world in PyeongChang.

And then Kim Jong-un stepped in and shocked the world in a way nobody could have imagined.

# PART ONE

# CHAPTER ONE
## Atlas Shrugs

The concourse inside the Kwandong Hockey Center resembled a crowded Seoul subway station during rush hour. The evening's game had been over for almost ninety minutes, but patrons were still milling about, buzzing from the impromptu postgame festivities. The highlight came when South Korean President Moon Jae-in took photos with Kim Yo-jong, the sister of North Korean leader Kim Jong-un. Together, they conjured up thoughts of peace and unity to the six thousand in attendance and millions watching around the world.

Having just met these two luminaries, goalkeeper Shin Sojung did not look starstruck, but dazed. She walked against the flowing arena traffic like a salmon swimming upstream, her sullen eyes hidden by the brim of a gray baseball cap. Because none of the fans really recognized Sojung, she was able to home in on the person she was seeking among the bustle, thrust her head onto her mother's left shoulder and begin to cry.

Sojung had just allowed all eight goals in Korea's Olympic debut in women's hockey. The game had drawn global inter-

est and created one of the most surreal atmospheres in sports
history thanks to its political undertones and unprecedented
intermingling of North and South Koreans in the crowd and
on the ice. But all Sojung could think about was the 8–0 loss
to Switzerland, which she felt responsible for. Throughout her
life, Sojung was an Atlas-like figure on South Korea's women's
hockey team, carrying the program's destiny on her shoulders.

A blowout was not how Sojung envisioned the script playing
out when, eighteen years before, at the precocious age of nine,
she began skating with South Korea's national hockey team,
dreaming of one day representing her country in the Olympics. Sojung may have been the only child in South Korea to
concoct such an ambition at the time. She was the rarest of
species in her homeland—a young, naturally talented female
hockey player.

*Shin So-jung began playing hockey at age seven and within two years was training with
the national team.*

Sojung had only begun training two years earlier, when she
was seven. In Seoul's plentiful street markets, one can find almost anything from fishing tackle to parts for knockoff watches.
However, hockey equipment, particularly for children, was as
rare in the city as red diamonds. During her first practices, So-

jung's head bobbled around loosely inside her oversized adult helmet and the blade of her stick was bigger than her legs, but the quiet, only child of Seol Kyoungrang and Shin Kwangsik was never happier than when inside a rink, stopping shots coming from men more than twice her size. To this day, written on Sojung's bedroom wall is the phrase "Life is simple. Eat sleep play hockey."

Sojung had barely turned fourteen when she made her debut for South Korea in 2004. She was so small that it seemed to be a competitive disadvantage to have her stand in goal, so she spent a majority of her time at forward. Some of her teammates were more than twice her age, but did not have a speck of Sojung's talent.

When South Korea formed its first women's national hockey team for the 1999 Asian Winter Games, the only requirement was that a candidate be female. They were mostly former figure skaters or speed skaters who had never picked up a stick. The goalie was a former field hockey player, and even included among their ranks was a defector from North Korea who had been a star for her former country's women's national team.[1] South Korea's first women's hockey teams were groups of misfits, the Bad News Bears on ice. But Sojung always wanted them to be known as more.

Unlike the wunderkind South Korean singers and dancers who are fawned over and bestowed with honorary titles like "Nation's Little Sister" for displaying talent at an early age, Sojung toiled in anonymity. Throughout her teenage years her contemporaries were ogling K-pop magazine covers, dreaming of which stars they would marry, while Sojung, who was moved back to goalie for the 2007 Asian Winter Games, received pain-relieving injections in her back after every appearance in net for South Korea. The pucks clashing against her still-developing bones left bruises, but did not sting as much as the feeling after regularly losing games by twenty or more goals. The most lopsided loss in the National Hockey League (NHL)'s 101-year history was when the Detroit Red Wings bested the New York Rangers 15–0 in 1944. In one of Sojung's first games against rival Japan, her team lost 29–0, and Sojung faced over one hundred shots on goal. The South Korean national team was treated like a punching bag by opponents, even in their scrimmages against elementary and middle school boys' teams (since there were no other girls' or women's teams to play). Sojung's family and friends often wondered what drew her to an activity that reaped no tangible reward. At times, Sojung wondered, too.

Sojung's mother originally tried sending her to ballet lessons, but she refused. Wearing leotards could never provide Sojung the feeling she had when putting on a goalie's mask. In her equipment, Sojung felt like a Transformer—a superhero on skates. "I was a tomboy," Sojung said. "My mom wanted me to be more feminine, girly. Because I was an only child, she had her own wishes for her only daughter. She eventually said you can do whatever you want. However, she still said that I should only play hockey as a hobby. She also said if you do any sport professionally it should be golf, because with hockey you can't go to university or make a lot of money."

Sojung's mother was correct. In 1998, twenty-year-old South Korean golfer Se Ri Pak took the LPGA Tour by storm, winning two major titles, including becoming the youngest-ever champion of the US Women's Open. Pak inspired a generation of South Korean girls to hit the links, where they'd amass hundreds of millions in dollars over the next two decades. Meanwhile, there were no girls' or women's hockey teams in South Korea at the high school, college or professional level. Choosing to dedicate one's life to women's hockey in South Korea was a career choice with almost no future. For her entire life, Sojung would battle for acceptance in a culture and nation that treated female athletes in unpopular sports like pariahs.

While Seol may have preferred her only daughter to gravitate toward less rugged activities like the ones that the other neighborhood girls were fond of, there was a part of her that admired Sojung's independence. When Seol was a child, she said girls envied boys who played hockey, an activity that seemed so cool and yet so inaccessible for her. Although she rarely attended games out of a fear that she would see Sojung get hurt, Seol knew that every time her daughter left for practice she was doing something that she herself never could.

Sojung showed so much promise at an early age that she was allowed to practice with Anyang Halla, a men's hockey team in the professional Asia League. But when the time came to report for her duties with the women's national team, the change was like going from performing on Broadway to a community summer stock production. Many women's players received hand-me-down equipment from Anyang Halla players, but those sticks were often cracked and the helmet visors were scratched. This regularly led to Sojung's teammates having to buy their own equipment, the quality of which depended on what they could afford. With hardly any of them holding full-time jobs, that meant substandard products. Quality hockey skates cost about $1,000 and many players were forced to wear dated brands from decades before that damaged their feet.

The entire stipend for a women's national team player was as little as $13 per day, with players making under $200 a month when they trained at their maximum schedule before international competitions. Practices often seemed to come and go on a whim and the team never knew from year to year if they'd travel abroad to compete in World Championship tournaments. Since they were not always allowed to access the government-funded training facilities offered to other South Korean national teams, the women's hockey squad's off-ice workouts usually consisted of running up and down hills, which was torturous during the summer when Seoul is either suffocated by hot and humid temperatures or flooded by monsoons. When the women's team was allowed to practice at the national training center in Seoul, they were banned from eating in the cafeteria among the other national teams. As a result, Sojung and others would order takeout meals of ramen or Chinese black bean noodles that they'd hurriedly slurp down in the hallway—that is, if the food hadn't congealed into cold clumps by the time it arrived.

"The rink was bad, the gear was passed down," said Han Do-hee, who joined the national team in 2005, when she was eleven, and grew up in the Suyu neighborhood of northeast Seoul with Sojung. "Overall the environment was maybe fifty times worse than it is now."

These poor conditions clearly left Sojung at a disadvantage. Other circumstances further hurt her budding career. Although most South Koreans had no idea that women in their country even played hockey, when she was still only in her early teens, Sojung's name had slowly been spread around the worldwide women's hockey community.

The annual World Championships are broken down into several divisions based on ability, with tournament winners able to earn a promotion to the next level up each year. Although few fans attended the lowest level World Championships—which South Korea played in regularly—the officials from the International Ice Hockey Federation (IIHF) and opposing coaches there took notice of Sojung's talent for deflecting pucks and making impulsive glove saves.

Sojung's name had reached the brick facades and manicured lawns of Phillips Academy Andover in Massachusetts. Sojung learned that Phillips's girls' hockey team was interested in cultivating her game at the prep school associated with F. Scott Fitzgerald characters and New England privilege, but the $55,000 in tuition was a nonstarter. Another institution, the Edge School near Calgary, Alberta, Canada, flew Sojung in for a tryout and offered her a partial scholarship, but the remaining costs associated with attending the school were still too much for Sojung and her parents.

The offers did not cease, though, and instead began arriving from even more prestigious institutions. Brown and Harvard approached Sojung about playing college hockey in the United States, but the cost and her lack of confidence in taking the exam for international students to attend American universities—Test of English as a Foreign Language (TOEFL)—once again left Sojung stuck. "I was afraid of the money," Sojung said. "I felt helpless. I really wanted to go, but at the time my family's financial situation had gotten bad—comparatively bad to before all these opportunities started coming to me. I had to give it up because the living expenses were so high. My family couldn't afford it. When I was nineteen years old, my father passed away, and since then my mom did everything on her own to provide money. I couldn't leave her when I had opportunities to go abroad. It was more than money; it was because I couldn't be there for her."

Sojung could have taken more time to study for the TOEFL after her father died, but she received a scholarship to attend Sookmyung Women's University in Seoul, which would allow her the possibility of finding a part-time job and contributing at home. With her mother working in real estate and struggling to keep the family afloat, Sojung knew that staying in South Korea was the proper choice, even at the cost of her hockey career. South Korea's losses in international games had gradually fallen from twenty-goal differences to the teens, but like upgrading from Fs to D-minuses, this improvement was hardly encouraging.

In February 2011, South Korea finished in last place at the Asian Winter Games, an international event that rivals the Olympics in popularity on the continent. All-time, South Korea was 0–15 at the tournament, outscored by a total of 242–4 in those contests. They were the laughingstock of women's hockey in Asia. Even North Korea, whose gross domestic product was more

than seventy-five times less than South Korea's, had enough resources to dominate their neighbors on the ice, evident when
they cruised past the South, 6–1, in the 2011 Asian Games.

After that loss, Sojung had already given almost a decade of
her life to the national team. When strangers asked her what she
did for a living, she would often pause, her face looking deep
in thought but actually hiding an acute pain. She was too embarrassed to say she was a hockey player. A majority of citizens
in South Korea wouldn't even know of the sport if Sojung answered truthfully. She was the most important piece of a team
that never was expected to win and had no resources to get better. Hockey was Sojung's passion, but it also agonized her. She
was turning twenty-one in a month. She still lived with her
mother—now out of Suyu and in a modest apartment on the
outskirts of Seoul, small enough that she had to store her goalie
pads outside her front door.

As she turned twenty-one, Sojung seriously began thinking
about retirement. First she had ankle surgery, a procedure that
she had put off for two years. Her body was tired and glory
seemed impossible. Sojung even began training in boardercross,
the snowboarding course race, with aspirations of becoming an
Olympian in time for 2014, but it did not provide the same rush
as hockey. However, that summer, it began to look as if Sojung
would not need to switch sports to fulfill her childhood dream.

On July 6, 2011, after narrowly missing out on hosting the
2010 and 2014 Winter Olympics, South Korea was awarded the
2018 Games, which were to be held in the ski resort county of
PyeongChang, about one hundred miles east from Seoul. Tradition has dictated in Olympic team sports that all host countries earn automatic spots to compete. But with South Korea's
women's hockey program in such dire condition, the International Olympic Committee (IOC) and IIHF were cautious in
just handing over the reward. The IOC and IIHF needed proof
South Korea would not embarrass itself or their own reputa-

tions. Sojung's ability in saving goals would be key. But Sojung was not sure if she could sacrifice another seven years of adulthood preparing to fulfill a childhood fantasy.

COURTESY OF SIMON CROSSE

*Sojung, seen here at the 2011 Asian Winter Games, thought about retiring when South Korea remained all-time winless in the tournament.*

# CHAPTER TWO
# Not Like Hannah

While Shin So-jung practiced in obscurity, Marissa Brandt grew up in Minnesota, the self-proclaimed "State of Hockey." Ice time, equipment and quality competition were never in short supply. Yet in spite of this environment, Brandt too felt out of place, never quite comfortable with her circumstances.

Brandt was born on December 18, 1992, in South Korea, as Park Yoon-jung. Her birth mother was around twenty-four years old, single, with an oval face and olive-colored skin. The woman went into labor prematurely, calmly entered the hospital to deliver Yoonjung, and then left before officials could formally interview her. That is about all that is known of Marissa's biological family.

More than 6,200 miles away, Robin Brandt, a retail business owner, and Greg Brandt, who owned a fire restoration business, were looking to adopt a child after unsuccessfully being able to conceive on their own. Greg's sister, Barb, had adopted a son and recommended South Korea's process as streamlined and safe. In January 1993, the Brandts received an adoption referral—acceptance to become parents of a Korean child—and soon were given Yoonjung's picture and a report on her background. Then, just as the Brandts began finalizing paperwork for Yoonjung, Robin learned she was pregnant. The Brandts should have notified the Children's Home Society, an organization they worked with that found families for orphaned and abandoned children. But the thought of losing Yoonjung, who already felt like their own daughter, seemed unfathomable.

"What they do is they put your adoption on hold," Greg said, "and if you successfully have a baby then it's—"

"We wouldn't have had Marissa then," Robin said.

"It's like we already had her," Greg added. "We knew that was our baby."

Robin understood that because of her age, the pregnancy carried high risks. Her doctor suggested it might be best not to tell the Children's Home Society of her condition. "She said it's a bit of a stretch to think that this is going to work," Greg said of getting two daughters. "Both did."

In May 1993, Park Yoon-jung, now Marissa Brandt, arrived in Minnesota, greeted at the airport by thirty friends and family with balloons, presents and a cake—one of more than 2,000 South Korean children adopted around the world that year. From 1953 to 2008, almost 110,000 South Korean children were adopted by American families alone, with the biggest boom occurring during the 1980s.[1]

"She came off the plane and was sound asleep and just beautiful," Robin said. Six months later, the Brandts celebrated again when their second daughter, Hannah, was born.

Despite the presence in many adoptive households of Cabbage Patch kids—the "adopted" plush baby toys popular in the 1980s and 1990s—and copies of the 1960 children's book *Why Was I Adopted?* by Carole Livingston, parents cannot prepare for every challenge in raising adopted children. And while the Brandts had Greg's sister as a reference for advice, much had to be learned through trial and error. After Marissa came off the plane, the Brandts gently placed her in their car seat and she began to scream. The outbursts seemingly did not stop for months. She cried so much that Robin and Greg nicknamed Marissa "Fussy Mussy." Once she became a toddler, the Brandts soon learned that Marissa, who was left behind by her birth mother in South Korea, did not seem comfortable outside of the care of loved ones. There was a local Korean school program that Robin enrolled Marissa in on the weekends that was supposed to be as much a respite for parents as it was to immerse children in a Korean environment. However, whenever Robin tried to exit, Fussy Mussy would go into fits. "Because Marissa was a cling-on, I could never leave," Robin said, laughing. "Most of the parents were able to drop their kids off, it was kind of a break for them. Oh no. I was there so much that people thought I worked there."

COURTESY OF THE BRANDT FAMILY

*Marissa and Hannah Brandt.*

As Marissa grew older, Robin and Greg enrolled her and Hannah in Korean culture camps during the summer, but she never took to them like her parents had hoped. It was Hannah, with her bowl-shaped haircut and porcelain skin, who loved the tae kwon do classes and kimchi cooking lessons, while Marissa felt repelled by these reminders of her heritage. This role reversal perplexed the Brandts. "I totally didn't understand she wasn't that interested in her Korean roots," said Robin, who has short, stylish blond hair and a recognizable Minnesota accent. "Now I kind of get it. She just really wanted to be part of the family and look like Greg and she wanted Hannah to look like me so they each had one to look like, and just be sisters and not be adopted."

Marissa eventually found a place of comfort at ice rinks, which define Minnesota's landscape the same way palm trees define Southern California. In Minnesota, being on the ice equates to normalcy. Marissa started out as a figure skater—even today, former hockey coaches marvel at her stride, saying it was among the most beautiful motions they've seen on the ice. But like the way Marissa clashed with Korean lessons, Hannah did not take to white skates and decorative skirts (her father occasionally points out how sometimes after scoring a goal, Hannah still lands on her butt). Instead, Hannah gravitated toward hockey, and because of Marissa's natural inclination to be a mother hen to her little sister, she left behind the grace of jumps and twirls for "bag skating" drills—going up and down the ice in a straight line until your legs feel as if they are going to give out.

As Marissa became deeply enmeshed in Minnesota's hockey culture, she did not ever really worry about identifying as Korean and had no reason to. But society was always ready to insert occasional reminders that her tanner complexion and distinct eyes made her an outsider despite her American name and citizenship.

The Brandt sisters were hockey prodigies, good enough to earn spots on prestigious travel teams early in their youth. One Under-12 team they played for based out of the Twin Cities had a fierce rivalry with the girls from Edina, Minnesota. Even for kids in elementary school, the two sides could play brutally hostile hockey. After one particularly prickly game, the two teams lined up for the customary postgame handshakes. Usually, after a hard loss, children will stick their hand out and be silent, not even looking at their opponents while they sulk as if they had just lost the Stanley Cup Final. One Edina player had a different tactic to cope with her feelings. She approached Marissa and snapped, "Go back to China."

Marissa's heart dropped. Her eyes instinctively welled up and her nerves hardened with anger. The verbal jab was a stinging one-two combination of racial animosity—the implication that Marissa did not belong—but also the ignorant assumption that all Asians look alike, lumping them together as an amalgam race who study the way of the samurai, wear silk qipao dresses and eat kimchi all the same. Such stereotyping has followed Asians throughout their history in the United States, and is not uncommon appearing in sporting environments. In 2016, when the Brooklyn Nets of the National Basketball Association signed Taiwanese American guard Jeremy Lin, Andrew Keh, a Korean American reporter for the *New York Times*—who had been mockingly called "Jeremy Lin" in recreational and professional environments—wrote about the effect of such statements:

"It's common as an Asian American to feel like an unwilling participant in society's lazy word association game: See someone Asian, say something Asian."[2]

"There's not many Asians here that play hockey, so of course I stick out like a sore thumb," said Marissa. "I did take those things personally because I just wanted to blend in."

The slurs were not an every game occurrence, but they occasionally popped up throughout Marissa's high school career. By then, though, opponents began choosing another tactic to make Marissa feel unwelcome on the ice. As the Brandt sisters flourished at Hill-Murray School just outside of St. Paul, Hannah evolved into a generational talent and would be named "Ms. Hockey" her senior year as the state's top player. Marissa remained a crucial leader for her prep team, but garnered less attention than her sister, and sometimes a bitter opponent would not hold back in letting her know that. What made matters more hurtful was that behind the scenes, college recruiters began hounding the Brandt household with calls and letters to entice Hannah. Some would feign interest in Marissa. "I feel like a lot of colleges, they reached out to me because they knew me and my sister wanted to go to the same college, so if they got me, they'd get her," Marissa said. "There was a college that was even like, 'Oh, we can't give you a scholarship, but we can give your sister a full ride.'"

COURTESY OF THE BRANDT FAMILY

*Marissa and Hannah were naturals on the ice and inseparable as children.*

"It was awful," Robin said. "I felt like they used Marissa to get to Hannah. It really hurt Marissa."

Like being called Chinese, the tactics were doubly cruel because just a few years earlier, an argument could be made that Marissa was the better player and the one destined for universities like Minnesota or Wisconsin, schools that are stepping-stones for the US Olympic team. Within the Minnesota hockey community, parents and coaches would debate over which Brandt sister would become the better player, the way barbershop patrons argue for hours if LeBron James has surpassed the talents of Michael Jordan. Marissa often had the larger constituency because of her textbook fundamentals. "People would say, 'I think Marissa's going to be the one that really goes far, because she's a better skater,'" Robin said. "Hannah was so terrible at skating, always on the ground."

When she started high school, Marissa got on the radar of USA Hockey, the sport's national governing body that selects players for its girls' and women's national teams, including the Olympic team. Bill Schafhauser, who had just taken over as coach at Hill-Murray, naturally was thrilled to have her.

"I started to hear rumors this Brandt family was going to come to Hill-Murray and I thought that's great because we need more players," Schafhauser said. "A colleague said, 'No, you don't understand. This changes everything.'"

In 2008, when she was fifteen, Marissa was invited to a USA Hockey select camp for top prospects at St. Cloud State University, where her group was coached by Mike Carroll from Gustavus Adolphus College. Carroll did not think Marissa would ever consider his school at the time, which is an NCAA Division III program in St. Peter, Minnesota, located about seventy-five minutes southwest of Minneapolis. At such a prestigious camp, most attendees have their dreams set on big Division I programs. "When it came to Minnesota state high school hockey, the Brandt sisters were a big deal," said Courtney Boucher, who played in Hastings, thirty minutes outside of Minneapolis, and later in college with Marissa. "They were kind of known to be above and beyond."

Some Division I schools had already shown interest in Marissa, but during her sophomore year of high school, she suffered a serious concussion off a hard body check. The head injury not only held her back from playing hockey for months, but prevented her from engaging in everyday tasks like studying or even watching television. The game's rules prevent body checking and fighting, but women's hockey is far from a game without contact. Concussions have become a prominent issue in the rapidly growing sport, where players are evolving stronger and faster than ever, creating more forceful collisions. A 2014 study among NCAA student-athletes found that women's hockey had the highest rate of self-reported concussions, coming in at 20.9 percent.[3] Some researchers speculate that the physiology of female neck muscles might be a contributing factor, but there is no conclusive reason as to why women's hockey players are experiencing concussions at an alarming rate.

When Marissa returned to the ice, she continued to contribute to her team, but was slowed by further concussions. "It was just unnerving to even watch her play," Greg said. "It wasn't even enjoyable."

"When that happened, that just really took the wind out of her, out of her confidence," Robin added. "Even today, I still say sometimes she doesn't have that confidence that she had when she was young."

While Marissa struggled to regain her top-level form, Hannah's stock continued to rise with a wondrous combination of a precise slap shot, immaculate vision and instinct, and brute power. She won a gold medal at the 2011 Under-18 World Championships with Team USA and became a stalwart on junior national teams. By her senior year in 2012, Hannah accepted a scholarship to play college hockey at the University of Minnesota, the three-time national champions.

Marissa considered attending Princeton and Union College in upstate New York, but was not fond of the idea of moving out east. One day, she admitted to her father that she had come to terms with playing Division III hockey. "She said, 'Dad, I'm not like Hannah,'" Greg recalled.

"Their first few years it looked like they very well could go to a powerful Division I program together," said Schafhauser. "Not that Marissa dropped off, but Hannah separated herself from everybody. It did kind of become clear and I think Marissa knew that. She's such a quiet, humble kid, I never saw it as a problem, but you felt bad sometimes. Like it'd be nice if she got a little more attention here or there."

Marissa attended Gustavus Adolphus, where there was less of a spotlight and fewer comparisons to Hannah, who was excelling in her senior year at Hill-Murray, garnering national recognition and being built up as a future pillar of USA Hockey and a possible Olympian with the 2014 Games approaching.

Meanwhile, during her first year on campus, Carroll saw Marissa playing tentatively on the ice and not tapping into the potential that caught his eye in St. Cloud when she was fifteen.

"I think he saw her lack of confidence and then he stopped playing her," Robin said. "Around Christmastime they had a game at the state fair and a bunch of people came and he barely played Marissa and she was crying after. All her relatives had gone. She's like, I don't want to go back. It was bad. She was very upset. I was kind of mad at Coach Carroll at the time, thinking, why are you doing this? There was a notebook they journaled each game. I started reading what he was writing and he knew exactly what was going on. He was just trying to get the most out of her and stimulate her. Although it was extremely painful for her to go through it, he really was trying to do the best for her. He saw the same kind of flaws we sometimes saw in her. Sometimes she didn't dig into that potential for every game."

Eventually, Carroll switched Marissa to defense, in part because he worried that her concussion history was affecting how aggressive she was on the ice. "Something I'm sure she was thinking, the next hit she gets she might not be able to play hockey again," Carroll said. "I thought she'd be better off playing defense for the reason most of the game is in front of you. You see the whole ice. On top of that she was a beautiful skater. Very good lateral movement, very good ability to skate forward and transition into backward."

The "Gusties," as the Gustavus Adolphus sports teams were

called, were perennial Division III national championship con-
tenders during Marissa's years, a notable achievement, but hard
to compare with the accolades Hannah was compiling at Minnesota. During her college career, Hannah won three Division
I national titles and she remains the program's all-time leading
scorer. "Players would come up and say, 'I know your sister,'
and 'Tell your sister I said hi,'" said Courtney Boucher, Marissa's
friend and college teammate. "It got old to an extent. Like it's
cool that you're a fan but I'm trying to do my own work here.
But Muss never threw a pity party. It never felt like woe is me."

"I sort of at the time not felt sorry for her, but felt for her because she was doing her own thing and doing well in her own
element," Carroll said of Marissa. "It never seemed to bother
her. She was very proud of her sister, but it had to be a hard time
for her in that regard."

The Brandts' household is covered in photos of Marissa and
Hannah together, in ballerina costumes or traditional Korean
gowns or patriotic-themed outfits. They seem to always be
smiling—Marissa with a full, pristine set of pearly whites, and
Hannah sometimes already resembling a hockey player with
a few teeth missing. Ask anyone who has known the Brandt
sisters—friends, teammates, coaches—and each will say with
full sincerity that Marissa never once felt like she was in Hannah's shadow. Robin and Greg would either split duty if their
daughters had a game on the same day, or would make sure to
at least catch one period of each. Courtney Boucher remembered Marissa would attend Hannah's games whenever she had
free time, and Hannah would do the same.

As Marissa's own hockey career seemingly came to a close,
she made peace with letting the sport go and began filling up
other aspects of her life, taking steps toward defining herself
individually. Marissa was always socially outgoing and continued to be popular in college with her ebullient personality; she
eventually met her future husband at Gustavus. As graduation

neared and Marissa began thinking of prospects for her future, she occasionally discussed with Hannah and Boucher a small itch to visit South Korea, perhaps teaching English there after she graduated.

An opportunity to test the waters was nearing on the horizon. During Hannah's sophomore year at Minnesota, she was one of the final cuts from the 2014 US women's Olympic hockey team. Motivated to fulfill her childhood dream, Hannah continued to improve and was on track for the 2018 Olympics in South Korea. Marissa, Hannah's biggest fan, circled February 2018 in her mind as a possible date to make her first trip back to the country where she was born to support her sister.

But then, to her astonishment, South Korea came calling for Marissa.

# CHAPTER THREE

## Phishing for Talent

The emails sounded like a phishing scam.

KIHA is looking for North America Hockey Player of Korea Dscent. We'd like to ask them if they are inrested in playing for Korea at 2018 winter olympic game.

Glancing over these messages that contained broken English and random Korean symbols, the American and Canadian college students who received them either marked the letters as spam or thought they were being pranked.

In actuality, the mysterious emails were the result of meticulous research. The IIHF mandated that South Korea prove itself worthy of an automatic berth in the 2018 Olympic hockey tournament. Despite a dedicated core of a few women's players at home like Shin So-jung, preventing total embarrassment remained a challenge. But a unit had to be forged together quickly much in the way South Korea formed as a nation. With so much on the line in reputation and national pride, the Korea

Ice Hockey Association (KIHA) didn't have time to slowly develop youth programs and build a women's hockey program the organic way. Strangely, a solution was to be found six thousand miles away across the Pacific.

Throughout its history, Korea has been of interest to foreign nations and the peninsula has been invaded over nine hundred times.[1] After warding off Japanese aggression in the 1500s, Korea became extremely isolated, closing off its borders.

In the nineteenth century, as Western nations turned their attention to Asia, Korea still resisted diplomatic relations with the United States, England and France. Japan, Russia and China also kept a keen eye on Korea, with the three nations eventually going to war over interests in Korea. Japan's rise as an economic and militaristic giant quickly transformed them into Asia's dominant power, leaving them unchallenged in their pursuit of controlling the Korean peninsula.

In 1905, four years before he became president, US secretary of war William Howard Taft reached an agreement with Japan's prime minister that paved the way for the unobstructed Japanese domination of Korea; in return, Japan recognized America's right to the Philippines.[2] Five years later, Japan officially claimed sovereignty over the Korean peninsula. Police and military forces brutalized any and all dissenters. Korean citizens were mandated to take Japanese names, change languages and religion, and forced to enter Japan's military.[3] Later, as fighting intensified in Asia during World War II, Japanese cruelty rose to extremes, with as many as 200,000 Korean "comfort women" made into sex slaves subservient to Japanese authority figures.

After Japan surrendered to end the war, there was no real discussion between Allied leaders and Korean citizens about the peninsula's future. The US and Soviet Union hastily decided to separate Korea into two sections on a supposedly temporary basis. Once again, a half-assed decision by American machers changed the course of history. According to authors Don Oberdorfer and Robert Carlin in the 2013 edition of *The Two Koreas*, a pair of US colonels used a *National Geographic* map to propose that American troops occupy Korea south of the thirty-eighth parallel, a border that lay just north of Seoul.[4] Soviet military settled in the North, while American troops in Japan were then deployed toward the southern end of Korea for occupation duty, an unpopular decision for many GIs. US General John R. Hodge was known to say, "There are three things American troops in Japan are afraid of: diarrhea, gonorrhea, and Ko-rea."[5]

The American-supported Republic of Korea was proclaimed on August 15, 1948, and the Soviet-backed Democratic People's Republic of Korea was created twenty-five days later. Koreans on neither side wanted to recognize the border and in less than two years, North Korea, backed by the Soviet Union and China, invaded South Korea in an attempt to take control of the entire peninsula. The two Koreas fought for more than three years and when an armistice was signed on July 27, 1953, nearly five million Koreans had become refugees, South Korea lost almost $2 billion in property[6] and almost half of all houses on the peninsula were destroyed.[7] Overall, estimates range that three to five million people were killed during the conflict, including civilians. American soldiers even massacred hundreds of civilians in the South Korean village of No Gun Ri and scores of servicemen abused women and left behind families after leaving Korean soil. Former US Foreign Service officer and noted Korea scholar Gregory Henderson wrote in 1974, "There is no division for which the US government bears so heavy a share of the responsibility as it bears for the division of Korea."[8]

The societal and economic chaos that followed the Korean War resulted in a sizeable population of South Koreans scattering. In 1953, four Korean children were adopted by families abroad, but over the next fifty years, more than 156,000 Korean babies were adopted around the world. Minnesota eventually became a de facto capital for South Korean adoptees thanks to its progressive social welfare programs. Numerous Korean families faced with an inability to make a living at home also found amicable lives settling in the US.

Almost seven million people of Korean descent live outside the Korean peninsula,[9] with the Pew Research Center reporting that 1,822,000 Koreans resided in the US in 2015.[10] The first collective of Koreans to arrive in American territory were sugarcane and pineapple workers brought to Hawaii in 1903. More than seven thousand Koreans arrived on the island over the next two years, many seeking an escape from the encroaching Japanese aggression and increasing instability back home. Another wave occurred after the Immigration and Naturalization Act, signed into law in 1965, dissolved quotas on migrants arriving from foreign countries. According to data compiled by the Migration Policy Institute, in 1970, 39,000 Koreans lived in the US; in 1980, there were 290,000, and by 1990, 568,000 Koreans resided in America. In 2015, the US had the largest South Korean immigrant population in the world.[11]

In 2013, officials at KIHA eventually realized because of this diaspora, there might be Korean-heritage hockey players in North America that could compensate for the low enrollment numbers at home. They hoped these young women were not only equipped with crisp skating skills and rattling shots, but that they'd be familiar with the kind of disciplined training and knowledge that have made the US and Canada the two powerhouses of women's hockey since it became an Olympic event in 1998.

The pressure from the IIHF to rapidly upgrade South Korea's hockey programs was building. In 2012, when the lowest level Women's World Championship tournament was held in Seoul, KIHA officials said IIHF President René Fasel attended without advance notice. When he arrived, he saw no media coverage and sparse attendances, exemplifying how unimportant hockey seemed to the nation at the time. Afterward, KIHA was told that they could only send teams to the Olympics if the men moved into the Top 12 of the world rankings and the women into the Top 18. Entering 2012, the women were ranked twenty-sixth.

The following year, KIHA named a new president, which helped alter the IIHF's strict stance on South Korea's Olympic participation. Chung Mong-won, a well-regarded businessman who at fifty-eight years old still had a chubby, childlike face, became head of the organization. In addition to being chairman of the Halla Corporation, a prominent South Korean conglomerate, Mr. Chung was the nephew of the founder of Hyundai. Mr. Chung's business background and desire to improve hockey in his country impressed Olympic decision makers. IIHF officials met with Mr. Chung in November 2013, telling him that if the men's hockey team performed well in their division at the 2014 World Championships, both of South Korea's national hockey teams would qualify for the PyeongChang Games.

The men faltered, going winless in five contests.

KIHA was given another chance at qualification on three conditions: find a new program director for their men's and women's teams, preferably from Canada; invest more funding into the national teams; and add foreign players who could become naturalized citizens in time for 2018. The Korean Olympic Committee and Mr. Chung—whose family is worth nearly $15 billion—had no problem pumping in $20 million over the next four years to expedite growth. KIHA had already begun interviewing Canadian coaches with NHL backgrounds in late 2013 to reform their national team programs. The men also had the benefit of a professional hockey league in Asia, where many North American players hanging on for one last go-round or those who never could quite cut it in the NHL latched on. Several played for Anyang Halla, the Asia League team based just south of Seoul that Sojung practiced with. Since they already lived in South Korea, their path to citizenship would not include as many hoops to jump through. Asking them if they'd like a free ticket to the Olympics was an easy proposition. Finding women to entice with the same offer, however, wouldn't be as simple.

Kim Jung-min, a former sports journalist who had just been hired at KIHA to head up their media relations department, knew the story of Jim Paek—believed to be the first Korean player in the NHL—who won two Stanley Cup titles with the Pittsburgh Penguins alongside Mario Lemieux and Jaromir Jagr in the early 1990s. Paek's father was a doctor in South Korea, but left due to the country's worsening conditions after the Korean War. Paek told the *New York Times* in 2014: "At that time Korea was still under martial law; it was a tough place to live, I guess. We immigrated to Canada because he had an opportunity to work at the Hospital for Sick Children in Toronto, and to give his family a better life."[12]

Mr. Kim began a search to find female Paeks. KIHA did not even know how talented college-level American or Canadian players were, but with a sudden swell of financial backing, they could invite some imports over to test them out. At first, Mr. Kim contacted American journalists to see if they had heard of any Korean female hockey players in the US. When those sources turned up dry, he went to the internet. Mr. Kim began scouring rosters of North American colleges. He looked for any names that sounded Korean, or where applicable, noted photos of players who looked to be of Korean heritage. His first finds were a Yang and a Woo, but they turned out to be Chinese. Such was the outcome for the first five or six players he contacted, until one of the rare cases where racial profiling proved to be beneficial started bearing results.

Mr. Kim stumbled upon the roster of Wilfrid Laurier University in Waterloo, Ontario, and saw a five-foot-five kinesiology and physical education major with Korean facial features and a smile that filled her entire face. Like any young girl who took up the sport in Canada, Danelle Im dreamed of wearing the red maple leaf crest on her jersey in the Olympics. A quiet middle child with untapped wanderlust, Danelle had never been on an airplane when Mr. Kim reached out via Facebook with one of his spammy-looking messages. Intrigued, yet suspicious, she forwarded the inquiry to an uncle living in South Korea, who contacted KIHA and confirmed the authenticity of their overture.

Hockey was one of the only activities that Danelle could wholeheartedly say she was passionate about in life, and she wanted to remain enmeshed in the game as long as possible. Danelle was a diligent student, but she did not have the best prospects of getting accepted into a top graduate program to study physiology, her professional goal. Instead, she applied to nursing schools, but was not exactly thrilled with the prospect of working in that field for the rest of her life.

"I didn't know what to do," Danelle admitted. "I don't know what I'd be good at is the problem."

The only certainty in Danelle's life was that she loved hockey. She was raised in Toronto, where her father's family settled after her grandfather fled South Korea because of his outspokenness against Park Chung-hee, the tyrannical South Korean president who ruled the country from 1961 to 1979. Her mother's family also left South Korea in search of a better life for their children. These two descendants of Korean refugees met in Toronto and raised a family of three children—Danelle and her two brothers. Playing in youth leagues in one of the hockey capitals of the world, a diverse city with approximately 70,000 Koreans,[13] Danelle didn't experience the kind of verbal assaults on her race that Marissa Brandt did in America, but she remained insecure about her physical appearance and never wanted attention put on her background. "I never really talked about this, but I did know I was different, that I was a minority," Danelle said. "I think generally I'm a self-conscious person. I can't deny that I didn't know I'm the only Korean person in my group of friends or my hockey team. I can't deny that didn't have any effect. Me being who I am, I was shy, too. Parties, team events, social things, I was on the back burner a lot. Just kind of be there and just be shy about it."

On the ice, Danelle was the antithesis of a flamboyant player, but still made top junior teams and was recruited by NCAA Division I schools. In December of Danelle's senior year, she accepted an offer to play for Wayne State University in Detroit. Five months later, on the morning of her senior prom, Danelle briefly checked her email in between styling her hair and making sure her dress was wrinkle-free, and saw an urgent message from her future coaches. "I received this email saying, 'Sorry, but due to budget cuts the women's program is getting cut,'" Danelle said.

Danelle was sent reeling. "I always dreamed of getting a D-I scholarship in the States," she said. Danelle had been accepted at some universities in Ontario as fallback options and hastily contacted programs to see if they had any open spots for the fall semester on their hockey rosters, a rarity that late in the year. By chance, Danelle found one at Wilfrid Laurier. "She was kind of devastated with the news she was going to lose her D-I scholarship," said Rick Osborne, the women's hockey coach at Wilfrid Laurier. "We were full, but I needed to make room for Danelle."

*A photo Kim Jung-min found of Danelle Im on the Wilfrid Laurier University website, which led him to contacting her with an offer to try out for the South Korean national team.*

Osborne knew that Danelle wasn't a superstar talent to change the trajectory of his program, but that she carried inside her the personality and fundamentals all coaches wished they could instill in their players. However, the reserved nature that Danelle exhibited in her social life could often extend to the ice, which was troubling. Wilfrid Laurier was a regular contender for Canadian national championships and Danelle was often relegated to earning her time on third and even fourth lines, lest she not play at all. "When she has confidence she can be a really good player," said Jessie Hurrell, Danelle's college teammate. "When she was on fire she was unstoppable. But at times at Laurier I think she lacked confidence in herself."

"She came into a pretty high-powered program, so she had to earn her stripes on the ice," Osborne added. "She feels really bad if she feels she offended anybody or let anybody down. She was a nice kid and sometimes she played like a nice kid. The first couple of years it was a struggle—'I'm sorry, Rick. You're right, Rick,' and I was like, 'Don't be sorry, I just want you to realize there's so much upside to your game and I'm going to have to push you harder than I've pushed you in your life to get that out of you.'"

In Danelle's final year at Laurier in 2015, her star power began to show. Laurier made the regional semifinals, where they faced the University of Western Ontario in a best of three series. After dropping the first contest, Laurier allowed a goal twenty-three seconds into the first period in Game 2. Just seventeen seconds later, though, Danelle propelled herself down the ice and took a pass from Hurrell, sending a wrist shot past a Western defender and their goaltender to tie the game. Later in the period, with Western pressuring on offense, Danelle swiped the puck away at the blue line and then sped down the ice, leaping over a defender that left her one-on-one with the opposing goaltender, whom she deked out and beat on the glove-side for her second goal of the game. Danelle also added a late assist in the third period that sent the game into overtime.

"We had some star players the other team was shutting down pretty well," Osborne said. "When we needed her most and I was appealing for people to step up, all of a sudden she got herself into some kind of optimal arousal zone I had never seen before. She turned into this assertive, aggressive type of performer for that sixty-plus minutes."

Wilfrid Laurier lost in a double overtime heartbreaker, ending Danelle's career there. But her whole life she has been busy handing out assists.

In college, Danelle was well-liked by teammates and on campus, but her postgraduation life contained much uncertainty. She would move back home to Toronto and didn't really have any friends in her North York neighborhood. Her family often worried about this lonesomeness and how it might affect Danelle entering adulthood. KIHA's contact presented Danelle with a life-changing opportunity.

When she accepted the overture, Danelle was asked by Mr. Kim if she knew any other Korean hockey players in Canada. It just so happened that a few years earlier, Danelle's father, Charles, was walking the family dog and noticed a Korean woman in his neighborhood wearing a women's hockey jacket. Charles Im approached Diana Park and discovered that not only did their daughters both play hockey, but they lived on the same leafy street about three minutes apart.

Before Caroline Park played at Princeton, her life was the antithesis of Danelle's reserved upbringing. Caroline starred on the teen drama *Degrassi: The Next Generation*, a twenty-first-century Canadian version of shows like *Beverly Hills, 90210*. Caroline was cast as a devoutly religious, spunky student with a button nose and glittering smile, starring alongside a young actor named Aubrey Graham, better known today as the rapper Drake. She also was featured in commercials for companies like Nike and Robitussin, but saw acting as more of a hobby and left the show in 2007, when she was seventeen.

Jeff Kampersal, the former Princeton coach, first watched Caroline play for the Mississauga Junior Chiefs and became enamored with her speed and feel for the rink. He deployed her in a multitude of roles—penalty killer, tenacious forechecker, and the energizing force he relied on to break up the doldrums of practices. Caroline devoted herself to Princeton Tigers hockey, but the rigors of the sport took a toll on her body. Injuries, particularly to her right shoulder, hampered her career. Despite several surgeries and otherwise keeping her body in peak physical condition, Caroline never fully evaded the injury bug.

COURTESY OF SASHA SHERRY

*Caroline Park (seen here, center, with college teammates Sasha Sherry and Laura Martindale) fought through a multitude of ailments in college.*

Sasha Sherry, a teammate at Princeton, recalled that Caroline's shoulder joint often popped out of the socket and had to be manually put back in by Caroline or the team's athletic trainer. Caroline tried wearing a constricting sling to keep the socket in place because the ligaments around her joint became strained and needed to be immobilized to heal properly. The obvious remedy was to take time off or to have another surgery, but Caroline was determined to not let her team down.

"The number of games she felt 100 percent was probably less than the number she was fighting through recovery," Sherry estimated. "In my opinion she never was able to really catch her stride with playing consistently. We did talk about the frustration about not being able to play and how the shoulder trouble would get bad at the most inopportune times."

After college, Caroline moved to Manhattan to work in clinical research at the Hospital for Special Surgery. She casually competed in a recreational men's beer league at the rinks at Chelsea Piers, but her hockey career was basically over. When Caroline was a child, she remembered watching the news one night and there was a clip about women's hockey in South Korea. She told her father how funny it would be if she played with that team someday. Caroline never thought about the moment again until Kim Jung-min contacted her upon Danelle's recommendation.

"When they first emailed me about flying out to Korea to skate with them, like, I thought it was a joke somebody was playing on me," Caroline said.

It was not. Two weeks later, Danelle and Caroline were on a plane to South Korea.

# CHAPTER FOUR

# Seoul Sisters

Not everyone was thrilled with the plan to import foreign players. With a steady roster of about twenty skaters, South Korea's women's national team was essentially a "no-cut" squad since its inception—once a girl was selected, members had no fear of losing their spot because there were no waves of young talent emerging as challengers. Players left of their own volition, usually when they reached their thirties and felt carrying on into obsolescence was not worth the hassle for something many considered a hobby.

Kim Jung-min's emails raised the possibility, though, that not only might demotions become possible, but that athletes could be in jeopardy of being eliminated off the roster completely if several new talents could be found.

"I didn't necessarily feel good when I heard about it because that means that my stance on the team would get lower," admitted Lee Yeon-jeong, a normally unobtrusive soul who debuted with the team as a forward in 2007, when she was thirteen. "I also used to think that foreigners are a lot more individualistic than Koreans."

Yeonjeong's preconceptions about non-Korean players were not unusual. The Korean peninsula has historically been a proudly homogenous land. Even into the twenty-first century, school textbooks strongly promoted the idea of "one blood" among Koreans as a source of national pride.[1] For decades, mixed-race and adopted children were treated as inferior for not being 100 percent, pure, premium Korean. Though none of the members of the hockey team openly expressed such sentiment, Yeonjeong was not alone in initially responding coldly to the idea of imports coming in to change the face of the tribe.

By its second generation, the young women that made up South Korea's national team shared a singular motivation—an unabashed love for what was considered a niche sport in their homeland. Yeonjeong and her teammates played hockey with the kind of passion that guides American children on sandlot diamonds and blacktop basketball courts far after the sun has set on hot summer nights. There surely wasn't any money to be made from their profession, but over time their obsession held its own unique value.

When Yeonjeong and others first joined the team, they were the targets of cold shoulders, cursing tirades that brought them to tears and outright bullying from older players who were almost twice their age. Part of this was due to Korean culture, explained Park Ye-eun, who was picked for the national team in 2011, when she was fifteen. "In Korea there's a huge hierarchy according to age," YeEun pointed out. "If somebody is just one year older than you, then you have to respect them. When players bump into each other on the ice, the older girls might get upset if the younger ones bump really hard and don't say sorry. Afterward they would scold the younger ones for doing it."

YeEun grew up in the city of Gangneung, the future site for the hockey events at the 2018 Olympics. Known for its luxurious beach resorts on the East Sea, Gangneung also has an abundance of lakes and forests; it is not unlike Vadnais Heights, Minnesota, the hometown of Marissa Brandt, in being an ideal location to raise a family. Boasting a collection of offbeat museums dedicated to coffeehouses and Alexander Graham Bell, Gangneung is also a city where residents can explore a variety of interests, but where few girls tried on hockey gear.

A bit of a bookworm and an introvert, YeEun began playing hockey at the age of eight, inspired by watching her older brother try the sport in an attempt to lose weight. There was one hockey rink in the basement at Gangneung Gymnasium—which later hosted the 2018 Olympic curling competition—and YeEun watched her brother huff his way around the ice, while nearby, Park Jong-ah, a young figure skater, occasionally futzed around with a hockey stick while her contemporaries practiced toe loops and lutzes around her. When Jongah turned nine, she joined a newly formed hockey club at the urging of her mother and met YeEun, one of the only other girls on the team. Over the next five years, YeEun made the five-minute walk to Jongah's house several times a week, where they'd continue on together another ten minutes to practice, usually holding hands the entire way.

YeEun's company was appreciated, since Jongah did not take hockey seriously at first. She grew annoyed having to repeatedly explain to teachers, adults and friends what hockey exactly was. However, Cha Bong-hwa, the coach of the Gangneung club team, saw a natural union between Jongah and hockey. She had raw talent that few players regardless of gender seemed to display on the ice. Since there were no hockey stores in Gangneung, Coach Cha ordered gear for Jongah whenever she needed it, encouraging her to stick with the sport. When Jongah turned fourteen, he even pushed her to travel to Seoul to try out for the national team.

Jongah did not get selected—future teammate Choi Ji-yeon

won the lone slot available—but she was not necessarily disappointed. "I didn't have any passion to be on the national team," she disclosed. "I was too young. It was not a big deal for me." A few months later, though, another spot opened up when an older player retired and Jongah was called upon to represent her country. That meant moving to Seoul alone, an endeavor actually supported by her mother, a former speed skater who saw hockey as an avenue for her daughter's maturation. The family likely could never afford to send Jongah abroad to a boarding school or an American college, and this seemed like a special opportunity.

And so Jongah, still only in the eighth grade, moved two and a half hours away from home to a single-room apartment in a complex that housed mostly college students near the Taereung national training center in northeast Seoul. Her friends were envious of the independence and imagined her living alone amid the city's neon-lit streets packed with movie stars. But the fantasized appeal of the nation's capital was never apparent where Jongah resided, near a military training base and rustic farmland. Jongah's schedule forced her to study and train until 11:00 p.m. Afterward, she'd walk by her lonesome, shivering and scared through the dark alleys near her dormitory until she found her way home, then rushed inside and locked the door behind her.

Jongah felt no less isolated when practicing with the national team. She had no friends and the older players repeatedly screamed at her for seemingly every action she performed on or off the ice. The only form of respite came when Jongah found time to reach out to YeEun, who was still living in Gangneung. "She often called me and told me how difficult it is living alone not knowing many people and she would ask me to come live with her in Seoul," YeEun recalled. "Back then I was studying really hard, but I really loved hockey, too. I told my dad I wanted to go to Seoul but my dad went against it. 'You're doing really well with your studies; why would you want to go for hockey?' he said."

It took one year before YeEun convinced her father to let her relocate to Seoul—the entire family eventually moved there— but that was not of immediate help to Jongah.

"I wanted to give up every day," Jongah divulged.

As Jongah debated going back home, one of the senior players on the team started to show sympathy to her plight. Han Soo-jin, who at twenty-three was nine years older than Jongah, was quite familiar with others looking down on her presence in the rink. In fourth grade, Soojin befriended a new student from the United States who played hockey, and together they joined a club team in Seoul for one year. But since Soojin was five, her focus had been playing piano—her mother told her that she began planning her daughter's career as a pianist while she was still pregnant with Soojin. For five hours a day, Soojin practiced scales and sonatas, developing a maestro's ability, even though she sometimes cried at competitions, unable to cope with the stress. The sacrifice eventually paid off. Throughout her youth, Soojin attended prestigious art schools and was accepted into the storied college of music at Yonsei University in Seoul. She had largely forgotten about hockey until one day at age eighteen, right before she entered college, when she was on her way to a piano lesson, she stopped by an ice rink in the Mokdong area of Seoul. Hearing bodies slamming against the boards and rubber pucks clanking off the steel pipes of the goal sounded even more angelic than the Chopin compositions she favored performing. The flashbacks to her childhood enjoyment in the game became as vivid as if it had occurred only moments before.

Soojin returned home and told her mother her desire to become a hockey player, only to be yelled at very much in the way the senior players on the national hockey team treated Jongah. Despite this reaction, Soojin regularly visited the small hockey shop near the Mokdong rink before piano lessons, perusing the gloves and helmets that she dreamed of wearing. Eventually, Soojin mustered up the courage to buy a pair of skates and she snuck them into her room and hid them beneath her bed. Before going to sleep, Soojin tore up the receipt to discard the evidence. During the middle of the night, though, Soojin's mother woke her up, having taped together the receipt shreds, and then confronted her daughter with more vitriol than ever before about this foolish idea she was concocting that was getting in the way of her musical talent.

When their argument was done, Soojin's mother, although furious, realized her daughter's feelings about hockey were not temporary. She knew that Soojin was never the kind to accept defeat easily, and behind her eyes lay determination. "I think there's something fun in surviving and being thankful of any difficulties that arise along a journey," Soojin said. "If I'm doing something that I like, I think I have the will to overcome any negative events that happen in my life."

Soojin's mother made her an offer—as long as Soojin finished her college piano studies, she could also play hockey. Soojin agreed and joined her university's club team for men. With the same commitment that she had given to piano for the first two decades of her life, she now invested herself in curving and taping the blade of a hockey stick. One year after falling back in love with the game, Soojin's efforts won her a spot on the women's national team.

Years later, Jongah asked Soojin why she was so kind to her when everyone else treated her like the runt of the litter. Soojin seemingly always carried a look of intensity that, compounded with her heavy eyebrows and strong facial features, made her quite physically intimidating. At first, Soojin hadn't even realized Jongah was on the team. But after a few weeks, she saw the young girl from Gangneung always with her head down, being berated by her peers. "She told me because I looked a little pitiful," Jongah revealed. "I was young and after the girls scolded me

I would often cry. That's why she wanted to reach out." From that point on, Soojin and Jongah became best friends.

*Han Soo-jin gave up a career as an accomplished concert pianist to play hockey.*

"I think it's better for the older players to show how things are done through their own actions instead of scolding the younger players," added Soojin. "This way, the younger players can naturally follow the lead."

Soon after Jongah decided to remain with the national team, the squad underwent a multitude of changes. The aging first generation of players began retiring. KIHA shuttled in newer, younger players they found on boys' club teams around the country. Eventually, the hierarchy based on age dissolved and veterans like Shin So-jung and Lee Kyousun—who joined the team in 2000, when she was sixteen—created closer bonds with younger players like Soojin had with Jongah. Having experienced abrasive treatment as youths themselves, the new leaders wanted to make sure that such behavior wasn't cyclical.

"Sojung, Soojin and Kyousun, they sacrificed a lot to be on team," said Susie Jo, a forward who joined in 2012. "They didn't get paid enough, the infrastructure wasn't great. Despite that they were still passionate about hockey. They dedicated all their time. People expect athletes to be healthy, but they always went beyond their limits. These three players were the key to the Korean hockey team's success. They were the reason why the team was able to grow so much over the years."

Operating as equals, the players not only shared the rarest of interests, but could relate to the experience of feeling like outsiders. Almost every member commuted at least one to two hours each way to practice. In those lonesome hours on subways and buses it was not uncommon to stare in envy at schoolgirls laughing with their friends, or at the aspirational young businesswomen in spotless white blouses and perfectly pleated skirts, and wonder what it was like to have an engaging social life or a promising future. Once they made it to the Taereung training center, the players commiserated over the standing of women's hockey players in their country, from the subpar equipment to the lack of recognition of their very existence. Jiyeon, the young upstart who initially beat out Jongah to make the team, had flat feet, and the substandard skates she was forced to wear for much of her career caused constant pain, since the inner lining caused friction against her ankles. Jiyeon came from a single-parent household—she was once offered the opportunity to attend a hockey academy in Canada, but she could not give up the small stipend she received from being on the national team, fearing that her family might collapse without it. Such a sacrifice did not matter to her close friends, who teased her by pretending that a women's hockey team did not even exist in South Korea.

"Whenever I heard that I felt sad and angry," Jiyeon said.

Before Jiyeon and Jongah's generation arrived, younger players were forbidden from showering in the locker room. After the older regime left, the newcomers turned their cramped confines on the third floor of the Taereung rink into a social club where the team sharpened the blades of their poorly conditioned skates and sewed South Korean flag patches on their equipment bags and numbers on their jerseys. The fact that they woke up at

6:00 a.m. for school and sometimes didn't get home until 2:00 a.m. did not seem to matter as much. Nor did the reality that the men's national team received new equipment all the time, earned higher salaries and were able to compete overseas against international teams, instead of against local schoolchildren. On the women's team, there was an irreplaceable warmth from each other's company that compensated for their place in the lowest caste of South Korean sports society.

COURTESY OF CHOI JI-YEON

*Family, friends and classmates did not recognize how much the women's hockey team meant to its members.*

"We don't think about the age," Yeonjeong said. "We consider each other as older or younger sisters."

Yeonjeong, YeEun, Jongah, Soojin and their cohorts were able to make a grassroots passion into their livelihood. It was the reason they gave up sleep, friendships and better job prospects. They were part of a group of friends who loved hockey and those with whom they played above everything and would do anything in their power to protect that. The imports, however, risked upending all that they'd worked so hard to build.

# CHAPTER FIVE

# The Junger

The first time Danelle Im and Caroline Park were brought to Taereung in the summer of 2013, the Canadian duo were chaperoned by KIHA staff members who had not even introduced themselves. They cautiously entered the national team locker room and were greeted with unwelcoming stares by the South Korean players. That was followed by mumbles that turned into whispers that soon elevated to clearly articulated Korean words. Danelle did not understand the commotion, but sensed neither she nor Caroline was exactly welcome. Even Lee Kyou-sun, the amiable and quiet veteran leader who had been on the team since 2000, was not overjoyed with their presence. Danelle and Caroline were interlopers who had stumbled upon a small but tight-knit secret society.

Unbeknownst to the room, Caroline grasped every slanderous word being said. She absorbed a few more quips before piping up and announcing in the second language she had spoken since childhood that she wasn't necessarily a fan of the rude welcome. Suddenly, the gossipers fell silent. Caroline's message not only shocked her new colleagues, but motivated her to prove that she was not just here for a free vacation. "When I first went there, I mean both parties were sort of unsure," Caroline acknowledged. "They didn't think I understood Korean at all. I think once they found out I could—it wasn't like I was raised completely apart from the Korean culture—that kind of helped with getting along with the team."

The awkward introduction was also eye-opening for Danelle, who immediately turned sympathetic to her new teammates' plight. "I'm trying to put myself in the shoes of the South Korean players that have been here with this team training all year round," Danelle said. "If I were them, I'm not sure how I would feel toward an import player coming in and just walking in. I wouldn't necessarily think that's fair."

Although they could not voice it initially, not everyone was unenthusiastic about meeting the new arrivals. Susie Jo studied English in Vancouver from 2009 to 2012, where she also picked up hockey, eventually becoming captain of the girls team at Kitsilano Secondary School. In Canada, Susie learned firsthand the benefits of competing alongside women who since birth had been indoctrinated into a flourishing hockey culture. Susie privately knew that Danelle and Caroline would create healthy competition and push her teammates to perform better.

As well as Susie, Shin So-jung was intrigued by the imports, despite being shut out of international opportunities years earlier due to her financial challenges and language barriers. Still harboring an overwhelming desire to train abroad, Sojung was unable to communicate much with her new teammates, but nevertheless quietly trailed Danelle and Caroline.

Each summer, KIHA had an informal camp for female hockey players from around the country. In 2013, the year the imports first arrived, there was a tournament, with the winning team earning five million won, or about $4,400. Money was not supposed to be the motivating factor of the recreational tourney, so to keep competition fair, the national team members were expected to be spread among the competing squads that also included young girls and other novices. One coach, however, became greedy at the prospect of a cash bonus and stacked his roster with Caroline, Danelle, Park Jong-ah and Han Soo-jin. When they played Sojung and a team of beginners, the star-studded side won 6-0. Embarrassed by this performance, Sojung discreetly approached Danelle. She had yet to really connect on a personal level with the new additions, but she saw how fluidly Danelle competed in all aspects of the game and became tantalized at the possibility of playing in Canada. While many top-level Canadian prospects gravitated towards college hockey in the United States, Sojung could see the Canadian leagues were still vastly superior to what was available at home (and much cheaper than the Ivy Leagues). Tired of the beatings in net, she was determined to get better.

"It was after one of the practices, we were in Taereung in the locker room," said Danelle, who was about to enter her third year at Wilfrid Laurier. "In her very broken English at the time she asked, 'Could you help me with something?'"

With the assistance of Danelle and Danelle's mother, Hye-jin, who visited South Korea that summer, Sojung contacted almost every college in Canada with a women's hockey program, not unlike how Kim Jung-min had scoured North American rosters looking for players of Korean ancestry. David Synishin, the coach at St. Francis Xavier University in Antigonish, Nova Scotia, was intrigued when he received a random email from South Korea. He pulled up a video clip Sojung attached and forwarded the seven-minute highlight reel to his coaching staff. From a stationary camera located on the bench during one of the practices for Anyang Halla, Sojung turned away shot after shot even though her head barely stood above the crossbar of the goal.

"We said, 'Holy God, let's get in contact with this kid,'" Ben

Berthiaume, an assistant coach on Synishin's staff, remembered thinking.

"You can tell almost right away by how a player looks and how they play," Synishin added. "Just her movement and how she carried herself, we knew she was going to be a very good goalie." Synishin offered Sojung an athletic scholarship to come to Antigonish, a town with fewer than five thousand residents. Sojung immediately accepted. Ten days after first sending off her emails, Sojung left South Korea for Halifax Stanfield International Airport, where Synishin was awaiting her arrival.

Looking out the window of Synishin's Honda Pilot, Sojung gaped at the vast swaths of countryside that seemed so different from the bustling streets of Seoul. During the two-hour ride, Synishin tried to make small talk, but was only met with silence. "I was very nervous because training camp was going to start the next day," Sojung said. "I didn't speak any English at all. Coach tried to talk to me and I didn't understand."

Sojung, in searching the internet for information about Antigonish, learned that its demographics were overwhelmingly homogenous. Sitting in Synishin's car, Sojung worried about encountering cultural insensitivity in North America. As a child, she once watched a television interview of pitcher Chan-ho Park, the first South-Korean-born player in Major League Baseball, signed by the Los Angeles Dodgers in 1994. Park relayed a story about eating kimchi in the clubhouse and his teammates mocking him because he smelled like garlic. "That's why when I went to Canada, I didn't bring any Asian food," Sojung said.

Rumors of a new arrival from South Korea quickly spread around the St. Francis Xavier (StFX) community. Jenna Downey, who played defense for the university and is from the small city of Stratford, Ontario, admitted that most teammates had no idea South Koreans even played hockey. It was like finding surfers from Nebraska. Sojung was projected to be a backup goaltender, but the coaching staff decided she needed reps as soon as possible, to test if their hunch about her skills was valid. At a preseason tournament at Queens University in Kingston, Ontario, Sojung was put into her first game for St. Francis Xavier, whose female athletic teams are nicknamed the X-Women. As players swooshed by her in a blur, skating faster than the opponents she was used to back in South Korea, Sojung nervously tried to adjust. She called out to her teammates, *"Pikyeo, pikyeo,"*—literally "get out of the way"—which only registered bewilderment among her colleagues, none of whom spoke Korean. "There were times of just utter confusion, who was saying what," Downey recalled.

Finally, a defender came back to the bench and informed Berthiaume that their new goalie kept shouting this phrase that none of them could comprehend. Sojung sounded as if she was imitating a Pokémon character, not a goaltender calling out directions. Berthiaume pulled Sojung aside in between periods and asked her what she was saying. As best as she could relay in English, Sojung told him that she could not see past the Queens forwards. "So that became an ongoing thing; she would say *'Pikyeo, pikyeo'* when she was being screened and to move them out of the way," Berthiaume recounted.

Sojung could follow along with the diagrams the coaches drew on dry erase boards during practice, and since the South Korean national team used English words for hockey-specific vernacular, she understood bits and pieces of their instructions. Her teammates compensated for the rest. "The Canadian players told me, 'Teach us the Korean words and we'll learn,'" Sojung said. "That helped me a lot."

While Sojung could wing communication on the ice, the classroom proved to be a different challenge. Only about half of Sojung's credits from her university in Seoul could be transferred, and she felt overwhelmed by Canadian textbooks that seemed to be three times as thick as they were in South Korea.

During her first semester, it took Sojung forty minutes to read one page because she had to look up every word in her English-to-Korean dictionary. She did not understand why she had to attend classes if she spent her time there just staring blankly ahead.

ST. FRANCIS XAVIER ATHLETICS/ERICA ROBERTS

*Despite a language barrier, Shin So-jung quickly became her university's starting goaltender.*

Observing her struggle to ingest lectures, teammates shared their notes from classes and readings, which cut down on the excruciating task of translating each word in a textbook. Sojung then realized that as she was translating the notes, she formed her own thoughts on the subjects, which she jotted down separately and rote-memorized for exams.

Sojung hardly found time to sleep her first year in Canada. Aside from studying and learning English, the coaches wanted her to completely change her goaltending style. For example, in South Korea, goalies are not usually taught to emphasize stickhandling and playing the puck off the boards. With bigger, faster and more talented players ripping powerful slap shots at her, Sojung also had to refine her instincts and reflexes, learning how to better read smarter opponents.

Sojung proved to be an erudite learner on the ice, much faster than in the classroom, and became the team's starting goalie that first season. She posted a 12–4 record with a miniscule 1.44 goals against average, leading the X-Women to a conference championship.

While Sojung was finding success in Canada, KIHA decided to send additional players overseas to build up their skills. A few years earlier, the Canadian International Hockey Academy (CIH) in Rockland, Ontario, contacted Canada's embassy in South Korea and suggested having some players sent over to attend the school in a goodwill gesture. At the time, KIHA did not believe there were any worthy players and the prospect of having their girls compete against Canadians seemed daunting. But after watching Caroline and Danelle slowly mesh with the team during the summer of 2013, and with Sojung now succeeding at StFX, KIHA decided to circle back around on the offer. Jongah and Park Ye-eun were selected as the test cases.

Jongah was ecstatic about the offer. Hearing from Sojung made her yearn to play hockey at a Canadian university. Jongah's command of English was not good, but unlike when she moved to Seoul alone, her childhood friend would be accompanying her to ease the transition. However, the girls' time at CIH was not what Jongah had fashioned in her mind.

"It was our first time living abroad," YeEun said. "It was really scary. We didn't know how to react to other kids when they came up to us and talked to us in English because we weren't used to it. It was a difficult time."

Instead of recognizing their language deficiency and helping amend the gap like Sojung's college teammates had, YeEun and Jongah said some of their teammates mocked them. Early in the season, the team attended an off-site training camp and Jongah roomed with three Canadian girls who all shared the same bed. Shy and afraid to converse in the little English she knew, at night, Jongah curled herself on the edge of the mattress and turned away while the trio laughed at her.

"They would tease me about not speaking English," Jongah said. "The three girls were talking about me behind my back. One girl finally said, 'Jongah isn't sleeping.' The other girls said, 'She's not going to understand, anyway.' When these things happened I was really frustrated, but couldn't say anything."

The harassment continued on throughout the school year, particularly from some of the wealthier students. YeEun said she was called "ching chong" and other derogatory comments about Asians. On campus, each housing unit had two bedrooms. YeEun and Jongah lived with two French-Canadian girls who they later learned constantly mocked them in French. Whenever the dorm became dirty, they'd blame it on YeEun and Jongah. The worst incident occurred when, after returning from Christmas break, YeEun and Jongah discovered that all of their clothes were missing. "We found the clothes in their room," YeEun said. "We would think, 'Why are they doing this to us?' Back then it was very hurtful that they were so mean."

YeEun and Jongah went to the school's dean and their coach to report the pranks. There was a team meeting, but no further repercussions. By the end of the school year, the girls couldn't wait to get as far away from Canada as possible and back home to South Korea.

Meanwhile, as Sojung began to thrive at St. Francis Xavier, Antigonish started to feel like home. The more Sojung communicated, the more her teammates became fascinated by her story of how she moved halfway across the world, leaving behind her mother in an attempt to send her country to the Olympics. Originally, she only planned to stay two years in Canada, but when the coaching staff asked her to commit to three, she readily agreed. Sojung, who liked to part her shoulder-length hair slightly to the right and had a smile that scrunched up her face whenever she recognized someone, quickly endeared herself to many on the small campus, including Brenda Berthiaume, Ben's mother, who worked as an advisor for international students.

Berthiaume helped Sojung sort out the minutiae of administrative paperwork and credit requirements, but more importantly she remedied her battles with homesickness. Berthiaume regularly invited Sojung over for spaghetti and meatball dinners—when Sojung couldn't attend, she made sure to bring her a plate of leftovers.

Sojung began spending so much time at Berthiaume's house that her three-year-old grandson, Oliver, became fixated on Sojung and began mimicking her moves in net. For home games he'd wear one of Sojung's jerseys to the arena, which was so big that it drowned his little body. One day, Oliver cautiously told his grandmother that he wanted to become a goalie, too, but worried he wouldn't be successful. To Oliver, only girls and girls as good as Sojung could play the position with such beauty and aplomb.

ST. FRANCIS XAVIER ATHLETICS

*Sojung became a popular student in the St. Francis Xavier community.*

Even after Sojung returned to South Korea, her picture resided on a mantel in Brenda Berthiaume's house. Looking at Sojung's soft eyes and dimpled smile triggers a flood of memories for Brenda, like the hand-woven mitts the girl liked collecting from Hudson Bay, or how Sojung regularly invited the family to drive with her to Halifax two hours away for Korean meals. "She was so self-assured," Brenda Berthiaume said. "Just think of the courage to come here. She has more courage than she knows what to do with. She's an ambassador of all things that should be in the world."

Brenda gave her the name Sojung Berthiaume because of how close they became, but Sojung acquired other nicknames, as well. At St. Francis Xavier, there were occasions where students took pictures with Sojung and pulled back their eyelids, to pretend to look Asian. Sojung was unaware of the derogatory implications of the gesture until she showed the photos to friends back home who had also spent time abroad. And although she worked diligently to improve her English, there were many moments of discomfort as she acclimated herself with her second language. After finally feeling confident enough to regularly speak English, Sojung changed her Twitter handle to @golri31—a portmanteau of her jersey number and the pronunciation an Asian speaker might use to say "goalie." It was both a reclamation and winking nod to her journey in becoming bilingual.

The most popular of Sojung's new monikers was "Junger," a version of a nickname regularly given to hockey players by adding "-er" to their surname. It was a simple title, but an affectionate one that gave Sojung a sense of belonging among her Canadian cohorts. "Junger" followed Sojung to every stop of her career from that point on forward, an affirmation of acceptance by teammates from around the world.

Everyone at StFX began to recognize that behind Sojung's soft voice was an iron will to save women's hockey in her homeland. Although Sojung wanted to win desperately for the X-Women, others around the team knew that she was also competing for a greater glory. "She had this pressure above and beyond what normal student–athletes deal with," Downey said. "For her, a game wasn't just a game. It was something extra she was working toward."

If South Korea's women's hockey team was granted acceptance into the Olympics, the pressure would be colossal compared to facing off against Queens University. In South Korea, sports fanaticism reaches levels that makes English soccer hooligans seem tame. Sojung knew that throughout her country's history, sports have not only helped the nation blossom, but have the influence to turn potential national heroes into national villains.

# CHAPTER SIX
# The Hen Crows

For generations, sports have inspired Koreans through periods of despair. During Japanese colonial rule, Sohn Kee-chung became the first Korean to win an Olympic medal while forced to compete for Japan, taking gold in the men's marathon at the 1936 Summer Games in Berlin. Nonetheless, this victory boosted Korean patriotism to such an extent that several newspapers ran photographs with the Japanese flag removed from the chest of Sohn's uniform.[1] The offenders, of course, were swiftly punished, but the rebuttal to imperial oppression seemed almost worth it. (The Japanese do not seem to respond well to displays of Korean pride. Many Koreans swear by a long-standing rumor that their country was supposed to be spelled with a C, but the Japanese changed the first letter in order to be first alphabetically.[2])

Sports were further used to foster patriotic identity once the country was released from Japanese rule, even helping to shape modern South Korea. When Park Chung-hee became South Korea's leader in 1961, he believed sending athletes abroad and having them achieve success at international sporting events would provide more to the nation than "hundreds of our foreign diplomats spending large budgets ever have."[3] President Park, a tough-looking figure who once wore sunglasses while meeting John F. Kennedy, also saw athletics as an avenue to gain an ideological advantage over North Korea, if his country could out perform their neighbors.[4] As a result, in 1966, he established the Taereung national training center in Seoul.

Just as important as the government's support in South Korea's sports ascension were *chaebols*, a combination of the Korean words *rich* and *clan*. Many of these family-owned business conglomerates have extended beyond Korean borders to become recognized worldwide brands—Hyundai, LG and Samsung being among the most prominent.[5] Once South Korea started using sports as an avenue for international attention, *chaebols* were encouraged by the government to sponsor teams and organizations. Chung Ju-yung, the founder of Hyundai, was known to have quite the favorable relationship with President Park, receiving cheap loans and desired contracts in return for cooperation in helping to boost the nation. Euny Hong, author of *The Birth of Korean Cool: How One Nation is Conquering the World Through Pop Culture*, described Hyundai, along with Samsung, as one of the *chaebols* that "have clothed and fed the nation since the 1960s," adding in her book that a *chaebol*-centralized economy increased South Korea's per capita by almost 1,700 percent during President Park's term.[6] At one time, twenty-five of South Korea's thirty-three national sports organizations were led by *chaebol* figures.[7]

Sports increasingly became associated with South Korean identity under President Chun Doo-hwan in the 1980s. Analysts at the time believed that this was likely meant to shore up legitimacy in the presidency after Chun took power during a tumultuous period in South Korean history, which included a coup that followed a massacre resulting in hundreds of deaths in the city of Gwangju in May 1980.

After witnessing the success of the 1964 Summer Olympics in Tokyo—just nineteen years after World War II obliterated Japan—and a positive response to the smaller-scale 1978 World Shooting Championships in Seoul, President Chun felt emboldened enough to bid for the 1988 Summer Olympics. Part of the reason the country's citizens stood behind the endeavor was that South Korea's bid went up directly against one from Japan. In 1981, Seoul, which had promised to spend $2.3 billion on the Games, beat out Nagoya, Japan, by a margin of 52–27 in a vote by the IOC.[8]

It is important to note just how unlikely it seemed at the time that South Korea could ever hold a prestigious international sporting event. The country was nowhere near like it is portrayed today, as the wired nation on the cutting edge of technology. Hong lived in Seoul in the early 1980s, and remembers the city as being overrun by counterfeit goods and lawlessness, with men even urinating on the street in broad daylight.

New roads, parks, public transportation systems and tourism efforts were all rapidly put into place for the 1988 Olympics. Richard W. Pound, a vice president for the IOC, called the Seoul Olympics "the most successful in modern Olympic history," and said that "Korea, the country that had been vilified in the media for its political instability, had pulled together in a manner that astounded the world."[9]

The Games were a triumphant success and marked a turning point in South Korean history, when the nation refurbished its global perception and boosted patriotism to unprecedented heights. Rising from the war-torn ashes that colonialization and conflict impressed upon the land for the first half of the twentieth century, South Korea reintroduced themselves on the world stage as an emerging economic giant of budding ingenuity. The 1988 Olympics not only legitimized South Korea, but helped fulfill Park Chung-hee's wish, distinguishing the country as the polar opposite of North Korea, which since the end of World

War II had become the black sheep of Asia—increasingly isolated, decrepit and transforming into a communist state run by
a cult of personality.

Daniel Tudor, author of *Korea: The Impossible Country*, has
called South Korea "arguably the greatest national success story
of recent times."[10] But since oppressive circumstances have defined Korea's history, the emotions from those events have created a lingering, unshakable rawness, as often happens in nations
built out of wars. As much as South Korea has glossed its exterior with Samsung phones, Kia cars and world famous K-pop
groups, there seems to be a deep-seated pain still buried inside
each citizen.

*Han* is a uniquely Korean term that captures the psyche of the
nation. *Han*'s genesis is hard to pinpoint, but its impact was described by Hong. "Karma can be worked off from life to life,"
Hong wrote. "With *han*, the suffering never lessens; rather, it
accumulates and gets passed on." Despite this feeling of infi-
nite oppression and sorrow that many Koreans believe they are
born with and cannot escape, Koreans are also wonderfully re-
sourceful in the face of such perpetual woe. As Hong noted,
"A race that has been under constant threat knows it can survive anything."[11]

One challenge to *han*'s power over Koreans has been athletic competition. As seen in the success of marathoner Sohn
Kee-chung, Koreans become galvanized by triumph in major
sporting events, and athletes who achieve worldwide success
can become national heroes. The most well-known example is
figure skater Kim Yu-na. At the 2010 Olympics in Vancouver,
Kim Yu-na won gold with what were described as "unforget-
table, nearly perfect performances."[12] Since then, even after retiring from competition, Kim Yu-na has remained the South
Korean equivalent of Beyoncé.

As South Korea continued its ascent in the twenty-first century, its citizens sought out an opportunity to further legitimize their worldwide standing and host the Winter Olympics. Once again, it was no surprise that *chaebols* played a crucial role. The campaign for the 2018 Winter Olympics was led by a triumvirate of highly powerful business leaders: Lee Kun-hee of Samsung; Cho Yang-ho of Korean Air; and Park Yong-sung, who formerly headed Doosan Group, a conglomerate with a focus on manufacturing and construction. Mr. Lee was a member of the IOC. Mr. Cho was chairman of the bid committee and Mr. Park was president of the Korean Olympic Committee. To truly understand the power of *chaebols* in South Korean sports, just know that all three leaders had been convicted of corruption while running their businesses, but never earned more than a slap on the wrist; Mr. Lee was even pardoned in 2009 so he could lobby to bring the Winter Games to South Korea.[13]

Among *chaebols*, few entities have played as crucial a role in shaping South Korean sports as Hyundai and the Chung family. Chung Ju-yung was chairman of the committee to bring the 1988 Summer Olympics to Seoul and reportedly bombarded voters with beautiful airline hostesses, free airplane tickets and cash totaling in the millions.[14] Chung Mong-gyu, a Hyundai scion, leads the Korean Football Association. And of course, Chung Mong-won, a nephew of Chung Ju-yung, is president of KIHA.

In 2018, not hockey but speed skating was expected to be the centerpiece event to captivate the nation's emotions. At the 1992 Olympics in Albertville, France, speed skater Kim Ki-hoon won South Korea's first ever gold medal in the Winter Games, obliterating the field in the 1,000-meter with a world record effort. Kim Ki-hoon helped set another world record in the men's 5,000-meter relay final, setting off a frenzied interest in the sport at home. Today, it is not uncommon for hundreds of nine-year-olds to train in three-hour sessions, six days a week, in the hopes of becoming the next speed skating superstar.[15] Sixty-four of the seventy medals South Korea has won at the Winter Olympics have come in speed skating, and just about every prime slot at rinks around the country is blocked off for speed skating training. In contrast, out of a total population of fifty-one million, South Korea had 319 registered female hockey players in 2017. But if they could earn their automatic berth to compete in the Olympics, the women's national team hoped the elevated spotlight could change their standing in South Korea's sports ecosystem and maybe garner more attention from the Chungs of the world.

That the team felt so neglected was not particularly shocking. Even with all of its rapid advancement, South Korea can often seem like a culture stuck in the Dark Ages. This is particularly evident when examining the nation's dated views on gender equality, which are heavily influenced by Confucian teachings that dictate women should be subservient to men through all stages of life and focused on raising and preserving families. Estimates gauge that South Korean women earn almost 37 percent less than men, more than double the gender wage gap in the US.[16] Women are also sometimes expected to quit jobs once they marry or if they become pregnant. There is an old saying in Korea about women deemed too assertive: "If a hen crows, the household collapses."[17]

"The elderly definitely has a fixed mind-set about the distinct roles between men and women," explained Ko Hye-in, a forward on the women's national team studying nanotechnology, with aspirations to patent inventions. "I have friends interviewing for jobs and they'd be asked, 'When do you plan on getting married?' or 'When do you plan on having kids?' I think Korea's far from changing."

In 2012, it seemed as if a monumental moment in gender rights occurred when Park Geun-hye, the daughter of Park Chung-hee, was elected the nation's first female president. But many South Koreans believed that her victory was more a confirmation of the country's patriarchal society, as older voters gravitated toward romanticizing her father's legacy (which included banning miniskirts with police officers measuring the length of them with rulers) than Geun-hye's own merits.[18] As Oberdorfer and Carlin wrote in their book on the Koreas, even in the mid-1990s, "Park was remembered less for his conflicts with Washington and successive waves of political repression than as the father of his country's remarkable economic progress."[19]

Park Geun-hye never fully became the bastion of feminist empowerment that some thought she could represent when she was voted into office, at a time when women accounted for only 3 percent of government officials. Instead, the circumstances of her reign proved to somehow be even more outlandish than her father's.

One of Park Geun-hye's closest friends was Choi Soon-sil, the daughter of Choi Tae-min, a spiritual leader who claimed he could heal disease and provide wisdom straight from the mouths of Buddha and God.[20] Ms. Choi developed a reputation as a Rasputin-like figure with access to President Park's decision-making, and in November 2016, Ms. Choi's influence proved costly when she was arrested for extortion. Using her authority from within the president's inner circle, Ms. Choi demanded from businesses almost $70 million in donations to charities she controlled.

As the story captivated South Korea, scores of protestors took to the streets to call for President Park's resignation. South Korean media began reporting that Ms. Choi's sway extended beyond the president's office to the Ministry of Culture, Sports and Tourism, a body that controlled the operation of organizations like KIHA. Dozens of reports followed alleging that President Park had dissenters in the arts blacklisted, imprisoned or fired, drawing to mind the ethos of her father's authoritarian regime.[21] This drew particular ire from young generations. The largest

ever protests in South Korea ensued, with a majority of march-
ers being young women.[22]

On December 8, South Korean parliament voted to impeach
President Park, suspending her authority. Four months later,
after South Korea's economic and government foundations were
shaken to their cores, Park Geun-hye was removed from office.
As the verdict was announced, one elderly pro-Park supporter
died of a heart attack and two others were killed in chaotic dem-
onstrations outside the courthouse where the decision was made
to banish South Korea's first female leader.[23]

Others were in a more congratulatory mood, feeling as if a
new day was coming. Among the candlelight protestors that
took to the streets were twenty-one-year-old Cho Mi-hwan,
twenty-year-old Park Ye-eun and fifteen-year-old Lee Eun-ji,
members of the South Korean women's national hockey team.

"She undoubtedly had to be impeached," YeEun stated. "Everybody agreed with that. We felt like we were correcting something done unjustly. In the past, I think people followed the
advice of adults a lot more. Now we're more willing to break
that. This is my life."

Before the marches, YeEun and her friends were already challenging social norms by simply playing hockey, representing other
contemporary South Koreans willing to buck the conventional roles
for women that centuries of history had ingrained in the culture.

If a South Korean businesswoman saw dire prospects in climbing a company ladder before she ever entered an office, women's
hockey players never even dared to dream of making careers as
athletes. Rachael Miyung Joo, author of the 2012 book *Transnational Sport: Gender, Media, and Global Korea*, noted in an interview that only female athletes like Kim Yu-na could become
celebrities through extended success, as long as they conform
to Korean standards for women. "The other athletes are really
invisible for the most part," Joo said. "They only emerge into
the public eye in the context of international sporting events

and only if they do well. Kim Yu-na is the paragon of women's sports. She has transcended the sport to become a national icon. She sort of embodies the idolized Korean female in a global context with K-pop and Korean beauty products and soap operas, and a lot of these image-based media become part of the way Korea is marketing its sort of national brand. Kim Yu-na becomes a perfect example of Korean femininity and competitiveness and cosmopolitanism and national loyalty."

Lee Kyou-sun never wanted to become the next Kim Yu-na. Genuine love for hockey is what kept her motivated into her thirties when she worked mundane part-time jobs such as a waitress or stocking shelves at convenience stores and Daiso, the Japanese dollar store franchise. "No office or company would understand missing time for ice hockey," Kyousun lamented. "So I often thought of quitting." Kyousun never did give up, though, playing until she literally could not stand any longer due to back injuries that even in retirement affected her day-to-day life.

The South Korean men's national hockey team had no such quandaries. While KIHA was searching for female imports, the men were boosted by foreign players that had previously competed in the professional Asia League—"mercenaries" as some on the women's team called them. These American- or Canadian-born Caucasian players earned salaries of at least $200,000.[24] One of those contracts alone surpassed the amount the entire women's team made during a full year of training. "Although women have become stronger in Korean society than in the past, I think women in Korean ice hockey are still living in the patriarchal era that's reminiscent of the sixties," said Han Soo-jin, the oldest member of the team after Kyousun retired.

Since many players were still in school, their schedules prevented them from holding even part-time jobs. Choi Yu-jung wanted to become an engineer and had to pass up attending a prestigious high school for the sciences to train with the national team. University student Choi Ji-yeon had the inconvenience of taking all of her classes in the morning to be able to reach Tae-reung for practices that began with weight training at 4:00 p.m., and usually ended six to seven hours later, causing her to return home at midnight.

Younger players like Eom Su-yeon had even more straining regimens. Many South Korean students engage in study sessions at 7:00 a.m. or earlier before classes begin. The school day doesn't end until 5:00 p.m. and then after a short meal, they go to private academies for further classes from 6:00 to 10:00 p.m. That is followed by time spent studying at home or at libraries to midnight or later. Because Suyeon had to attend practices, she often fell behind in her classes and had no time to catch up.

"When I'm on the ice, I get a feeling of accomplishment because I'm not good at anything else," said Suyeon, who would turn seventeen just days before the Olympics.

COURTESY OF EOM SU-YEON

*With teammates like Shin So-jung (top), teenager Eom Su-yeon felt pride playing hockey, which was absent from the rest of her life.*

Suyeon's teammate, Park Chae-lin, tried her best to keep pace in high school by going to the library after hockey practice until

2:00 a.m. The pressure of attempting to excel in both school and athletics led some girls to retire prematurely. Mia SeungEun Lee fell in love with hockey at a young age, but for as long as she played, could not stop wondering if there was any future in it. Every day as her mother drove Mia the two hours each way to practice for the national team, they debated whether or not she could continue on as she entered her final years of high school.

"To be very frank, I knew there's not a promising future at all for female hockey players in Korea," said Mia, now attending Cornell University in Ithaca, New York. "We all came to the conclusion it was the best decision to quit. It was hard because I also knew that was the right decision. It's basically impossible for girls to do both. If they want to be athletes, they basically have to give up on their studies. It's extremely different from the culture here in North America."

Balancing hockey and school created other obstacles. There were hardly any social lives to speak of—while studying after midnight may not seem like the most fun activity, it does allow many students to still be around their friends. Devotion to hockey often fractured or alienated other friendships. Chaelin, a fashionable teenager with stylish brown bangs who displayed the confidence of a ringleader while around the team, was unable to maintain relationships with her schoolmates; later, in her teen years, Chaelin began visiting karaoke rooms by herself, singing sad ballads about remorse.

Aside from feeling distant from their classmates, many players felt pressure from their families, teachers and society in general. Originally, Chaelin's mother told her to quit hockey and wouldn't let her join the national team because it interfered with school. Jiyeon, after repeatedly trying to convince her friends that a women's hockey team even existed in South Korea, regularly questioned her commitment to the sport. "At times I asked myself, 'Why do I have to do this?'" Jiyeon said. "If I didn't do hockey, I would have more time to study and I could go to a better university. When game results weren't as good as I expected, my parents told me I have to choose one. Don't just be mediocre in both things. Choose studies or hockey and dedicate yourself."

Despite her better judgment, Jiyeon selected hockey, just like every one of her teammates. After having made similar life choices, hearing comparable taunts and having the same doubts, the players on the women's national team formed their own social circle. They decorated the locker room for Christmas and birthday celebrations. Instead of attending K-pop concerts with friends, they sang and danced to routines before practice. They teased and pinched the cheeks of teammates' brothers and played jokes on their friends' mothers, who watched their daughters share umbrellas and dye each other's hair like they were sisters.

"In my ordinary things in life, I'm usually doing things on my own," said Kim Hee-won, the youngest player on the national team. Heewon was noticeable for her short bowl haircut that resembled the top of an acorn, a style that might have drawn heckling at school, but was adored by her teammates. "I feel happier exponentially playing hockey."

Heewon was not the only younger player who was able to ward off the encroachment of teenage angst through hockey. Yujung defined herself as "fourth-dimensional," a term she explained Koreans use to describe someone weird or eccentric. But she was instantly put into a better mood upon feeling the cooling sensation of entering a rink; in her hockey life, she was a socially active seventeen-year-old who deftly bounced among the team's various cliques, stuffing her face with pizza with the imports one day, and going to the movies with other teammates the next, just like regular teenagers.

Hockey was not the only source of their bonds. Almost one in five players on the team came from a single-parent household. Together, they could relate to the economic, social and emotional struggles that this environment created in South Korea, where single parents, particularly mothers, remain heavily stigmatized.

Their bodies tingled when they wore the South Korean flag on their chests, representing a country they were proud of even if it didn't always take care of them in return. For as much as the South Koreans prided themselves on their dedication to their sport, they consistently wondered how they could improve their standing in a nation where they were viewed as anomalies. They had almost nothing to show, no recognizable trophies or bona fides. For this they sacrificed blood, their bodies, relationships and the formative years of their lives to play hockey, a sport that made them feel less blue and like they finally fit in.

COURTESY OF MARISSA BRANDT

*Together, South Korea's women's hockey team formed their own family.*

# CHAPTER SEVEN
## The Coach with the Blue Eyes

As a child, Sarah Murray was not particularly fond of hockey. Her mother, Ruth, recalled that whenever peewee coaches pointed out that Sarah, with her blond hair poking out of her helmet, should be proud to be the only girl on their teams, her daughter replied that she was only playing because "my dad makes me."

Sarah's father, Andy, is recognized as one of the game's most esteemed minds. During his four decades of coaching, Andy Murray molded players at the youth, international, college and pro levels. During Sarah's adolescence, he coached ten seasons in the NHL with the Los Angeles Kings and St. Louis Blues. This nomadic lifestyle left one constant during Sarah's youth—hockey—whether she liked it or not. Unlike the way Sarah's future pupils were drawn to the game by a romanticism found in the thudding sound of pucks bouncing off pads or the skate blades piercing the ice ever so slightly, hockey, to the young Sarah Murray, was a routine like eating vegetables, not exactly born out of passion.

Still, despite her early antagonism toward the sport, Sarah displayed a keen understanding of the game. When she was about four, Sarah's coaches asked her to play goalie. The boys on her team had proved they could barely balance themselves on skates, let alone stop pucks. When Sarah was placed at the position, she looked at her new surroundings and then lay down in front of the goal, barely covering the space from post to post. Sarah realized that four-year-old players weren't yet equipped with the capacity to elevate shots off the ground and so she lay there unfazed as puck after puck slid against her body.

"The coach was just screaming at her to get up because he was scared she would get her arm cut or her fingers cut," Ruth Murray relayed. "They were all pounding away at her and she's laying straight across the ice not letting a goal in."

Despite the ingenuity of her strategy, Sarah's time in net was short-lived. Back at forward, she spent much of her time fighting with her brother Jordy who is two years younger. Coaches became so distraught at their constant bickering, swinging sticks and throwing their little fists at each other, that Sarah was relocated to defense. It was at that position she spent the next two decades, winning national championships in high school and college and becoming the metronomic force for every team she played for. Her natural habitat, it turned out, was indeed on the ice.

"There wasn't whining," said Shannon Miller, Sarah's college coach. "She wasn't 'Mrs. Tough Guy,' but she wouldn't be a baby about an injury. She'd rather suck it up. She worked hard, she listened. She did whatever it takes."

Sarah Murray first gained a reputation as a hard-nosed, reliable defender at Shattuck-St. Mary's, America's top high school hockey program that produces Olympians and NHL players with the rapidity that Apple releases new iPhones. Murray played on a star-studded team with future Olympic gold medalists Jocelyne Lamoureux-Davidson, Monique Lamoureux-Morando and Brianna Decker. Although she did not post gaudy stats like her teammates and was undersized at about five feet three inches and just over 100 pounds, there was no questioning her importance at Shattuck.

"I was intimidated by her at first," said Sasha Sherry, Murray's teammate for three years in high school. "She had this cold stare that made me think she hated me.

"She was extremely competitive and slightly stubborn, which are two good qualities in the hockey world," Sherry added. "She was on the smaller side, but you didn't want to get stuck in the corner with her because her toughness might land you on your butt."

Murray also played for Team Manitoba, a top Under-18 youth travel team (she was born in Canada, but bounced around living between there and the United States, depending on where her father was working). During one game, Murray was knocked down and flipped over twice, causing her helmet to bounce off her head. But like a gymnast finishing a tumbling routine, Murray sprang back up in one motion, plopped on her helmet and kept skating without missing a beat. In attendance to witness this display of pluck were coaches from the University of Minnesota-Duluth, the three-time national champions, who later told Ruth Murray that after that moment they knew they wanted Sarah on their team.

After Andy Murray briefly coached at Shattuck and Sarah and her brothers attended school there, the family settled near the campus in Faribault, Minnesota. The house is decorated in hockey memorabilia collected throughout the family's journeys across the world, but Sarah always had interests outside of the sport. She wanted to study marine biology and at an East Coast college, with Maine her top choice. The Maine Black Bears women's hockey program has never qualified for an NCAA hockey tournament, but Sarah saw an opportunity to play on a top line and be ensured lots of ice time while focusing on her academic interests. Her father, though, leaned toward the pedigree of Minnesota-Duluth, led by Miller, a family friend Andy Murray had known from his days coaching with Canada's national teams.

Sarah knew at Duluth she'd be a third- or fourth-line defender and might not dress for every game. Thinking she only had four years left of hockey, she wanted to play as much as possible and for the sport to not be so much of a grind. But her father implored her that there were no benefits playing for a losing team; at Duluth she needed to force herself to work harder and earn her spot on a perennial contender. In the end, her father's influence swayed Murray and she committed to become a Minnesota-Duluth Bulldog.

Once again, Murray's team was crowded with Olympic-level talent. She found herself at the bottom of the depth chart, but after ingesting the game under her father's tutelage, Murray was equipped with a different understanding of the sport than most college players. There was a maturity she exuded that immediately won over teammates on a roster that had been in disarray the year before.

Jessica Koizumi was a senior at Duluth during Murray's freshman year. With almost one quarter of the team having left during the previous season, Koizumi thought about transferring. But the incoming class, led by Murray, reinvigorated her commitment to the sport. "I was really unhappy with the personnel," said Koizumi, who was raised in California by a Korean mother and Japanese father. "She, along with some others that were recruited that year, really turned the program in a complete 180 from the previous year."

Koizumi, now a coach for the University of Vermont's women's hockey team, saw Murray determined to prove her worth from the first practice. "I do think that could be attributed to her dad and his background in coaching, to kind of give her that sense," Koizumi said. "As a coach, there's a lot of times you have players that aren't necessarily the stars of your team, not getting all the ice time and glory, and they have trouble with that. They have trouble trying to be happy with the role that they're in. Instead of working harder and having the mentality of they're going to help the team, they have a different one. Sarah certainly came in; you could see she was one of the hardest workers. Every single practice or a meeting she was talking different tactics. She was extremely engaged and always a sponge willing to learn."

In her office at Vermont, Koizumi keeps a team photo from her senior year, taken on the blue line with all of the Bulldogs' arms linked. The only unusual aspect of the picture is Murray standing on crutches with a broken ankle. At the time, the injury was a crushing blow to Sarah's confidence, but it forever changed Miller's impression of the quiet middle child of Andy and Ruth Murray she thought she knew. After suffering the fracture, Sarah instinctively knew the extent of her ailment. Instead of coming to the bench dejected, she suggested concocting a *MacGyver*-esque solution to get back on the ice by fashioning a small boot and adjusting her skate. That is what they did in the NHL. It is what Andy Murray would have done.

"I was like, 'Oh, my God, I love this kid,'" said Miller, the head coach at Minnesota-Duluth from 1999 to 2015.

"As soon as they took her skate off, her ankle swelled up and her dad said she should have left her skate on so she could have finished the game," Ruth Murray said, laughing. "She's tough. I think being small and having two brothers, that just made her more tough."

Unfortunately, Duluth didn't have the same kind of medical resources available as an NHL team and Sarah missed the remainder of the season. Still, she finished her career ranking second all-time in games played at Duluth and won two national titles. Despite all of her intangibles, though, Murray never landed in the plans of Hockey Canada, the organization that selects members for Canadian national teams. For women's hockey players who want to continue playing competitively after college, options have always been sparse. The National Women's Hockey League was founded in 2015, with four teams in the northeastern United States. Originally they paid players up to $25,000, but that figure has dropped by more than half since. The Canadian Women's Hockey League, which was founded in 2007, only began paying salaries in 2017, maxed at $10,000 annually.

*Sarah Murray's grit and work ethic made an immediate impact in college and helped change the culture at Minnesota-Duluth.*

Without steady North American–based options after Sarah graduated from college in 2010, she moved to Switzerland to play for HC Lugano (Andy Murray coached Swiss pro men's teams during stretches of the 1980s and 1990s). Sarah knew, though, that she was playing on borrowed time. Semipro women's hockey in Switzerland was not a sustainable job—more like one last hurrah—and so she became resigned to the reality that her career was reaching its finality.

In 2012, Murray accepted a position to teach English in Beijing. Her parents did not want her to go and at first their worries proved prescient. Without any support system to fall back on and no knowledge of the native language, it was the first time in her life Murray felt vulnerable.

"I would call my mom crying every night and then she'd start crying talking back to me," Murray said. "We'd end the conversation saying, 'Don't tell Dad. Don't tell Dad.' Basically I had decided by Chinese New Year, if I didn't like it I was going to come home."

In Beijing, Murray soon stumbled upon a hockey league that enabled her to make friends. Pretty soon, China no longer seemed as overwhelming. Hockey had saved her and Murray realized how much the game was still a part of her. But a recreational beer league could not satisfy her thirst for competition. She could bide her time going back to Switzerland, where her brothers Brady and Jordy were now playing, but that path had no clear ending. Coaching was never in her plans, either, and she had no real experience besides helping out at a few summer clinics.

Murray came back to the United States in 2014 and decided to rejoin the Swiss league. By then her father was coaching at Western Michigan University and she could train there during the summer. Shortly after Murray returned to the Midwest, in July, her father was at the wedding of Spiros Anastas, a former assistant of his, and ran into Jim Paek, another old colleague from the coaching circuit. During the 1990s, Paek was a rugged defender with a flowing mullet that matched the zeitgeist for hockey hair at the time. Andy Murray learned that Paek, now with a cleanly parted look, was recently hired as director of South Korea's hockey programs.

During his adolescence, Paek occasionally returned to South Korea with his father and later helped conduct hockey clinics there for the small populations interested in the game. But after his career ended, he had largely been out of touch with KIHA. With pressure on KIHA to find a North American director to lead their Olympic push, Paek was invited to Seoul in July 2014. Inside the five-star Park Hyatt Hotel, KIHA wined and dined

Paek and offered him the job of revamping ice hockey in his homeland. Not only would Paek be provided any and all resources, but he could hire whomever he chose to help cultivate the men's and women's teams.

Paek had been coaching in Grand Rapids, Michigan, and was preparing to head back to South Korea shortly after the wedding. He and Andy Murray discussed the fork in the road that Sarah had come upon, and Paek mentioned how he needed someone to take over his women's hockey team. Within days, Sarah was sitting in her father's office at Western Michigan, interviewing to become the head coach of South Korea's women's national hockey team.

Murray didn't hold back in her ambitions, saying that her end goal was to try to win gold in the Olympics. It was a facetious boast, but represented the kind of vigor she hoped to inject into the program. Murray left, encouraged by the interview, and Paek told her they were interested in having her involved in some aspect, even if not as coach. Weeks passed without a response, though, and by the end of summer, Murray decided she did not get the job and moved back to Switzerland to see where the winds of life directed her next.

Those gusts stormed in rather briskly. Murray played three games in October 2014 before she received an email from KIHA—attached was a contract to become the women's team's new coach. She immediately left Switzerland and flew back to Michigan to shadow her father for a week and then boarded her first flight to South Korea, which had recently been the recipient of fortuitous news. One month earlier, Paek and KIHA had won over the IIHF with a presentation and, having fulfilled their assignments for qualification, were guaranteed host's berths into the 2018 Olympic hockey tournament.

Murray was exuberant over the opportunity, but her family worried. They frequently watched CNN and saw news of nuclear threats and missile tests coming out of North Korea. But

Murray didn't agonize over such boasts from her new neighbors. There were more pressing issues at hand, like molding a hockey program accustomed to mediocrity. Murray didn't even know what ingredients she had to work with. The clock was already ticking.

*Murray could handle any challenge at home, but moving to South Korea would present uncharted waters.*

Murray was about to enter a nation so futuristic and backwards, both wonderfully chic and yet weird beyond her imagination. In Seoul, posh hotels employ robots and elderly women openly spit on the street under the belief that doing so ejects the bad elements from their mouth after smoking cigarettes. As Euny Hong noted in her comprehensive examination of Korean pop culture, within a few decades, South Korea went through changes that most wealthy nations take hundreds of years to achieve, so that they still had customs like testing schoolchildren's fecal matter for internal parasites. "If Korea were a person, it would be diagnosed as a neurotic, with both inferiority and a superiority complex," Hong wrote.[1]

Understanding Korean dynamics was going to be no simple task for Murray. She was already intimidated upon learning there were adults on the team older than her. Some KIHA members not only worried that Murray, at twenty-six, was too young, but also fretted given her status as a foreigner (upon being introduced to the local media, Murray was nicknamed by the press, "The Coach with the Blue Eyes"). "In Korean culture, especially hockey, age is very important," one KIHA official asserted. "We were very surprised at her hire." Through no fault of her own, Murray was at a disadvantage before she even met her players.

North American coaches have had varied success leading international teams. Sometimes, the ability to connect to another culture never materializes. Then there are cases like manager Bobby Valentine, who achieved glory he never had in Major League Baseball when he directed the Chiba Lotte Marines to a Japan Series title. The idea of a foreign savior has been a common trope for Hollywood—the team that overcomes hurdles to become champions, taking on some of the Western flair of the outsider coach, while imparting life lessons to him or her through their customs.

Such a formula wouldn't be so easy with the South Korean women's national team, which was formed and operated under the most unique of situations. Spending six days per week with her players for eleven months of the year, Murray would be more than a coach. She needed to be a motherly figure; as the team grew, the right tone had to be found, being both stern and caring for two dozen maturing hockey players. Murray also had to traverse a tightrope, balancing the personalities of women that at times could be fragile, hardheaded, insecure, stubborn and overwhelmingly proud. She not only had to convey orders to some players who were older than her, but also younger ones craving to be treated like adults. Above anything else, the South

Koreans longed for a coach who respected them, whether they be Korean or Canadian.

Murray learned that previous coaches engaged in behavior like commenting on social media posts of the players, somewhat blurring the lines between being an authority figure and their friend. This was a convenient relationship since so many of the South Korean players came up in a hockey environment where elders and authority figures treated them like miscreants. But Susie Jo thought that the team wasn't always structured properly, a sentiment shared by Park Jong-ah. "I liked the ex-coaches, but they don't really teach us anything," Jongah said.

However, the style of leadership that Murray had learned from her father would likely not go over well with the South Korean team, either. Her experience around the game was positive, but if a foreigner came in and tried to undo everything the South Korean players had learned at once, it could cause chaos. The players surely knew they needed to improve tremendously in time for the Olympics to avoid a colossal embarrassment, but they were a close-knit group, some of whom had been responsible for maintaining the only women's hockey team in South Korea for over a decade.

After Murray landed, her first stop was a Canadian-themed sports bar in Itaewon, the Seoul neighborhood popular with expatriates and foreign military. The Canadian Olympic Committee and a contingent from Hockey Canada were there, in town to make their first site visit in preparation for the 2018 Olympics. Melody Davidson, a two-time gold-medal-winning coach and the general manager of Canada's women's Olympic hockey team, had known the Murrays for decades. While Davidson was already preparing Canada to try to win its fifth straight gold medal, Murray was equipped with the knowledge of her team only from a few Wikipedia articles and grainy video clips. Murray did not even know if her squad had proper equipment.

"She definitely was excited, maybe a little bit curious as to what she got herself into, what it was all about," Davidson remembered. "She always portrayed strong confidence. I admired her courage, a young woman just starting her career and diving in to coach the host team, that's no small feat. Sometimes naivety is better in those situations."

Afterward, Murray arrived for the first time at Taereung. One of the first players she laid eyes on was Eom Su-yeon, then only thirteen, pedaling away on a stationary bike. The sight of Suyeon at just over five feet tall stunned Murray. As she pumped her feet, Suyeon's large round-framed glasses constantly slipped off her nose and she simultaneously had to pedal while pushing her glasses back up on her face.

"I was like, this girl is not going to be good at hockey," Murray assumed. "She got on the ice and she had her big glasses under her helmet. But then I saw she can move. She can skate. I was like, okay, never mind. Can't judge a book by its cover."

On the ice, Suyeon is an audacious defender, a bundle of nonstop energy who will shove a player six inches taller than her in the face if she sees her approaching Shin So-jung's crease around the goal just a bit too closely. She has a sharp, accurate shot and knowledge of the game beyond her years. She's an anchor on South Korea's top line, a tireless worker who never stops pushing.

She is the embodiment of the way Murray was as a player.

"She has that edge not a lot of our players have," said Murray.

Suyeon's ability was a pleasant surprise and proved that there were commonalities to be found between the South Korean players and their Canadian American coach. But Murray soon realized her roster was deficient in surprising ways. Murray watched from the rink's aging stands while the team skated and observed many of her new players engaging in a peculiar act. In hockey, the five players on a line usually stay on together for less than one minute of ice time before replacements come in. The frenetic nature of the game forces player substitutions to occur rapidly while the puck is still moving—there are no long stoppages like in basketball or baseball. Murray's new team had yet to learn this one basic tenet of the sport.

Murray became concerned as she watched each player line up single-file during shift changes, as if waiting for lunch in a cafeteria, and then slowly walk through the waist-high door near the bench before allowing the oncoming players to reach the ice in the same slogging manner. At peewee levels in the United States, players are taught to hop the boards on and off the ice, to make substitutions snappy and to avoid penalties for having too many players on at once. Some imports later noticed during their first practices with the team that some of the drills taught skills they had learned on Under-12 teams back in North America. It also seemed that a majority of the South Korean players did not have the sixth sense of knowing how to read the whole ice and feel out where their teammates were with pinpoint precision. This made their appearance not only stiff, but quite rudimentary.

Murray knew there were certain principles she had to immediately instill, but given the diverse composition of the roster, changing the culture of this team was going to be vastly more challenging than doing so on a high school or even college program. Still, there were only four years left until the Olympics. It could normally take two generations before a country like South Korea could be expected to compete with European powerhouses like Sweden or Switzerland. It could take half a century before they even came close to competing with the US or Canada. The South Korean national team had still not won a single game in the Asian Winter Games even against weak programs like Kazakhstan and North Korea.

Murray's first inclination may have been to approach her team as if she were renovating a house from the bottom up. But there was a solid foundation to work with. The team was raw, but the players worked hard and did not gripe about practicing late at night for little pay. Many couldn't speak English, but they were eager to learn and were keenly smart. There was talent lying beneath their green exteriors. They could skate well and fast and already had a natural chemistry with each other.

Unbeknownst to the team and coach, they also had much more in common than they imagined, in particular sharing a burning desire to be respected. It was hard for Sarah to shake her father's reputation early on. Andy Murray had been the one to secure Sarah's job interview in the first place. "I really wanted to show it was me that got this job," Sarah said.

In March 2015, Andy Murray traveled to watch his daughter coach in her first tournament at the IIHF Division II Group A World Championships in Dumfries, Scotland. South Korea, competing with the fourth tier of teams, struggled in its first game against Kazakhstan. Watching his daughter's disciples labor on the ice, Andy Murray left his seat in the stands in between periods and followed Sarah, talking strategy beside her as she walked to the locker room. "She really had to kind of set up boundaries because her dad really wanted to help her," Ruth Murray said. "There was some conflict there because he did want to interfere a little bit and she wanted to make it her team. I'm sure it hurt his feelings because he just wanted to help. At first there was a lot of tension. I had to kind of keep him away from her."

"He wanted to get on the ice and do it for me," Sarah added. "He just wanted to help so much. I had to remind him. We had a big fight about it and then I was just kind of like, 'No!'"

As much as she yearned for separation, Sarah's father's influence was hard to escape. There were little tactics she found herself implementing, like setting practice time for thirty-seven minutes after the hour to keep players on their toes—a page straight out of the Andy Murray playbook. "My first year I realized I want to be super intense because that's my dad's coaching style," Sarah said. "He's very intense, very demanding, very hard. But you can't do that for eleven months for four years."

Over those next four years, Murray constantly tinkered with finding the correct balance. There were times when she perhaps overplayed her hand, like naming a new captain in place of Han Soo-jin, who did not speak English well and could often be stubborn to change. "When Soojin was the captain, she wouldn't necessarily accept everything Sarah told her," said the forward Lee Yeon-jeong. "Soojin would gather everyone's opinion and suggest that to Sarah. I think in Sarah's opinion the captain should be delivering the coach's message to team members and Soojin wasn't doing that."

Susie, a fluent English speaker, could understand Murray's instructions during practice, but she knew others couldn't. Susie is quiet and usually respectful, but also has an inquisitive, abrupt way of approaching people without tiptoeing when she wants to speak her mind. Wondering why Murray seemed so callous puzzled her and she worried how it might affect the team in the long term. Susie approached Murray about this.

"My first year I was really worried about them," Murray said. "I was very close to their age and I was really young and it was my first full-time coaching job. So I was trying really hard to make a fine line between I am the coach, you guys are the players, there's no intermixing. It was almost to the point—I remember Susie came up to me and she was like, 'Do you hate us?' I was like, 'No, I don't hate you guys, but I can't be friends with you.'

"I got kind of lazy my first two seasons because I had a translator attached to my hip," Murray continued, explaining why she didn't dive into learning Korean. "Sometimes players look scared when I talk to them. There's so much I want to say to them, and I do want to have a very personal relationship with my players. Sometimes it's hard to say with someone else saying it for you. That gets frustrating."

Although Murray did not outwardly show it, she had grown fond of the team quickly. Away from the rink, Murray missed home but did not have the same kind of struggles she initially encountered in China. She had found a chance to define herself, and of all places, in South Korea.

*Murray quickly became devoted to representing South Korea. Sarah (right) is pictured here with assistant coach Kim Do-yun (top left), and fans Christine Soojung Kim and Ryan Minjae Kim.*

# CHAPTER EIGHT
# Babos

One of the first people to email Sarah Murray to congratulate her on being hired was Rebecca Ruegsegger Baker. A former high school teammate, Ruegsegger Baker was working as a goaltending coach at St. Cloud State University. During her campus visit in middle school to Shattuck-St. Mary's, Ruegsegger Baker remembered Murray letting her borrow a jersey to skate with the team. Before the South Koreans made their first training camp trip to Minnesota during the winter of 2014, Murray, now back in contact with Ruegsegger Baker, again extended a hand and invited her to volunteer.

In the summer of 2015, Rebecca's husband Mitch, with whom she ran a goaltending school, was helping out at the University of Minnesota. One day, while shooting the breeze with the school's coaching staff, Baker mentioned his wife's recent work with the South Korean national team and how they were still looking to expand their ranks in time for the 2018 Olympics. With Hannah Brandt on his roster, Minnesota head coach Brad Frost knew her family well and regularly saw Marissa Brandt at home games wearing her sister's maroon-and-gold jersey. After Mitch passed this info along to his wife, it wasn't long before Rebecca called Marissa to explain the mind-boggling state of affairs that could possibly make her an Olympian. Lee Ji-yoon, the South Korean women's team manager, followed up with an email to formally invite Marissa to the annual girls' and women's hockey summer camp in Seoul, beginning in July 2015.

"It was surprising at first, because you don't really know if this is real or not," Marissa said. "I thought my hockey career was over and I was fine with it. Being contacted by Korea, though, it was something I kind of couldn't say no to. I hadn't been back since I was adopted."

COURTESY OF THE BRANDT FAMILY

*Adopted in 1993, Marissa Brandt did not return to South Korea until 2015.*

There are few direct routes from Minneapolis to Seoul, so Marissa had a scheduled layover in Dallas before heading to Incheon International Airport. Waiting for her connecting flight, the prospect of going to South Korea suddenly did not seem like the dreamlike scenario some adoptees conjure up when they think of returning. A series of questions began infiltrating Marissa's thoughts. She wondered how good the players were and if they would accept her. Outside of hockey, what would it feel like to represent a nation she had an unmistakable relationship with, but no emotional investment in? She didn't even know who was picking her up at the airport or where she was going to stay. "I was sitting in the airport just crying," Marissa remembered. "I call my mom and I'm like, 'Mom, I don't think I can do this.' I'm so scared and nervous. I don't know anybody there."

Despite feeling sick during much of the fourteen-hour flight, Marissa made it back to South Korea for the first time since she was four months old. After wandering around the airport, she saw a stranger holding a sign with her name. Marissa agreed to follow the man and for an hour, she rode in the back of his car, looking at the skyline of Seoul's high-rise apartment buildings that jutted into the air like a crowded bar graph. Just like when Shin So-jung arrived in Nova Scotia, Marissa did not speak a word to her driver, whom she later learned was the equipment manager for the men's national team. Upon arriving at her hotel, Lee Ji-yoon passed along a message that there was another import player staying on the premises and encouraged Marissa to say hello. But Marissa was still so petrified that she did not leave her room. "Of course it was Danelle, like, the nicest girl ever," Marissa lamented.

After her jet lag waned, Marissa was taken to meet the national team players at Taereung. It was like being introduced to class on the first day of school—if everyone else spoke a foreign language. "I remember meeting the team for the first time in the locker room and I was so overwhelmed," said Marissa, who spoke no Korean. "All the names like YeEun and Chaelin, how was I going to remember who's who? With the language barrier, I was like, I'm not going to survive here. I don't know what is going on at all. I have nobody to talk to. It was really hard. I really didn't know if I was going to make it."

Marissa wasn't the only new arrival that summer. Another Korean American decided to see what kind of concoction KIHA was cooking up for the Olympics. When Randi Griffin, whose mother is Korean, was initially contacted by Kim Jung-min, she labeled his offer as spam. As the messages continued to come in, Randi, who was then twenty-five, realized the inquiry was valid, but was not as gung ho on the idea of playing hockey for South Korea. Physically, she felt out of shape, having been away from the game for almost four years. Her conscience carried an even larger burden.

Much like how Jim Paek and Danelle Im's families sought to escape the dilapidated conditions overtaking South Korea after the Korean War, Randi's mother Elizabeth Heesoo Kang emigrated with her parents to Minnesota before eventually settling in Chicago, searching for the American Dream. But for much of Kang's early experience in the United States, her life was less than ideal, bordering on the torturous for the psyche of a young Korean girl trying to find her place in a foreign country. South Korean immigrants quickly developed a reputation for being unable to speak English and hoarding low-wage jobs, which created pushback in the largely Midwestern communities they settled in.

"She talked a lot when I was growing up about how kids harassed her, called her names," Randi said. "I think for my mom it's a pretty classic kind of immigrant experience where they want to pass almost this rage down to their children and, I don't know, use it to motivate them and sometimes to guilt trip them. Like, 'This is what I went through to bring you here.' That kind of thing. Almost anytime we got into some kind of conflict it somehow came back to her talking about how hard it was to transition to life in the US."

Ignoring the awkward glares and verbal barbs as best she

could, Kang strove to create better circumstances for her future children. While in college, Kang met dental school student Thomas Griffin. They married and together raised two daughters and one son in North Carolina.

Like many of her future teammates, Randi never took much to so-called traditional activities for young girls. She was enamored with hockey and showed a penchant for the game at an early age. Kang did not necessarily like the sport, but hoped that her daughter's talents could open doors to better education opportunities. "She even says now that sometimes she wishes she hadn't supported it as much as she did," Randi said, "because I was a little crazy about it and it was like this all-consuming thing for me where my happiness would ride on how my hockey career was going in a way that was a little unhealthy."

Although Randi was obsessed with hockey, it did not always create the most forgiving of atmospheres. Usually, Randi was the only girl whenever she played and she disguised herself in subtle ways such as tucking in her ponytail, lest she be treated differently. During one youth summer camp, Randi, as usual, excelled and outplayed the boys, even setting the camp record for the one-mile run. Later during practice, one teammate sidled next to her and asked if she heard that "some Chinese dyke" had won the mile race.

"I'm like, 'You mean me?'" Randi snapped back. The boy's face turned bright red and he fled in embarrassment. About twenty minutes later, Randi was sitting on the bench when the same boy, unsure of how to react to her presence now, spit on the back of her neck and ran away. The altercation was not the first time Randi was targeted in a hockey rink for being different.

"It was usually just people calling me Chinese," Randi said. "I've been called a chink a few times. Everyone just thinks I'm Chinese. People don't take racism against Asians as seriously because it's seen as sort of a joke or not that big of a deal."

See someone Asian. Say something Asian.

For Randi, the racial taunts from Americans weren't as painful as being picked on for being a girl playing a supposedly male sport. However, her race did lead to complicated feelings when interacting with other Koreans. With a white father and Korean mother, Randi always felt unaccepted by Koreans in the US. Whereas Marissa just simply did not like Korean food, Randi's family shied away from going to Korean restaurants because her mom could hear the waitstaff talk about her children.

"It was less 'I didn't want white people to make fun of me' and more I knew Korean people would never see me as Korean and they might even see me as something offensive because I'm mixed and sort of diluting the Koreanness of Korean people," Randi explained.

Despite her outsider status, Randi never viewed her genetic traits as handicaps. It was partially through defining herself as a ferocious attacking forward that Randi became such a strong-willed and resilient woman, confident that she could outperform almost everyone who crossed her path. During her teenage years, Randi attended national camps run by USA Hockey and was accepted to Harvard, where she joined the women's hockey team. A fiercely introspective and independent soul—she once lived in a tent for an entire school year—Randi was a rock on her college team, led by legendary coach Katey Stone.

Randi was all but done with hockey after Harvard and began studies for a PhD in evolutionary anthropology at Duke. But as KIHA's search for female Korean hockey players continued, Caroline Park's parents remembered seeing a fellow Korean mother in the stands when Princeton played Harvard. KIHA contacted Randi, who ignored their advances for over a year.

Randi focused on her doctorate, but friends and family occasionally tried to convince her to at least take up the offer for the free trip to Seoul. However, it was more than the authenticity of the offer that worried Randi. "My first reaction was that it was maybe wrong to think about playing for a country I didn't grow up in," said Randi, having spent years training with the world's best women's hockey players on junior national teams and in college. "Maybe it was unfair to a player who did grow up in Korea and also unfair to kids who are better athletes than me who grew up in the American system who don't have a chance to go to Olympics. I think about a lot of great athletes growing up that had a dream playing for Team USA and Team Canada and a lot got really close and didn't get there. I felt like I'm getting something that's sort of unfair and am concerned people I know wouldn't understand that and be mad at me."

Randi's selflessness was often on display at Harvard, but her other behaviors in college could sometimes be confusing to those not close to her. During one of her first practices with the team, the players received new equipment. Christina Kessler, another incoming freshman, remembered Randi taking her gear and immediately finding a pair of scissors to cut open her gloves and the knees of her pants, styling herself more like Sid Vicious than Sidney Crosby. "I think it was more of a grip thing and she didn't want to spend the time breaking in her equipment, but going about it in a very nontraditional way," Kessler relayed. "That's just how she was in high school and how she was going to start her freshman year. I remember the look on everyone's face when she stepped into practice in brand-new equipment just sliced open. Everyone was very taken aback.

"I think that's just a reflection of who she is. If she's determined to do something or get there, she's going to do what's necessary."

Randi, a blue-collar freshman with a streak of rebelliousness who enjoyed late-night debates and deep conversation, differed from much of the roster at Harvard. Much like how there were girls from wealthy families at CIH who took their status as carte blanche to tease Park Jong-ah and Park Ye-eun, many of Randi's teammates carried a sense of privilege that clashed with her style. Those like Kessler, though, not threatened by Randi's independence, became charmed by her enigmatic personality, including her infamous decision to live in a tent. Along with three other students, Kessler and Randi decided to room together their sophomore year. But their apartment in Eliot House at Harvard did not have enough rooms for everyone to live in a single. Randi, adamant about needing her space, pitched a blue-and-yellow tent in the living room, put her mattress inside and slept there the entire year.

"That was her way of having her own privacy," Kessler said, adding with a laugh, "It definitely smelled, that's for sure. I don't think I ever went in there."

"I could be a weird kid," Randi said.

Eccentric or not, no one ever doubted Randi's commitment to the sport. Kessler, who first met her when they were teenagers and attended an IIHF camp together, believed Randi was in the best physical shape of any player she encountered. In addition, she had very firm opinions on how the game should be played and what was the optimal way to deploy her skills, which sometimes presented a problem for Stone. At first, their strong mind-sets clashed. It wasn't until Randy's junior year that Stone finally began to understand her way of thinking; after that, she became among the most trusted players on the Harvard roster, the kind of forward able to withstand the pressure of a penalty shot or any big moment as if it was mundane.

"It wasn't always free-flowing dialogue between the two of us," acknowledged Stone, who also coached the 2014 US Women's Olympic team. "I think there were times when I probably questioned if I was reaching her as a coach. I think over time we gained a better perspective on each other and how to communicate well. It happened over a lot of trial and error.

"I don't spend a lot of time in the locker room, but I would hear from her other teammates that regardless of whether it was an act or a comment, that her timing was impeccable," Stone added. "She's really an observer. She's constantly processing what's going on in given situations. To assess certain things and when to insert a comment or action, she was really great at it."

*Randi Griffin was one of the most dependable leaders for Harvard's women's hockey team.*

Whether or not Randi could have the same impact in South Korea, given the cultural and age differences, was debatable. When Randi arrived later in the summer of 2015, she initially tried to stay in the background and not step on any toes. She was so quiet that it made some players wonder if she was a recluse. Having experienced a range of encounters with the first batch of imports and Coach Murray, the locker room was not exactly sure how to welcome Randi when she entered the fray.

Meanwhile, after her first few weeks in Seoul, Marissa had yet to feel a part of the team. Not only were there cultural and language barriers, but only six spots available on the roster for players on defense. Park Chae-lin, then a brash sixteen-year-old defender who joined the team one year earlier, seemed threatened by Marissa's presence, making her feel like an intruder. During team meetings or in preparing for practices, Marissa just sat in the corner staring at the players, not knowing what was being discussed.

Despite feeling uncomfortable, she never gave less than optimal effort on the ice, which gradually caught the attention of Chaelin and others.

"In the beginning, it was inevitable to feel tension because we played the same position," Chaelin admitted, "but after all it's a team sport and I saw how good Americans were."

Chaelin and other players began asking Marissa small questions, like how would she play against the boards in a certain situation or other tactics about positioning. Marissa began to understand just how much the idea of establishing women's hockey in South Korea meant to her new teammates and became determined to help. "When you're there, everybody's so proud to be Korean," Marissa observed. "It was definitely an eye-opener."

As the new imports slowly became accepted into the team dynamic, they still had to deal with assimilating into Korean life outside of Taereung. When they'd explore Seoul, their looks of bewilderment sometimes drew snide looks from locals. If Marissa tried to hail a taxi, drivers sped off upon hearing the first syllable of her speaking English, even if the passenger door was still open.

"The imports look Korean, but we are really bad at being Korean," Randi wrote in an email early in her tenure. "Consequently, we often surprise people in Seoul with our constant confusion, refusal to read signs, and inability to carry on a basic conversation. We like to joke that due to our Korean appearance, people must assume that something is mentally wrong with us."

There is a term for this behavior in Korean—*babo* or *fool*. As time went on, watching the imports engage in *babo*-like activity—which was virtually any moment outside of the rink—some of the South Korean players began to feel sympathetic to the position they were in.

"We started calling them *babo* because whenever we'd talk to them in Korean, they wouldn't understand us," Lee Yeon-jeong said. "We'd try to teach them, but they'd forget quickly. Then, Danelle and Marissa would be like, 'I am *babo*.'"

Like Shin So-jung owning the idea of "golri," the imports

began using *babo* as a term of endearment for each other. *Babo* was a small but potent way for both sides to connect to each other—particularly for Canada travelers Jongah, YeEun and Sojung, who could relate to what the imports were experiencing. The *babos* proved not to be all that different after all.

Though she couldn't communicate all that well with them, Han Soo-jin saw the imports beginning to make an effort to integrate themselves into the team. As a team leader, her thawing attitude was vital. Soojin invited Danelle and Caroline over to her house on weekends, where they'd cook Korean meals and visit Korean spas, and began regretting not studying English seriously in school.

"She's like a mom," Kim Se-lin, one of the youngest defensive players on the team, said of Soojin. "A very comforting person. If she cares for somebody and something happens, she worries for them as much as if it was her own problem."

Other players soon began following suit in showing more outward appreciation of the imports. Ko Hye-in and Cho Mi-hwan, two veteran South Korean players, took Danelle and Caroline out drinking and introduced them to blood soup, which they told the imports could cure hangovers. Sojung's mother invited Marissa over for dinner, where she and her daughter gently laughed at Marissa's cultural faux pas like not taking her shoes off inside, and then taught her about such Korean customs.

"I knew exactly how they felt," Sojung said. "They didn't speak the language and I remember I was supported by my teammates when I was in Canada. So while I'm not very expressive in my emotions, I wanted to be like a family with the import players."

As the imports learned more about Korea and the South Korean players absorbed information about hockey from them in return, a common thread began to become apparent to both sides. In the end, they were all young Korean women who simply strove for the same thing: acceptance.

# CHAPTER NINE
## The Boy Crying Wolf

In the summer of 2016, a motion picture hit South Korean theaters based on the country's early women's hockey teams. *Run-Off** was a feel-good, underdog tale that showed the strength of teamwork in overcoming adversity and the emotional pain suffered from separation and implicit feelings.

The main character, played by popular Korean actress Soo Ae, was loosely drawn from the story of Hwangbo Young, a North Korean hockey player who escaped in 1997, when her family of seven snuck into China via the frigid waters of the Tumen River near the northern border of North Korea. When they defected to South Korea in 1999, Young was asked to join the nascent national team program, which had been formed only one year earlier, patched together from a mishmash of former athletes— basically any woman KIHA could find with ice skates. "People would say you can become a member of the national team as long as you have the gear," Han Soo-jin said.

---

* Also known as *Take Off 2* in English, named after an unrelated film about Korean ski jumpers.

In the film, Soo Ae's sister is left behind when her family flees. During the penultimate scene, North and South Korea square off at the Asian Winter Games and Soo Ae sees her sibling for the first time on the opposing team. However, Soo Ae's former linemates receive her frigidly and they spurn her hand during pregame handshakes, an event that actually happened to Young in 2003 (Young's sister did not play for North Korea, however.) After the game, Soo Ae chases after her sister in the airport. She hands her a box of Choco pies, their favorite childhood treat, and they share tears while saying goodbye. *Run-Off* ends with Soo Ae at the face-off circle in a game the following year and looking up to see her sister across from her, smiling.

The symbolism made many audiences weep. But given the history between the two nations and North Korea's sudden aggression, defiantly showing off its militaristic force under Kim Jong-un and testing ballistic missiles throughout the summer of 2016, the implied meaning of togetherness between North and South seemed only possible in the movies.

"It's a fairy-tale-like story that we really need right now," Soo Ae said of the film, adding that she hoped it "will have a healing effect"[1] for the increased tension on the peninsula.

Before Sarah Murray, North Korea regularly bullied South Korea just like every other women's hockey team in Asia. During Lee Kyou-son's first Asian Winter Games in 2003, opponents didn't bother warming up before playing South Korea. When Kazakhstan led them 19–0 after two periods and South Korea did not come out for the third period due to a dispute with referees, the Kazakh team cursed vehemently at the officials since goal differentials helped decide tiebreakers in the tournament standings and they wanted to run up the score as much as possible.

However, North Korea often showed a sliver of sympathy while storming the South Korean net with goals. That was not lost on the players who stayed through two generations of the national team. When the two sides met at the Asian Winter Games in 2007 and 2011, North Korea won both contests relatively easily, 5–0 and 6–1. Soojin noticed that her opponents did not seem to be trying their hardest and sensed they were trying to help South Korea save face. "They went easier on us," Kyousun remembered. "Even if they could score directly, they would pass around a little bit to waste some time."

In their limited interaction together away from the ice, the North Koreans were not as cordial. At the 2007 Asian Winter Games in Changchun, China, Cho Mi-hwan, then only eleven, recalled briefly seeing members of the North Korean team before a game. "Their faces never had any emotions and we couldn't even make eye contact," Mihwan said. "Although we speak the same language and we're the same people, it felt as if they were from a completely different country and simply unapproachable. So it was scary to face them during a match and I was convinced that we could never become close to each other."

Ko Hye-in, then only twelve years old, stood in line one day with some North Korean players in the dining hall in Changchun and had a similarly uneasy encounter. "I told the North Korean player in front of me, 'Please, go first,'" Hyein said. "She was a younger player and in front there was an older player who yelled at her, 'Don't listen to her!' That really terrified me."

The South Korean players could not figure out why North Korea was so forgiving of their neighbors' lack of hockey experience, yet so chilly in person. The team did not know much about North Korea as a country at all. One day over lunch, Lee Min-ji relayed to the imports a popular rumor that former North Korean leader Kim Jong-il had been quite the women's hockey fan, an eccentric taste along with his affection for Hennessey cognac and collecting a movie library of over 20,000 VHS tapes.[2] Kim Jong-il, Minji relayed, enthusiastically provided financial support to his country's women's hockey team until his death in 2011. Other players believed North Korea only showed interest in women's hockey because the country's leaders could boost their confidence by regularly beating their Korean rivals.

Both theories may have held some validity. Before South Korea formed a national team and emerged as a foe, it appears North Korea's hockey conditions were extremely dire. While in the program, Hwangbo Young's training began at 5:30 a.m., six days a week, while also being tasked with doing the chores of older teammates. In whatever spare time they had, Young and other junior players sewed their own underwear from scraps of cloth they found. They practiced without the luxury of Zambonis, manually coating the ice with tanks of water, and had to utilize one outhouse, which in the winter became frozen with overflowing feces.[3]

Canadian Scott Howe is one of the few people outside of North Korea with an inkling of knowledge of the sport's history there. After traveling to North Korea with a voluntary non-governmental organization in 2014, he created the Howe International Friendship League, a goodwill organization based around sports. In 2016, Howe began making hockey trips to Pyongyang, the capital city where North Korea's men's and women's national teams were based.

According to Howe, there are two ice rinks in Pyongyang— the women's team's official arena is equipped with a weight room and even a museum archiving the country's hockey history. Howe observed photographs on display labeled from as far back as the 1910s, featuring missionaries and expatriate groups playing games in what is now North Korea. Traditionally, the best players hail from north of Pyongyang, where the weather is colder and makeshift outdoor rinks can be crafted. As a player reaches adulthood, they may be invited to try out for the national team, which often means a better quality of life.

"They get looked after well and their family gets looked after well," Howe said, adding that a national team member can sometimes be given an apartment and car in Pyongyang. "Any chance to improve, they take it seriously. I would say even more so with the women than the men."

Still, life on North Korea's women's hockey team is far from paradise. Because the Pyongyang rinks must be shared with speed skaters and figure skaters, the players' days began early in the morning for practices, followed by dry land training and then a night session. Few North Koreans are aware the team even exists. Howe noted the women's players as eager to learn and fast, but at an obvious disadvantage. Sanctions forced the team to train with lower-grade or older equipment—at some international tournaments the North Koreans borrowed newer models and had to return them before departure. "We don't do it, but sometimes a visiting delegation will leave equipment behind and ask people to look the other way," Howe said.

Since Howe's annual trips are based around goodwill, friendship and peacebuilding, it is possible that some of what he witnessed in Pyongyang was staged, although the reality for women's hockey players in North Korea is likely not as harsh as during Young's days on the team in the 1990s. But after the death of Kim Jong-il, it appears the interest in women's hockey in North Korea, at least from people in positions of power, declined.

By the time the two Koreas met at the 2016 IIHF Division II Group A World Championship, their first game since 2011, North Korean hockey was trending downward, while South Korea was reaching unprecedented heights two years into Murray's tenure. Shin So-jung and the girls attending boarding schools were showing vast improvement after playing in Canada, and the team benefitted from seasonal trips to the United States, where they received specialized training and scrimmaged against local colleges, competition light-years ahead of what was available at home.

South Korea finally defeated North Korea, 4-1, at the game

in Bled, Slovenia, led by an assist and a goal each from Park Ye-eun and Choi Ji-yeon. South Korea also outshot their rivals, 39–20. But while North Korea had clearly fallen in stature, they left an impression on Murray. She was still trying to coerce her own players into the habit of blocking shots with their bodies and was envious of the way the North Koreans didn't flinch as they threw their faces in front of pucks.

The Koreas were scheduled to meet again the following April at World Championships, although that game took on added significance. In preparation for the Olympics, Gangneung, South Korea, was selected as the host for the tournament, meaning that North Korea versus South Korea was going to take place for the first time on Korean soil. The North Korean presence did not go unnoticed. A local civic group promoting unification sent almost three hundred members to each of their games. The proxy cheerleaders banged inflatable thundersticks and chanted messages of hope: "We are one!" or "Go Korea!" They also waved a white flag with a significant light blue symbol—a unified Korean peninsula—and wore sweaters with the same striking geographical image.[4] "We should be unified as one," Lee Chang-bok, the head of the cheering squad, told the South Korean news outlet *Yonhap*. "We hope our enthusiasm can reach the hearts of the North Korean athletes and help lay the foundation for unification."[5]

In 2013, the United Nations declared April 6 as the International Day of Sport for Development and Peace. It was only fitting that the 2017 North Korea versus South Korea game fell on that day. Despite this harmonious background, the contest was played shortly after the North Korean government tested another ballistic missile, exacerbating worries throughout Asia. Amid the geopolitical tension, KIHA officials appeared moments before the face-off and approached Murray with a message of good luck, shook her hand and then pulled her in to menacingly whisper: "Do not lose this game."

"Hearing 'North Korea' was frightening during World Championships," Mihwan said, the memories of the 2007 Asian Games encounter still fresh in her mind. "But I was determined to win against them and the Korean people's attention was all on us. It was the first time that the stands were full of people. I thought, 'This must be a very important game. We have to win no matter what.'"

That a women's hockey game in South Korea could ever hold such significance was a preposterous thought just a few years earlier. But a near-capacity crowd filled the newly built ten-thousand-seat Gangneung Hockey Center for a once-in-a-lifetime event. In a special ceremonial puck drop, Kyousun and North Korea's Kim Kum-bok met at center ice with IIHF president René Fasel and Lee Hee-beom, president of the Pyeong-Chang Organizing Committee. Kyousun allowed her opponent to win and silently skated back to her teammates while Mr. Lee waved to the audience for an extended period.

South Korea was without Sojung, who was inactive through the majority of the tournament due to injury. With Han Do-hee filling in admirably in net, South Korea jumped out to a 2–0 first period advantage with power play goals by YeEun and Susie Jo. Lee Eun-ji, who at five foot one, 106 pounds, was the smallest player on the team, but displayed its biggest smile, added an insurance goal in the second period, and Dohee made twenty-six saves to secure the shutout. Afterward, the two teams lined up on opposite blue lines for postgame ceremonies, which began with the playing of the South Korean national anthem. At the conclusion of the final note, two men in suits walked onto the ice and handed both sides white cards, meant to symbolize the belief that sports can bring peace and make the world a better place. However, many of the South Koreans did not take away any added significance from the moment.

Some held them in bewilderment, not being informed of their meaning or the purpose for this improvisational act. Jung Si-yun,

Mihwan and Soojin fanned themselves with the cards, looking bored. Then an official signaled both lineups to merge. As the two Koreas cautiously converged, a delegation of eleven men and women in dark suits walked onto a red carpet that had been laid at center ice, to give further direction for a planned photograph. Once the crowd pieced together what was happening, they clapped and banged noisemakers as the group melded together into one. The game's referees and the officials squeezed into the photo, telling the players to hold their cards high. Jiyeon helped a North Korean player position her card facing the cameras. Once the pictures were complete, there was no chitchat between the teams and they went their separate ways. Only the suits milled around, shaking hands on a successful staging.

"It was just for the media," Jiyeon said of the postgame snapshot. "I think there was no other purpose."

Once again, the interaction between the two countries was subdued, although the tables had turned. Whether subconsciously or by plain coincidence, the sixty minutes of competition lacked the scrums of roughhousing and cheap shots that normally accompany the moments after a stoppage in play is called—a shove to the face or an elbow to clear space from an opponent. In the waning shifts, the South Koreans were coasting in second gear, not unlike how the North Koreans would pass around to help their opponents save face in contests a decade earlier. Upon heading to their locker room, North Korea declined to talk to reporters and many of their players left the ice in tears. Seeing this, some of the South Korean players felt empathy. Park Jong-ah hoped to share a few moments with her opponents, but observed that they looked too upset. "I wanted to put my arm around their shoulders, but I just couldn't do that," Jongah said after the game. "I'll try to do that the next time we meet."[6]

Unbeknownst to Jongah and her teammates, plans were already being formulated for that meeting to occur much sooner than any of them expected.

COURTESY OF SIMON CROSSE

*North Korea often showed sympathy for South Korea when they struggled to provide competitive games. Here at the 2011 Asian Winter Games, South Korean player Kim Eun-jin walks off the ice, briefly talking to North Korea's goaltender.*

In June 2017, South Korea appointed Do Jong-hwan as the new Minister of Culture, Sports and Tourism. Do was already a well-known, sympathetic figure, and he took over an office that had been plagued by scandal when it was discovered the previous administration blacklisted 9,473 artists critical of the government and President Park Geun-hye.[7] Do was a late bloomer in politics; he began in 2012 at age fifty-six, after leading a simple life mostly as a writer and schoolteacher. In 1985, his wife of two years died of cancer, just months after giving birth to their second child. In mourning, Do wrote a collection of melancholic love poems that sold over one million copies and gained him national recognition.

Do used his fame to push for education reform but was met with fierce resistance by old-guard politicians. Weakened by this conflict, he drifted into seclusion, focusing on his poetry and teaching middle school, only to reemerge decades later as a member of the South Korean National Assembly, where he advocated for increasing his country's devotion to the arts. Within days of becoming minister, Do, with his toothy smile, publicly announced hopes that North Korea would participate in the 2018 Winter Olympics. To achieve such a grandiose objective, Minister Do suggested forming a unified Korean women's hockey team, a shocking proposal that had never been broached publicly before.

The North's participation, Minister Do argued, would help promote inter-Korean peace during the Olympics and jibed with newly enshrined President Moon Jae-in's manifesto of pushing for better relations with the North. Days later, President Moon echoed Minister Do's sentiments in forming a joint Korean team, saying that sports "are a powerful tool to demolish walls and separation."[8]

Insiders at KIHA were perturbed with the development; it was the first time they had heard of such talk. While Minister Do and President Moon's intentions seemed noble, what went unsaid was that ticket sales for the Olympics were lacking and no real hook or celebrity athlete had emerged to drive attention to PyeongChang. Naturally, the IOC and IIHF backed the idea of a joint women's hockey team.

Rumors only intensified when President Moon and Olympic officials from both Koreas met at a tae kwon do event in Muju, South Korea, on June 24. KIHA told Murray to begin watching video from World Championships and to make a list of North Korean players she liked, just in case a unified team came to fruition.

Although the Koreas had collaborated before for athletic events, getting them together proved to be a headache. The minutiae—who would coach, how many participants there would be from each side, where they would train, which flags and national anthems would be used—often stalled talks before they ever gained steam. But President Moon, a human rights lawyer before entering politics, long held dreams of a unified Korean peninsula. His parents escaped the North during the Korean War. Serving under President Roh Moo-hyun in the early 2000s, Moon was a key proponent of the "Sunshine Policy" that aimed to provide aid to North Korea and hold dialogue on further collaboration.

Despite their antagonistic feelings often displayed in public, leaders from both Koreas have long yearned to be joined back together. Don Oberdorfer and Robert Carlin wrote in *The Two Koreas* that Kim Il-sung—Kim Jong-un's grandfather—had a burning ambition to reunite his country and that South Korean President Syngman Rhee had a messianic belief that he was destined to unify Korea under an anticommunist banner.[9] Kim Jong-un, however, had never publicly shown any inclination to bring together both Koreas, more focused on increasing the reputation of his sliver of the peninsula.

The olive branches offered by President Moon and Minister Do discomfited the South Korean women's hockey team. Although KIHA had told Murray not to discuss any possibility of a joint team with the media, her players were not given any directives and fumed to the press, who for the first time suddenly took a keen interest in their existence. "I find the idea of a joint team difficult to accept this close to the Olympics," Jongah, who recently had been anointed captain, told South Korean news media in late June. She pleaded with government officials to "see things from the athletes' perspective."[10]

Many of the imports, who had now joined the team full-time to train for the Olympics, fretted about the talks of a unified team. Dohee was the team's comedic personality, hiding behind corners or sneaking up behind unsuspecting teammates to scare them or jokingly kick them in the butt on a daily basis. But when the issue of North Korea arose, she turned serious and told the imports a merger was not going to happen. All of her life Dohee had witnessed grandstanding from the North—it was a Korean tradition seemingly as old as salting kimchi.

Dohee and much of her generation had almost become immune to North Korea's mood swings. In a truly millennial fashion, their response to North Korea could be summed up as *meh*;

whenever talk of North Korea came on the news, they put in their earbuds and blocked out the noise. Some players believed there was a less than 1 percent chance a merger would happen. "It felt like the government and IOC wanted to hijack our team for a pointless political stunt," Randi Griffin said. "But the girls never seemed to take the threat too seriously. From the beginning they said North Korea would never agree to it."

One of the first lessons the imports learned about living in South Korea was that the best way to continue on with daily life was just to ignore North Korea, as if the country were a schoolyard bully seeking attention. Originally, Marissa had worried about potential war breaking out, but found comfort in her teammates, who had lived through this dance their entire lives. "It's like the girls didn't bat an eyelash; no one seemed panicked," Marissa said. "If they weren't concerned, I'm not going to be concerned."

The current young generation of South Koreans surely sympathized with the reports of poor living conditions in North Korea and had heard the stories of smugglers risking their lives just to sneak black market video cassettes into Pyongyang. But they did not have the direct memories that their elders did of once being able to interact with friends and family from the North. Park Chae-lin hardly ever thought about North Korea at all before the talks of their players joining her locker room. Others on the team had developed subtle opinions of North Koreans, although none were glowing. Susie, who ironically was cast as an extra for the North Korean team in *Run-Off*, only thought of them as "oppressed," she said.

"Not so good, communist," Jiyeon added.

"Depressed and poorer than us," Dohee snarled.

For much of the late 1990s and early 2000s, Kim Jong-il and North Korea became a punch line to Americans, who only saw his awfully permed hair and heard the tales of him shooting 38 under par during a round of golf. In reality, North Korea was a country not made just for cheap quips by late-night talk show hosts, but ravaged by famine, starvation, corruption and torture. The nation kept hundreds of thousands of political prisoners in camps and brainwashed the rest of the population with state-controlled media, disallowing any information from outside North Korea's borders to infiltrate the regime.

*Susie Jo (left) portraying a North Korean hockey player, poses with actress Oh Yeon-seo on the set of* Run-Off.

While Kim Jong-il may have become more of a caricature than serious threat toward the end of his life, his successor was very much a wild card. Kim Jong-un was educated in the best schools in Switzerland and was a fan of basketball, especially Michael Jordan. He seemed to be cut from a different cloth than both his eccentric father and grandfather, Kim Il-sung, who, according to Oberdorfer and Carlin, not only had special fruits and vegetables produced solely for him, but traveled with a toilet with built-in monitoring equipment to analyze his fecal matter for any potential health problems.[11] However, once Kim Jong-un came to power, Westerners who predicted the new North Korean leader's appreciation of American superstars might lessen his pledge to communism were as wrong as those who thought Jordan could become a successful professional baseball player.

Kim Jong-un's commitment to strengthening North Korea's military arsenal became paramount. Changing the popular perception that North Korea's nuclear capabilities were equivalent to toy rockets, Kim Jong-un's scientists rapidly fashioned a successful cache of weapons. One of the more harrowing worries about Kim Jong-un's rise was the arrival of a new loudmouth in the international political scene, United States President Donald J. Trump. When Trump was elected in November 2016, his penchant for belligerent statements did not spare any targets, including Kim Jong-un. Never one to back down from a fight—Kim Jong-un allegedly had his uncle and half brother killed for insubordination—the North Korean leader responded to being called such preschool names like "Rocketman," by describing Trump as a "dotard" and a "frightened dog." With each passing day, they proceeded to boastfully claim they could wipe each other off the face of the earth in a verbal machismo contest that convinced many around the globe that World War III was imminent.

Despite all of the rhetoric, a September 2017 Gallup poll found 58 percent of South Koreans didn't believe North Korea would ever initiate war.[12] "Me and my friends would talk about Kim Jong-un to the extent of, oh, why is he acting like that again?" Choi Yu-jung, one of ten teenagers on the national team, said in an exasperated tone.

"I don't think our generation really gets the division of the Korean peninsula," Sojung posited. "Rather, we tend to think of the North and South as two different countries."

Underwhelmed with the idea of playing with North Koreans whom they felt no relation to, the South Koreans continued their counteroffensive in the press. Soojin, the oldest player on the team at twenty-nine, claimed adding new players would be like breaking up a family.[13] Susie discredited the idea that the North Koreans could even help the team, pointing to the widening gap in talent between the two sides, just months after South Korea's 3–0 win. The *JoongAng Ilbo* daily newspaper conducted a poll in which 95 percent of 1,182 voters did not agree with forming a joint team.[14]

But support from influential decision makers continued to grow. In early July, Thomas Bach, the president of the IOC, endorsed President Moon's idea after meeting with him in Seoul.

Murray, although instructed to not stoke the fires in the media, privately was appalled at the idea. "It is kind of insulting," Murray admitted. "It just totally takes away from what our team's been doing. To have the imports come in and have the players accept that and now you're going to add North Korean players? I don't know. It doesn't sound good. I keep telling the players because they get so stressed about it, don't waste your energy until we figure out exactly what's going on."

Previous instances when the two nations actually joined together for sporting events had mixed results. After about six months of planning and twenty-two rounds of talks, the Koreas finally agreed to field joint table tennis teams for the 1991 World Championship tournament in Japan.[15] That year also saw a joint boys' soccer team compete at the 1991 FIFA World Youth Championship in Portugal.

For the opening ceremony of the 2000 Summer Olympics in Sydney, Australia, athletes walked together under the white-and-blue unification flag (blue was chosen as a solution after South Korea wanted green symbolizing peace and North Korea nominated brown as a nod to its agricultural history). That led to other ceremonial appearances at the 2002 Asian Games in Busan, the 2004 Summer Olympics in Athens, Greece, and the 2006 Winter Olympics in Torino, Italy. North Korea also sent trained cheerleaders or "beauty squads," as they were labeled by South Korean media, to attend major sporting events held in the South. But the bright beams from the Sunshine Policy soon dimmed as more conservative forces won control of the

South Korean government and favored a hard-line approach to interaction with their neighbors.

KIHA president Chung Mong-won made assurances to protect his athletes, but conceded that his organization ultimately had to follow government protocol, whatever that may be. "We have to think of the nation's big picture," Mr. Chung told the press, perhaps not wanting to rile up his close comrades in government offices whom his family had sturdy relationships with for decades.[16]

Such a stance did not go over well with the players and coaches on the national team. Murray thought she needed three to four years to optimally and successfully train a joint collaboration of North and South Korean players. Behind the scenes, KIHA officials told Murray not to worry, though, believing, much like Dohee, this is what happens with North Korea. There's always bluster and no bite. They are the boy crying wolf. The unified team would never happen.

And indeed, just like Dohee predicted, after the initial hubbub, talk of a unified team quickly died down. The two Koreas somehow always seemed to contradict the basic laws of magnetism—on the peninsula, a North end and South end repelled each other, never joining together.

# CHAPTER TEN

# Boss-Ass Bitches

A bass-heavy beat reverberated against the den walls in Robin and Greg Brandt's home in Vadnais Heights, Minnesota. This sleepy suburb of the Twin Cities is the kind of town where children gallivant freely across neighbors' lawns and each summer, residents look forward to the annual ice cream social. Vadnais Heights presents about the starkest contrast possible from the nightclubs in Seoul's Hongdae and Gangnam neighborhoods, where chicly dressed twentysomethings leave directly from work to enter a world of fluorescent lights and booming music, ready to release their inhibitions.

Yet somehow, the South Korean hockey team transformed the downstairs log cabin decor of Marissa Brandt's childhood home into a VIP-only dance floor. Not only was there pulsating music, but the sweaty air of dancing in a confined space even came with the effect of strobe lighting, created by players taking turns flickering the light switch on and off in rapid succession. Occasionally, someone tried to escape upstairs to catch their breath, but as soon as they turned the knob and emitted the smallest sliver of daylight, the door was slammed shut and they'd be dragged back down into the shrieking chaos. Amid this ruckus, as lamps and family pictures teetered near destruction with bodies bouncing off them, Robin and Greg Brandt could not have been happier.

Two years after Marissa was first contacted by KIHA, the team was in Minnesota for a training camp and her parents invited them for dinner. After devouring plates of spaghetti and meatballs, Caesar salads and what was described as a purely Minnesotan concoction—a dessert salad made with marshmallows, fruit and vanilla pudding that the South Koreans largely avoided—Greg introduced the girls to the home entertainment system downstairs. "Oh, man, it's crazy down there," he said, chuckling and beginning to sweat, just barely able to emerge unscathed from the impromptu dance party.

Decades earlier, the Brandts had envisioned that by sending their daughters to Korean culture camp, Marissa would connect to her homeland, perhaps scratching an itch that seemed impossible to reach from Minnesota. Hannah, too, could learn about her sister's heritage, making questions from strangers less awkward. "When I was in the States, I didn't want to be Korean—I wanted to be like everybody else," Marissa said. "It was not like I was ashamed before, but I never really owned that I was Korean."

Marissa's feelings about her heritage are not uncommon. While every Korean adoptee develops a unique attitude toward their biological parents and place of birth, there come definitive moments in each child's upbringing that are sure to cause discomfort—like when that opposing player told Marissa to go back to China—leaving them to feel as if they only occupy a place in a no-man's-land. But after making successive summer trips to Seoul in 2015 and 2016, and then relocating there full-time in 2017, Marissa developed a different view of her birth country. "Coming back, I am Korean," Marissa beamed.

Being asked to play in the Olympics was an inimitable offer, but the fringe benefits were even more enticing. The opportunity was not lost on Marissa's parents. Robin and Greg had known many of Hannah's teammates on the United States national team for years. Whenever someone needed a place to stay near the Twin Cities, the Brandts always had a spare bed and breakfast ready in the morning. Listening to the South Korean team screaming and gyrating with joy one floor below them was an experience that neither Korean culture camps nor Robin or Greg could provide. "I feel like she maybe kind of walked away from it at times," Robin said of Marissa and her Korean roots. "She just wasn't that interested. This would give her that piece, kind of put it together for her and just have an appreciation for the country that you came from."

Before Marissa left her first summer hockey camp in Seoul, she and Danelle Im bought friendship bracelets for every player. It was a small gesture, but one the team overwhelmingly appreciated and kept over the years. Cho Mi-hwan, outside of occasionally singing and dancing to her favorite K-pop group BTS, was often solitary, finding solace in practicing amateur photography. She wasn't able to communicate well with Marissa, but was touched by the convivial trinket and wrote her and Danelle a note.

Thank you :) Marissa&Danelle
I will miss you
See you soon
I can't English well. sorry haha

Originally, Mihwan was vehemently anti-import, having been on the roster since middle school. "Of course it's necessary to improve our team's record, but suddenly bringing in imports meant that someone on our team had to be excluded," explained Mihwan, who normally dyed her chin-length hair blond or auburn-brown. "I really didn't like it. I thought I wouldn't get attached to them.

"But after going to places together and eating together, I grew very attached to them. I felt sad when it was time for them to go back to the US. I was thankful because they gave me that gift, although I should've been the one to give a gift to them."

Mihwan did not recognize that she and her teammates provided something to Marissa that could not be encapsulated in wrapping paper. When she returned from South Korea, Marissa told her family about climbing Bukhansan, the highest mountain near Seoul, and taught them Korean words and talked on and on about the food and music, particularly K-pop, which was devoured by the team in a fanatical fashion. In future years, when the team traveled to the US, Marissa eagerly introduced them to her family and friends, whom the players already felt they knew intimately. During one excursion in January 2017, the South Korean team watched an exhibition game between the University of Minnesota-Duluth and the Minnesota Whitecaps, a semipro team made of several US Olympians past and future, including Hannah Brandt. After the game, the South Korean players waited eagerly by the locker room area. When Hannah and her teammate Kendall Coyne emerged, in unison the team started screaming out, "Han-nah! Han-nah! Ken-dall! Ken-dall!" as if they were meeting with old friends at an airport. A few days later, when South Korea played the Whitecaps at an outdoor rink in Stillwater, Minnesota, Marissa joked with her sister before the game to make her look good in front of her friends. It did not take long for Hannah to get the puck in the open and dance past Marissa for a goal. Her teammates' natural reaction was not to console Marissa, but celebrate Hannah. "Marissa, did you see?" they exclaimed. "Hannah just scored a goal!"

The South Korean team adored Hannah—she and the members of Team USA were idols to many of the younger players—

and she was equally appreciative for what Marissa's teammates had begun to mean to her sister. One time when the Whitecaps played Shattuck-St. Mary's, Hannah approached Grace Lee, a junior forward who recently held the interest of Sarah Murray. "I just wanted to let her know I had a sister on the team and that she was having a great experience," Hannah said. "Since Grace was so young I didn't know if she would be nervous to go there."

*Returning to Seoul, Marissa Brandt, seen here atop Bukhansan with Danelle Im, began immersing herself in Korea's rich culture.*

The South Korean coaching staff first became informed there was a girls' hockey player of Korean descent on campus, because one of Grace's teachers had been classmates with Murray and kept in touch with her. During their first visit, though, Grace had a concussion five days before South Korea arrived and spent the entire week recuperating. When Grace returned to the ice the next year, she introduced herself with flair, scoring the game-winning goal in an exhibition match. The coaches thought Grace, who carried the confidence of an NHL All-Star, could be the perfect injection of bravado and skill on the South Korean team.

★ ★ ★

In the 1980s, Grace's mother Eliza emigrated with her family to the US at age sixteen. Her father owned a business in South Korea that was struggling due to the dire economic conditions throughout the country. An aunt already in Colorado told Eliza's parents it made for a good location to start anew. In college, Eliza met her husband, Albert, a Korean American who lived in Seoul before returning to the Denver area to work as a computer engineer. The Lees acclimated well to living in suburbia, but did not know much about the sport their youngest daughter became fixated by. "Neither of us were into hockey nor had been introduced to the hockey culture before Grace started," Eliza said in her gentle voice.

That meant in addition to shuttling her around to practices, Eliza had to wash Grace's sweat-stained gear, which did not mix well with the odor of kimchi, the fermented cabbage dish she regularly cooked. "I could not believe that girls could smell that way," Eliza said, laughing. "I had not smelled anything like that before. My parents who live here had given Grace a ride from the hockey rink to home once and my parents commented that for the longest time they could not figure what the smell was. They were so afraid that they were going to offend Grace to ask if it was her. They were trying to describe the smell, but it was so bad they could not find the right words.

"Even though it smells that bad, Grace loved it so much that she didn't mind putting it on again and again. In Colorado, it gets colder in the winter when hockey is in full season, so Grace comes home and sprawls her hockey gear all over the floor. Between the Korean food smell and hockey smell, oh, boy."

When Grace wasn't proudly wearing redolent hockey pads, she spent her spare time engaged in other sports or building bike ramps in her driveway. Grace clearly enjoyed living out a bucolic, all-American childhood, but in this realm her parents began to worry about her lack of connection to her Korean heritage. Whenever Eliza and Albert spoke Korean to Grace and her older sister, the girls replied in English. At one point, the Lees evaluated if they should continue attending a Korean church, or switch to a more American-style congregation, where their daughters might make more friends and understand services better. When they approached Grace with the idea, her answer surprised the Lees. Korean church, Grace told her mom, "is like going home." It appeared Grace still had a nose for the aromas of Korea, as much as she did for hockey.

Presented with the opportunity to join the South Korean national team, Grace's parents' ultimate hopes weren't that she would score goals or win medals, but like Robin and Greg Brandt, they wanted their daughter to gain something out of the journey she couldn't ever get in America. "Going deeper into the culture and learning the Korean history and how we came to be as a people, our absolute hope is that Grace can get a feel for it and prides herself as a Korean and of her heritage," Eliza said. "As much as she's learned about America and American history having education here, through friendships and living there and representing the country, the hope is that she would gain more of knowing the culture and political issues, and how far we've come from where we were."

The Lees flew to Minnesota to visit Grace during her first US training camp with the team and were invited to the Brandts' house for the team dinner. Seeing their daughter amid young Korean girls who may not have spoken the same language as she did, but shared Grace's passions and interests, was equally as resonant for the Lees as it was for the Brandts. At the end of the night, Shin So-jung put her hand over her mouth, overcome by emotion watching the Lees say goodbye, hugging Grace and then Robin and Greg.

Grace's parents were not her only family members smitten by her new interest in South Korea. Living abroad, Grace was able to cultivate a stronger relationship with her paternal grandmother, who lived in Seoul. As she turned eighty, Grace's *halme-oni* did not drive or leave her apartment much, but she mustered the energy to hail taxis or hop on the subway to spend time with her granddaughter near Taereung. "Before this whole thing started, I didn't really care about Korea or being Korean," Grace said. "That didn't really matter to me. I know my grandma that lives in Korea really pushed for me to learn Korean and to kind of come in touch more to my Korean side, but before this it never really happened. I was never really into it, just because I was always on a team with American kids, I lived with American kids.

COURTESY OF ALBERT LEE

*Her Korean parents knew nothing about hockey when they emigrated to the US, but Grace Lee quickly fell in love with the sport.*

"As soon as I moved and a couple months of being there I realized how special and cool it was. I felt definitely more in touch with my Korean side and definitely more in touch with my grandma because I understand now why she wants me to do that."

Eliza added that the newfound bond "means the world to grandma."

★ ★ ★

Grace was not the only import with relatives abroad. Genevieve Knowles, a seventeen-year-old from Vancouver, was added to the roster in early 2017 as the team's third goaltender and stayed with an aunt in Seoul. Living in South Korea also allowed Danelle Im to become closer with her older brother, Justin, who moved there after college to work for the International Vaccine Institute, an organization that works in developing countries to treat infectious diseases. Justin lived in the chic, boutique-laden Sinsa area of Gangnam, where players frequently met up with Danelle. They took her to fancy Korean salons and spent evenings together at cafés drinking Americanos or went to barbecue restaurants, talking for hours over the crackling sounds of skewers of meat cooking over open flames.

To Justin, observing his little sister embraced in such a manner was particularly meaningful. At home, Danelle was shy and not very outgoing. After college, when her friends from school dispersed around the country, Danelle spent much of her time in her room in her family's quiet suburban two-story house in the North York area of Toronto. However, in Seoul, she suddenly transformed into a bundle of energy and a social butterfly, among the most popular players on the team, willing to explore the city with anyone. Dressing up in a ceremonial *hanbok* dress decorated in red silk and white flowers or running along the Han River, she was no longer encumbered by the forces of fear and timidity.

It took much longer for Randi Griffin to become more comfortable with her circumstances. Although she eventually decided to join the team for summer camp in 2015, she still had a bevy of concerns.

"I was nervous about them sort of being disappointed in how not Korean I am and maybe having some resentments or something along those lines," Randi said. "I was nervous about just the whole concept about being brought in as, like, a ringer, a special person. I was worried girls would feel threatened or jealous. I was nervous about the fact that I couldn't understand what they were saying about me, but I was sure they were talking about me—like I'd hear my name or I could see they were looking at me, but I don't know what they're saying. That's a very intimidating situation."

*Canadian Danelle Im grew closer to her brother, Justin, and her Korean roots while living in Seoul.*

Having witnessed moments like when the Korean restaurant owners gossiped about her family in the US, Randi worried about acceptance not just by the team, but from South Korean residents in general. A few news outlets eventually picked up on her story and she spent hours translating all of the Korean comments through Google. Randi, however, was surprised that out of hundreds of replies there was only one negative response claiming she wasn't really Korean—that user was quickly downvoted and then attacked for his close-mindedness.

"That actually made me feel a lot better," Randi admitted. "They saw me as being Korean enough that they saw my participation as legitimate and appreciated it."

The fact that all of the women's team imports had Korean blood meant a lot to their teammates. They saw the men's national team being stocked with white players lavished with Korean passports and exorbitant salaries, and did not think that their motives for wearing KOREA across their chest were the most altruistic. Choi Ji-yeon described the men's team imports as "blue-eyed foreigners."

"I'm glad they reached out to people of Korean heritage because it means more to us and our families," Randi noted in an email in 2017. "Importantly, having Korean heritage athletes return to Korea to represent the country also means something to the average Korean spectator, which matters because it gets people interested in our stories and brings positive attention to the team and the sport. Koreans are curious about our family stories, our experiences living in Korea, and why we dropped everything and moved to Korea for this weird game. You can debate around in circles ad nauseam about the relative importance of genetics versus language versus culture in determining racial versus ethnic versus national identities, and whether me or any of the imports are truly Korean enough to call ourselves 'Korean,' hold Korean citizenship, slurp our kimchi soup, or whatever. But at the end of the day, if we pull off a shocking win against Japan at the Olympics, I believe Korean people will still feel that sense of pride because Korean people did that. And when it comes to athletic representation, I think that perception counts for a lot."

Shortly after her first trip to Seoul, Danelle began taking Korean lessons in an effort to better connect with her teammates. She did not become fluent, but the effort was not lost on the South Korean players, particularly those uncomfortable speaking English. After practices, it became a habit that Danelle met with Lee Yeon-jeong or Mihwan and they'd study Korean and English together. Occasionally, Han Do-hee tagged along for a special curriculum, teaching Korean curse words.

While the imports slowly dipped their toes deeper into Korean society, Dohee and other South Korean players had keen interest in learning about Western culture. The influence of hip-hop, street wear and American youth style can be seen throughout Seoul's trendiest neighborhoods. The imports proved to be a firsthand window into that lifestyle.

Mia SeungEun Lee was only on the national team for one year, but because she previously lived and studied in Vancouver, she became an instant target of curiosity for Dohee, a rapscallion who often wore a New York Yankees cap or one with the logo of Thrasher, a popular American skateboarding brand. When Mia arrived to practices with a full book bag that included an SAT prep guide, Dohee asked her to read words just to hear her American pronunciation. Eventually, thanks to Dohee, the team began calling Mia "Neutrogena." In South Korea, the skin care company ran a popular commercial where a model overemphasized each syllable of the product— "Neu-tro-ge-na. Deep Clean!" and Dohee constantly asked Mia to recite the tag line, which she obliged to uproarious reviews. With the prodding of her import teammates, Jiyeon frequently used American slang, texting the imports with sayings like, "OMG girl" or #YOLO—an acronym made famous by rapper Drake that means "You Only Live Once." Grace particularly encouraged the proliferation of American dances like "dabbing" in addition to the team's regular repertoire of K-pop moves that were performed prior to practices.

The imports also began forming relationships with girls not as interested in keeping up with trends in popular culture. Marissa watched Kim Se-lin spend hours playing video games, entranced by shooting zombies and criminals with a look of wonderment.

In return, Selin soon became comfortable dragging the imports to haunted houses, a favorite pastime, and Danelle and others would clutch onto Selin's arms as she guided them around a maze of monsters and ghouls.

The South Korean players understood that the imports were not coming over for the cheat code to Olympic entry. Yeonjeong, one of the early dissenters to the idea of their inclusion, appreciated that whenever she ate alone at lunch, Caroline Park always invited her to join her table. "I noticed throughout their time with the team they started taking care of our team members," said Yeonjeong, whom the imports came to lovingly call "YJ." The imports also didn't mind making fun of themselves for YJ's and others' delight. In her spare time, Grace traveled to Itaewon in a dinosaur costume to make videos terrorizing locals, clips that the South Koreans thoroughly enjoyed.

Amid their charms, the South Korean players, like any group of teenagers and twentysomethings, had their petty moments. One of the younger players, Jung Si-yun, was often left out by the other South Korean teenagers on the team. When Grace noticed this, she instinctively began talking to Siyun, despite her lack of English proficiency. "She's one of my best friends," gushed Grace, who enjoyed racing go-karts with Siyun. "I knew maybe she was a little bit of an outsider on the team, so I wanted to be friends with her. She's actually super funny."

Over time, this group of twenty-four women from America, Canada and South Korea realized they shared a common heritage and a pride in themselves that shuddered at the thought that they were undeserving to be in this position. Despite incongruences in language and culture, they each strove to belong, to cultivate a deeper sense of self in environments in which they'd never truly fit in. They had much to learn from and share with one another, about not only hockey but, more profoundly, their differing impressions of womanhood, ethnicity and identity. Seeing the North American women at work gave their South

Korean teammates confidence, and together they dreamed that they could actually change the future for generations of young girls in South Korea through their sport. The Olympics presented the perfect platform.

As the night wound down at the Brandts' household, Grace and Marissa sat at the kitchen table, providing another impromptu lesson in American slang. That night's tutorial seemed to take more time than usual to resonate. Grace paused for a moment, then explained succinctly: "So a 'boss-ass bitch.' Like us. What we're doing. We're all 'boss-ass bitches.'"

The South Korean players nodded in approval.

# CHAPTER ELEVEN
## Be Who You Are

An early-autumn nighttime breeze swung through as the team bid farewell to the Brandt family and loaded onto a charter bus full of sodium and sugar. When they had arrived earlier that afternoon, Greg Brandt arranged for a local fire truck to escort them to the front of his house, where the mailbox was adorned with white, blue and red helium balloons, and miniature flags of South Korea decorated the freshly manicured green lawn. After the team was greeted by about thirty of Marissa's family and friends, Bob Fletcher, the mayor of Vadnais Heights, read a proclamation dedicating Hannah and Marissa Brandt Day. The rest of the team was not left empty-handed; Fletcher passed out to each one a replica sheriff badge.

Lee Min-ji, with her high cheekbones and sharply curved eyebrows that gave her a look of knowing wisdom, did not have any need for a toy costume accessory. In visiting Marissa's house, she took away something much more profound by seeing the manner in which Greg showed affection for his daughter. "You could see her father was very proud of her," said Minji, who was born in 1992, just four days before Marissa. "When I went to the house and saw the photos and saw the way her parents were treating her I could see she was incredibly loved. My perception of adoption changed."

Minji had never met an adoptee before she became Marissa's closest friend from South Korea. The team knew that Marissa was born in South Korea, but many never broached the topic of her biological family with her. "In Korea, there's this perception that an adopted child is unfortunate because of the situation," Minji said, "but also maybe because of the influence of Korean dramas."

South Korea's history with adoption is not featured in school textbooks, so most of Marissa's teammates' knowledge of the subject was indeed formed by television. Cho Mi-hwan, a pop culture connoisseur on the team, agreed that most Koreans viewed adoption in a negative light, noting that adopted characters on television dramas or in movies often try to hide their past. Choi Ji-yeon added that the only time the topic entered her consciousness was when an adopted child became famous later in life and then was lavished with attention by the South Korean media. Such was the case with skier Toby Dawson, a bronze medal winner for the United States at the 2006 Olympics. One year later, Dawson met his biological father in a Seoul hotel, part of a live news conference covered by a passel of journalists.

As they became more comfortable around each other, the imports and South Korean players shared more than just slices of culture. Their conversations evolved to a point where they began to change each side's ways of thinking.

Many of the South Koreans were fascinated that Marissa had gotten married shortly after graduating college, yet still she chose to join the national team of her own volition. Having made such momentous life decisions at what to them was such an early age, Marissa's opinions rose in their esteem. "In Korea, when we think of marriage we think a lot of things are going to change," said Ko Hye-in, who was a year and a half younger than Marissa. "For example, you start belonging to the man instead of the family and you lose a part of your voice. It's also related to how prepared you are in life. Housing is so expensive and childcare is so expensive that most people can't afford to do it until their early or midthirties."

Hyein and Minji were among the few players on the team in relationships and saw in Marissa someone who could empathize with the peaks and valleys of dating. They also learned that Marissa wouldn't betray their trust with a proclivity to gossip, something Minji found to be a problem among women her age. "In Korean culture, if you say something to somebody, words go around pretty differently," Minji noted. "These import players weren't going to hear something and tell it to the Korean players."

"She's kind of like a mom on the team," Susie Jo added of Marissa. "She looks after the little details and all the players. A lot of the members can go up to her and ask her advice on those kind of things because she's married."

When Randi Griffin became more comfortable engaging her teammates, she also noticed a general curiosity about how life for women in the US differed from South Korea. If Marissa became a de facto team mother, Randi was the family's wise sage, willing to discuss taboo topics in Korea like sexuality.

"As they started getting more comfortable with me we would have these Q&A sessions where they wanted to know all kinds of personal stuff," Randi said. "For example, some of them were very, very curious about being gay. They asked me about that and asked me questions I would be very offended about if anyone here asked me, but because it was them and I realized they probably never met a gay person before—their questions were completely genuine because they never thought about this and they don't come from a place where people talk about that."

Through their late-night chats, Randi also began to realize

the extent of South Korea's strict societal and family mandates, observing that "the pressure for women in Korea to be feminine and submissive feels much more oppressive than it does in the US." Over time, Randi sensed a simmering desire to push back against such conventions, even though her teammates may not have known exactly how to do so yet.

During these intimate conversations, players became comfortable diving into deeper emotional waters with the imports, who provided a sympathetic ear that was not always easy to find. One day, Randi was lounging on her bed when she was taken aback by a random question from her roommate, Park Ye-eun. "Out of the blue we're just sitting there and she's like, 'Do you ever feel sad for no reason?'" Randi recounted. "I'm like, 'Yeah, sometimes. Do you?'"

"Always," YeEun replied.

YeEun explained to Randi how being with the team, immersed in the ritual and structure that hockey created, mollified her bouts of gloom. As soon as the season ended, YeEun experienced the "postseason blues," which Randi knew of quite well. "You get super down on yourself because you don't know what to do anymore," Randi expounded. "You don't know how to have friends. She was talking about that and saying, 'Sometimes I feel like I'm tired of hockey, I'm ready to do something else but hockey keeps me from feeling that way. I just keep going, otherwise I just get really sad.'"

YeEun is one of the most intellectual members of the team and was born with the kind of natural beauty that South Korean makeup companies fawn over. She is reserved, but even-keeled and well-liked by all for her empathy. Behind that seemingly flawless exterior, YeEun, who is eight years younger than Randi, occasionally wrestled with sadness and overbearing expectations, issues that afflict many young South Koreans, but ones that are too often kept closeted in Korean culture for fear of embarrassment. But to Randi and Marissa, YeEun's melancholy side was nothing unusual. "It was always very interesting questions she'd ask," Marissa remembered. "She has a lot of friends and you would never think that would come out of her. I think the pressure got to her a lot."

Kim Se-lin, although four years younger than YeEun, has always been quite adept at reading social situations. While spending a year in Canada during high school, she observed the open and casual banter her classmates engaged in, and could understand why YeEun felt more comfortable talking in-depth to girls not raised in South Korea. "I think it's true when something bad happens to someone, people around them when they hear about it, they exaggerate the story and also view the person negatively whether it's true or not," Selin said. "So it makes the person hide what struggles they're going through."

YeEun occasionally dabbled in discussing her personal concerns with older players, but not to the extent she did with the imports. "Randi and Marissa, I got the feeling were much more open-minded and they wouldn't view me negatively," YeEun said. "I don't really talk to the younger girls about it because I don't want to burden them. Randi and Marissa felt like older sisters to me that I could just open up to. In Korea, in general I do think people are a bit pessimistic about revealing their weaker and negative sides. People are generally more afraid of opening up. It's not like they don't open up at all, but only to very close friends.

"In America and Canada if it takes this long," YeEun added, showing a few inches of distance with her hands, "in Korea it takes a lot longer to get to the same point."

Before meeting Randi and Marissa, YeEun first realized that there was no shame in discussing her personal feelings during her second foray living in Canada. After the instances of heckling and teasing at CIH, YeEun was hesitant when KIHA asked her if she wanted to attend a school year at the Ontario Hockey

Academy (OHA). She had improved her English, but the scars of the racial slurs and stolen clothes still lingered. In Cornwall, Ontario, a small town whose hot spots for students included Pizza Hut, a dollar store and a Metro grocery store, YeEun learned that her experience at CIH was not necessarily the norm.

*Park Ye-eun (left) and Lee Min-ji (top) were able to open up about topics considered taboo in Korea to imports like Marissa Brandt (right).*

Kim Mongrain, an OHA student born in China but adopted by a family in Quebec, was assigned to a room with YeEun and Park Jong-ah. When Mongrain moved in, her dorm was still empty, so she spent the night at her parents' hotel. Coming back the next morning, she opened the door and saw YeEun and Jongah sound asleep, along with Selin. Seeing them huddled together on a tiny mattress like sisters, Mongrain immediately respected their bond and wanted to be a part of it. The girls often had that kind of effect on strangers.

Mongrain's first language was French, so YeEun and Jongah talked in simplified English to help her acclimate to her surroundings. Mongrain quickly fell in love with Selin's bright smile and flush cheeks, which always seemed to be stuffed with sweets, and the vigor with which Jongah—now known as Jojo around campus—always pushed Mongrain to her physical limits during weight training. But it was YeEun who became Mongrain's closest confidante, as they'd share their more intimate feelings during bus rides to away games. "Jojo was a little bundle of joy, very dynamic, curious and with a funny personality," Mongrain said. "Selin was the little sister I never had, would always seem to find the right moment to make us laugh. YeEun is one of the most down-to-earth people I'll ever meet, a friend to whom you could talk about anything without being afraid of being judged. We would basically talk about life. After a bad game I would sit with her and talk about it or if I had a bad day, she would be there to listen."

At OHA, classmates admired the camaraderie displayed by YeEun, Jongah and Selin, who locked arms while trekking in their flip-flops through heavy snowstorms just to hang out together at the local Tim Hortons doughnut shop, drinking iced cappuccinos and eating chocolate muffins. The Korean players' rooms became social clubs where Mongrain and others consumed Korean dramas and danced to K-pop videos on YouTube—a favorite among the students at OHA was "Good Boy" by GD X TAEYANG, a hip-hop song laced with an electronic dance music beat that reached number one on *Billboard*'s World Digital Songs chart. Girls even began sneaking into YeEun and Jongah's room after curfew to finish watching South Korean movies.

Selin also quickly became quite popular. One of the first people she met at OHA was Hanna Rose, a gregarious girl from upstate New York. Selin had less experience speaking English and was extremely shy at first. Recognizing this, Rose took Selin to shoot hoops or coerced her into acts of mischief, stealing friends' phones or throwing objects at other players from the back of the bus and then hiding behind their seats. Developing a streak of cheekiness, it was not long before Selin established a knack to inject inappropriate comments with perfect timing.

In history class, Rose occasionally asked Selin if she needed assistance with the lessons, to which Selin would slowly extend her index finger to pull Rose closer, lean over and whisper, "I have no idea what the hell I am doing," causing Rose to burst into laughter.

A favorite target of Selin's faux ire was Nicole Kaminski, a player on the older team at OHA with YeEun and Jongah, and Rose's roommate. If Rose and Selin were watching a movie and Kaminski asked Selin to move over or any other small favor, Selin often replied in a soft, almost soothing tone, "No, Nicole, fuck you," in a deadpan manner that would make Bill Murray proud.

Eventually, Selin's ability to randomly break up a room be-came legend around OHA. Rose and Allie Rodgers, another OHA teammate, played hip-hop music before games, and they'd explain to Selin some of the vernacular that couldn't be found in her English-to-Korean dictionary. One of Selin's favorite sayings became, "Fuck bitches, get money," which the team adopted as a rallying cry for the season.

"It was sort of a cheer they had and a way to get Selin to feel accepted and to enjoy being around the team," Kaminski said.

The time at OHA was also transformational for Jongah in that it made her life more colorful than before, despite living in a town she described as "just a big road with trees." Prior to arriving in Cornwall, Jongah had a mop-top style haircut and wore hooded sweatshirts. Teammates showed her how to apply makeup and she became curious about Western styles of fash-ion, dyed her hair a lighter shade of brown and gossiped about boys. Jongah also began to play a Western style of hockey that encouraged more individual flair, and she was named her team's captain midway through the season.

At home, Jongah once described herself as a "little chicken-hearted person," but her success in Canada, using the taunts at CIH as motivation, gave her the confidence to return to South Korea and define herself as a standout. "She was a lot braver as she got better in English," Selin observed. "Her personality became more outgoing."

YeEun and Jongah left OHA before the end of the school year to compete in the World Championships (Selin was still too young to play in the tournament). Their teammates woke up at 4:00 a.m. to say goodbye, and Mongrain promised to take care of Selin. "Their departure left me with a big hole inside," Mongrain said. "I will forever be grateful for all of the times we spent together. We made memories for a lifetime. No matter how far we are from each other, I know I will always be able to rely on them and I hope they know they can always count on me."

COURTESY OF KIM MONGRAIN

*Park Jong-ah, Park Ye-eun and Kim Se-lin left an indelible impression on their North American classmates, like Kim Mongrain, seen here.*

★ ★ ★

The way in which YeEun and her teammates were cared for at OHA made her sympathetic toward the imports. YeEun saw how a close-knit team could resonate on and off the ice. Despite apprehension from other South Korean players, she wanted them to feel accepted and not go through anything close to what she experienced during her first tour of Canada.

"In the beginning, the imports called everyone by their name instead of the Korean way of calling an older person with the term *eonni* which is *older sister*," YeEun clarified. "They broke all the rules and some people didn't like it, but I tried to make both sides understand each other by explaining in English and Korean."

Since YeEun lived near Taereung, she frequently met with the imports on off days, driving them around Seoul or taking them to eat at Italian restaurants for pizza and pasta so they could taste something from home. As the wall between the two factions dissipated, their desire to see each other grew even when apart. While on break from OHA, YeEun and Jongah stayed at Danelle Im's house in Toronto. Shin So-jung sometimes drove sixteen hours on the Trans-Canada highway from St. Francis Xavier to visit Danelle, too. One time, when Sojung's mother visited Nova Scotia, she brought her along for the ride. Han Do-hee liked to arrange video calls with Grace Lee back in Colorado. "I can't speak English at all so I probably sounded like a three-year-old, but I'd say things like, 'I miss you' and 'I love you' and she would say I'm embarrassed because my parents are next to me and then she would hang up," Dohee said, cracking up.

"The beauty of it was we had different people," Danelle said. "We each appreciated each other's qualities of being different. There was no kind of pressure to be a certain way, be who you are, and we just became a part of each other's lives."

Naturally, the team began performing noticeably better in competitions. Although a majority of the imports did not complete the process to earn their South Korean passports until 2017, their support in strengthening team chemistry yielded impressive results. Combined with Sarah Murray instituting overseas training camps and the help of Rebecca Ruegsegger Baker working with Sojung and Dohee in goal, in 2016, South Korea tied for first place in their division at the World Championships, only missing out on earning promotion to the next division due to having a lower overall goal differential in the tournament.

Their next major competition was the 2017 Asian Winter Games in Sapporo, Japan, where South Korea truly began to turn heads. They won their first game ever in the tournament, crushing Thailand, 20–0. Jongah scored five times and South Korea outshot their opponents 108 to 1, drawing to mind the way other nations routinely beat up on them during their early years.

The second game of the tournament was a much tougher task and arguably the most important, as South Korea faced Japan, ranked seventh in the world and cemented for years as the best team in Asia. After qualifying for the 2014 Olympics, Japan had been promoted to the top division of the World Championships, competing alongside the likes of the US and Canada, and were preparing for a run at a medal in 2018. For South Korea, Japan was both its rival and its measuring stick, even though it was hard for Japan to feel the same way, particularly after winning their previous four matchups against South Korea in the Asian Winter Games by an astounding combined score of 85–0.

The 2017 game started ominously. Less than two minutes after the opening face-off, a Japanese player cleared the puck from the blue line to initiate a shift change. Sojung went to play the puck from behind her net, but an awkward bounce off the boards deflected it back towards her crease. As she scurried back, Japanese forward Hanae Kubo lunged in and poked the puck past Sojung for a 1–0 lead. South Korea was able to refocus and over the next forty minutes clamped down and kept the game to a one-goal deficit, before Japan added two third-period goals to clinch the victory.

Despite the loss, many on the South Korean team felt that they now could truly compete with the world's premier teams. For Sojung, who was in goal for the most embarrassing losses in the program's history, including the 29–0 loss to Japan in 2007, the effort was heartening. "When the 29-goal loss happened, I actually felt more determined," Sojung said. "Back then our team didn't have proper hockey players—we had athletes from other sports. Our team didn't get past the defense zone. I remember thinking back then, in ten years I want to become a better player like them. After that game I found some joy noticing the decrease in score between us and Japan. Knowing we went from 29- to 3-goal losses made me feel really proud."

The rest of the team was also brimming with bravado as they prepared for their next test in China. After winning their first game against Thailand, media around the world wrote about South Korea breaking their eighteen-year losing streak at the Asian Winter Games, and outlets at home began covering all of their games, creating a temporary new enthusiasm for women's hockey. Players were shocked to see a sudden interest in their exploits. After beating Thailand, the contest against China was scheduled to be broadcast nationally, believed to be the first time a South Korean women's hockey game was televised. The players enjoyed finally reading about themselves online and in print; however, on Naver, the South Korean equivalent of Google, one particular antagonist kept commenting on articles about them, drawing their ire.

"There was a person whose nickname on Naver was Nike, and he'd always comment that China was going to win," Lee Yeon-jeong remembered. "He always sided with China and dissed Korea. So we decided to change our names to Nike Golf or Adidas or New Balance and each of us with our own nicknames talked back to him like, 'We're doing a great job. Don't diss us.'"

Injected with new mettle, South Korea climbed back from 1–0 and 2–1 holes to tie the game late in the second period on a goal by Caroline Park. With South Korea withstanding the Chinese attack, the game went to overtime and then a shoot-out. The two sides traded goals on their second attempts, and then Sojung and Chinese goalie Wang Yuqing each stopped the next seven shots, sending the shoot-out to an almost unfathomable tenth round.

China's Kong Minghui went first, approaching Sojung with a slick backhand move, but was turned away with a kick save in front of the left post. Murray then sent out Jongah to try and put the game away. Battered and tired, Jongah skated out to center ice. At the referee's whistle, she methodically skated to the left of the face-off circle, making a wide turn before cutting back closer to the center of the rink. Jongah then quickly cut right and then left, swerving in an S-shape before accelerating to the net. With the crowd standing, hushed in anticipation, Jongah chopped her stick in front of the puck and behind it, repeating this motion rapidly six times to throw off the goalie's timing, before letting fly a wrist shot that deflected off Yuqing and bounced into the net.

Before the crowd could register what had happened, Jongah's high-pitched scream signified victory. She looked behind one time to make sure she had scored and then floated toward the bench where Kim Hee-won jumped on top of her, Mihwan wrapped her arms around her neck and then the rest of team piled on top of her, crashing down like a pile of Jenga blocks. Together, the South Korean team lined up in a horizontal row, bowed and kissed the ice and then awaited the playing of their national anthem for the first time ever after a game against China. With their arms around each other's shoulders, they shouted the lyrics in unison. Choi Ji-yeon, unable to contain her emotion, put her left hand over her face and began to cry, and Caroline patted her on the head to make sure she was alright.

"My first game as part of the national team was when I was in sixth grade," Hyein said. "I played in the Asian Winter Games and I think we lost to China 20–0. Experiencing everything from losing then getting a chance to beat them, I think it's pretty crazy that one athlete could experience such a drastic change in a team's growth. In other sports, for other countries, it would usually be the next generation to experience this."

As the notes reached a crescendo and cymbals crashed at the height of the anthem, Hyein, Heewon and Park Chae-lin presented quite the contrast in emotions. Brimming with pride, they wiped away tears, smiled and coughed, trying to catch their breath from their uncontrollable crying. The Chinese national team even applauded in appreciation.

Two months later, after beating North Korea in the emotionally charged game in Gangneung, South Korea went on to capture the Division II Group A World Championship in resounding fashion, going undefeated and outscoring their opponents 21–3 in five games. After collecting their gold medals, the team lifted up Murray and the other coaches and tossed them in the air in celebration. Dohee sprayed the locker room with champagne. In the days that followed, players' mothers that still didn't know the difference between a power play and overtime proudly announced in restaurants their daughters represented the national team. With less than a year until the Olympics, South Korea somehow suddenly seemed like they were earning their right to be mentioned among the world's best.

The success at the World Championships was another kind of validation for Marissa, who had recently received her South Korean passport, thus making her eligible for the tournament. Just hours earlier, Hannah captured gold with the US national team at the highest-tier World Championship tournament in Plymouth, Michigan. Hannah stayed up all night and watched her sister achieve the same glory in her birth country. Originally, the South Korean players and Marissa herself did not know if she would ever shed her label as a *babo*. At the Taereung cafeteria, for months it seemed like she only ate white rice with soy sauce or chicken wings, ignoring more Korean dishes like *tteokbokki*, the spicy, stir-fried rice cakes.

Amid the celebration, Marissa had an epiphany. "It just hit me," Marissa said. "I remember the flag being raised and the Korean national anthem coming on. I thought to myself, 'Wow, I am so proud to be Korean.' That was the turning moment for me."

# CHAPTER TWELVE

# Under Pressure

On New Year's Eve 2017, a lunch was scheduled at Seoul Restaurant in New Haven, Connecticut, located just south of Yale University's campus. Owner Kim Sung-ye planned to close for the holiday, but when asked if she was able to host South Korea's national hockey team, she opened by herself that morning. "I can't say no because it's my country," Ms. Kim said.

Working alone and needing to serve thirty players and staff, Ms. Kim played the role of an *ajumma* down to a T, arranging six wooden tables together and placing various pickled side dishes along the row. For the main course, Ms. Kim served large metal bowls filled with *tteokguk*, a beef broth soup made with rice cakes that is traditionally eaten to bring good luck as the calendar turns over.

The team needed all the fortune they could muster after a demoralizing 4–1 loss the day before. Facing the Connecticut Whale of the NWHL, South Korea was schooled by an opponent that perfectly mimicked the physiques of those they'd encounter in the Olympics. The game was painted with chippy play instigated by the Whale, which rattled many of the younger South Korean players. The Connecticut roster was composed of mostly former college stars, and the seasoned skaters employed a series of wily veteran moves—throwing elbows when the referee wasn't looking and showing no restraint in pushing players down and away from the action—taking advantage of the overall lax enforcement of the rules by the game's referees. It was the kind of environment that triggers helicopter hockey parents to yell at officials from the stands, but here the locals ate up the ferocity like fans watching bodies going flying during a roller derby.

At one point Sarah Murray's players asked why she wasn't complaining about the lack of calls. Murray knew a game against Sweden or any other Olympic opponent could be this physical and thought her team needed to learn how to adapt to such a style. Finally, toward the end of the game, after Shin So-jung made a save and covered up the puck to stop action, a set of Whale forwards continued jabbing at her after the whistle as they had all afternoon. This time, Eom Su-yeon, the smallest player on the ice, skated in and shoved a Whale player in the back of the head, halting the fracas.

The girls originally wanted to travel to New York City on December 31, to take in the holiday ambience around Rockefeller Center and other tourist traps near midtown Manhattan, before heading to John F. Kennedy International Airport in Queens. But after the loss to the Whale, their bodies were too sore and tired, their psyches too demoralized to boost themselves into the holiday spirit. "I was tired of losing, and watching my teammates go through this made me feel sad," lamented Park Jong-ah.

After winning at World Championships in April, South Korea had gone into a downward spiral and had all but crashed by the time they opened their final American training camp eight months later. The team's spotlight was growing by the day, but so was the pressure to perform. Several exhibitions against international teams were planned throughout the summer, and with each loss, the tension among the players grew.

Sojung and other veterans long held a belief that the future of women's hockey in South Korea depended on their performance in PyeongChang. This became magnified each time a South Korean journalist asked them what the program's fate would be after February 2018. They did not need to win gold or even a medal necessarily, but they could not embarrass the nation. Why would KIHA, Chung Mong-won or the Korean Olympic Committee invest further money if the women's hockey team was wiped out by the competition? These high stakes became fixed in their minds as they ate, practiced and slept. "I would have nightmares," Sojung revealed. "Mostly about losing to Japan like we did by a 29-score difference."

In late 2016, in an effort to prevent such a result, Sojung signed with the New York Riveters of the NWHL, becoming the league's first Korean-born player. Similar to how she emailed colleges in the hopes of a tryout, Sojung contacted league commissioner Dani Rylan and sent a video highlight reel and résumé that bluntly proclaimed her goals. "I am the starting goaltender on the Korean Women's National Team, and I am preparing for the 2018 Olympics in PyeongChang and want to play with and against the best."

The NWHL not only featured several members past and present from the United States women's national team, but regularly scheduled exhibitions against Olympic-caliber opponents, as well. In a preseason match against the Russian national team, Sojung, in her first start with the Riveters, carried them to a 2–1 victory.

"When she was on her game, she was as good as anyone in the league," proclaimed Riveters coach Chad Wiseman.

Early in the season, Amanda Kessel became one of Sojung's closer friends. In 2014, Kessel won an Olympic silver medal with

Team USA and was driven to break Canada's vise-like grip over the gold, which extended back to 2002.

During their frequent discussions about the 2018 Olympics, even Kessel became amazed at the intense weight placed on Sojung's shoulders, which seemed to overshadow her own goals. "I can't imagine how hard it is," said Kessel. "On her off days she'll be at the rink. You see her put in all the work. She has so much pride in playing for her country. That's why she's over here right now, to train with the best people possible."

Many teammates became drawn to Sojung, just like they had in Canada. At the beginning of the NWHL season, the Riveters held a team party at Cadillac Cantina, a bar in Hoboken, New Jersey, lined with calavera skulls and other Day of the Dead decor. The 2016–2017 roster had a massive amount of turnover from the year before, and several of the newcomers weren't on the best of terms due to college rivalries that still lingered. As the Riveters tentatively stood in their different cliques, Sojung arrived carrying a bottle of champagne and one can of Budweiser. Sojung told her puzzled teammates that the champagne was for them and the beer was for her. It was not long before girls from Minnesota and Wisconsin began taking swigs together from the bottle, while Sojung quietly sat and enjoyed the atmosphere, sipping from her can of Budweiser. "She was just so happy," remembered Kiira Dosdall, who played defense for the Riveters. "I couldn't come up with a single thing that's not positive to say about her."

Unfortunately for Sojung, a foot injury suffered during the January 2017 national team training camp kept her off the ice for the Riveters more than intended. With less than a year until the Olympics, Sojung's body, which for almost two decades had withstood the workload of three to four careers, began breaking down.

Because she did not always have quality skates, Sojung's feet bent inward, which caused more pressure on her legs as she got older. "It was really painful," described Sojung, who also had ankle surgery in 2011. "I couldn't even wear my skates sometimes." Finally, Sojung received a bespoke pair to alleviate the soreness, but then in college she injured her knee and developed scoliosis. In one of her early games with the Riveters, Sojung also injured her wrist.

Over the years, Sojung repeatedly played through constant aching, understanding how important she was to the national team's success. It's surprising that the team did not keep her enclosed in bubble wrap. One time in Minnesota, the players were casually loading off a white passenger van. Sojung was the last person to exit and held her right hand against the door track as she stepped down. Not knowing that she was there, the team's trainer swung the sliding door closed.

"At the last second—she didn't even see it—she moved her hand back and the door slammed shut a moment after she moved her fingers," Randi Griffin recounted. "He turned around and saw what happened and looked like he had a heart attack. I think we all were processing what almost just happened, with Sojung almost breaking all her fingers and how much that one person if something happened to her would shatter our hopes of just keeping games less than double digits. I often had that thought about how precarious our lineup was. Losing one or two people could be devastating. If it was Sojung, I don't even want to think about what those games might look like."

With a mounting burden and a growing list of ailments, for the first time in Sojung's life, she became angry at hockey. Lee Kyou-sun knew that Sojung had a tendency to bury her concerns and not open up about her feelings, but as her oldest friend on the team, Sojung occasionally admitted that her love for the sport was waning, that it was difficult to be alone abroad and that she wanted a break.

Sojung's all-consuming pursuit of hockey glory worried those in her inner circle. Ahn Kun-young, her best friend and a former member of the women's national team, remarked how she seemed "lonely and sad" at home. Sojung's mother believed her daughter sacrificed "her beautiful twenties" for hockey, mournful she never had much of a social life or went on dates. Sojung also recognized her mortality as friends were getting married and being awarded salaried jobs, living much more stable lives compared to hers.[1]

*While playing abroad, Shin So-jung often questioned if she could handle the pressure of being the team's most important player.*

ST. FRANCIS XAVIER ATHLETICS/ SHAWN MURPHY

"My friends knew I was stressed," Sojung said. "They knew I wanted to give up and was just holding it through and trying to survive."

Kyousun (or "Q") was one of the few people who could truly relate to her plight. She first noticed Sojung as a child playing at the Mokdong rink in Seoul where Han Soo-jin fell back in love with hockey. Astonished by her skills, Kyousun had to find out the name of this preteen wizard.

Kyousun's career had also been battered by injuries, and by the time World Championships arrived in April 2017, she could no longer withstand the pain. Murray and the players saw her skill level deteriorating, a history of back injuries digging deeper into her physical frame, eliminating the spryness that used to be her calling card. She no longer was getting time on the top lines. Watching her play seventeen years after her career with the national team first began was like seeing a former great hanging on in the twilight of their careers—Willie Mays striking out with the New York Mets or Wayne Gretzky hobbling around with the New York Rangers. Kyousun's mother was a dancer and wished her daughter took up a more graceful sport. Perhaps she could have become like Kim Yu-na, whose magnificent sparkling outfits would have been much more fun to clean than blood-soaked hockey jerseys.

Kyousun's mother gradually accepted her daughter's wish to follow in the footsteps of her father, a former hockey goalie, but it was hard to watch her flounder to solidify her life in adulthood, instead always sliding around from job to job as she focused on the hockey team, where she was a necessary glue. Susie Jo called her the "big sister of the team and the one that holds the team together."

Almost two decades after Kyousun played in her first World Championship tournament, crying after South Korea repeatedly was demolished, she gathered the team in their locker room with a gold medal around her neck and made a speech. Though she was never a fire and brimstone motivator, a few players knew something was amiss. Her spine's decimated discs could no longer withstand the punishment. As Kyousun spoke to her teammates, she finally felt a relief that she hadn't in years.

"I'm retired," Kyousun, at thirty-two years old, announced. "I'm graduating from the national team. This is my last game."

The euphoria that had led the players to toss their coaches in the air moments earlier was now replaced by the sorrowful feeling of loss. The team enveloped Kyousun in a group hug and cried, paying their respects to their captain.

Kyousun did not know what to do next, but Murray demanded to KIHA that she remain with the team and hassled officials until they agreed to add a video coordinator position on the coaching staff. Kyousun and her teammates were elated that she could participate in the Olympics in some capacity, but it was hard not to feel a tinge of sadness watching her walk up dozens of flights of stairs to perch herself in solitude atop an arena, guiding the drag control handle of a small camcorder and not a hockey stick.

"I desperately wanted to participate in the Olympics," Kyousun said. "But I was mentally distressed because of my injury. I was in pain to the point where I couldn't stand up. I knew if I could continue for one more year I might have to back out if my injury came back. I would be taking somebody else's opportunity to play."

During South Korea's first game in 2018, at Minnesota State University, Mankato, Kyousun fretted as she watched her team struggle, falling into a quick 2–0 deficit. It ate at her, unable to march down to the locker room and lace up her skates, instead only being able to imagine what spots on the ice she could be filling if only her body had allowed her. Kyousun noticed an ennui in the team and did not understand the cause. After the game was over, a 3–0 loss, Kyousun could only stand in silence as the rest of the coaching staff ripped into the players for another poor effort. Their schedule did not get any easier. The next game on January 5 was against Minnesota-Duluth, the five-time NCAA champions and Murray's alma mater.

During their January 2017 training camp, South Korea made their first trip to Duluth's AMSOIL Arena for the exhibition game between the Minnesota-Duluth Bulldogs and the Minnesota Whitecaps. Traveling from their hotel through the Duluth Skywalk—an aboveground enclosed passageway that avoids the winter cold—they stepped foot into the new seven-thousand-seat facility that was similar in size to the venues to be used for ice hockey at the 2018 Winter Olympics, and immediately pulled out their cell phones to capture the immensity of the arena. After having their tickets collected, the team rushed down to their seats to watch the Whitecaps warm up. Lee Yeon-jeong walked all the way to the front row and stuck her cell phone against the glass to record the entire game.

*Lee Kyou-sun (right) struggled to adjust to retirement, pining to still be able to play.*

Murray always yearned for her team to be exposed to the highest levels of women's hockey, the kind of competition they'd meet in PyeongChang. Among the Whitecaps' stars were Hannah Brandt and the Lamoureux twins, Murray's teammates at Shattuck, and both two-time Olympic silver medalists. Inside the arena, photos of the Bulldogs' national championship teams decorated the arena walls. Scanning them like a *Where's Waldo?* puzzle, the South Koreans searched for Murray, joyously giggling and yelling her name when they found her. Later, during one stoppage in play, the arena scoreboard showed Murray and a message proudly proclaimed the former alum as the coach of the South Korean national team. Murray, sitting with her knees up to her chest, blushed and put her hands over her face.

The next time Murray entered AMSOIL in January 2018, she could not evade being the center of attention. Several local newspapers were on hand for South Korea's practices, ready to write about the former Bulldog with the unorthodox path to the Olympics. The familiarity with the environment seemed to relax the team. When the players arrived at the arena to drop off their gear, Duluth was in the middle of a practice. Kim Selin and others pressed their faces against the glass, looking to find Allie Rodgers, their friend from OHA who now suited up for the Bulldogs.

South Korea played a tight game against Minnesota-Duluth, buoyed by a sterling performance in net by Sojung. Losing 3–0 was not fully encouraging, but against the toughest team they would face before the Olympics, just one year after walking into the same arena with the wide-eyed look of children visiting Disney World, it was a sign that South Korea was slowly headed in the right direction.

However, losing their next game against Wisconsin-River Falls, an NCAA Division III program that on paper looked like a clearly beatable team, sent the team careening into an abyss.

Prior to each game, Murray and assistant coaches Kim Doyun and Rebecca Ruegsegger Baker entered the stands to watch the opposing team warm up. Inside River Falls' small barn-like rink, Doyun, a former player on South Korea's men's national team, needed only a few minutes to evaluate his opponent for the day before he hastily announced, "This team is fucking awful." That message was relayed in the locker room during a fiery speech, with Doyun expecting his players to respond with a blowout.

"Honestly, I think Doyun would say that more often than

he probably should," Marissa said. "You never want to underestimate any team."

That is exactly what Doyun's players did, though. South Korea took the scouting report as liberty to play more flashily, with more panache—more selfishly. Instead of setting up teammates, they took on two or three defenders at a time, trying to create highlights. The first goal of the game came on a sequence that drew "ooohs" from the River Falls crowd. On a power play, Jongah skated up the left side of the zone and behind River Falls' net. As the defense trailed Jongah, Han Soo-jin followed behind them. Jongah then flicked a no-look pass behind her as Soojin reached the left goalpost, and she easily slung the puck past the River Falls goalie still trying to follow Jongah's path.

This only inspired South Korea to further deviate from their systems, and the offense turned sloppy. Sojung was given the night off and River Falls rattled off four unanswered goals against Han Do-hee. With one game left on their pre-Olympic tour of the US, South Korea remained winless.

"I was, like, 'What's going to happen at the Olympics if we can't turn it on here?'" Murray worried. "'This is terrifying.'"

# CHAPTER THIRTEEN
## Lost and Found

Moments before her team scuttled out of their locker room, Sarah Murray paced around the bowels of Mars Lakeview Arena. Mars is a small, dated rink in Duluth, Minnesota, that seats a few hundred spectators and has a concession stand that sells hot chocolate in plain cups. In January 2017, Murray had scheduled a slate of games against small NCAA Division III programs, and today's host was the College of St. Scholastica. The St. Scholastica Saints were incomparable to the teams joining South Korea in PyeongChang, but Murray was not worrying about the level of competition at the moment. Staring out at the empty ice, Murray began sweating.

In South Korea's previous game, she noticed her players did not burst onto the ice for warm-ups, which gave off the appearance of a novice unit that slowly walked on one at a time and milled around before each member had surfaced. The night before playing St. Scholastica, Murray scrunched them up on a cot in her room at the local Radisson Hotel to watch video of how NHL teams entered the ice to begin their pregame routines.

When South Korea finally skated onto the sheet at Mars with fluidity, circling around in formation like a college marching band, Murray shot a smile of relief and briefly celebrated with Rebecca Ruegsegger Baker.

Now, one year later, Murray could no longer worry about mundane cosmetic features of her team's pregame ritual. With the unsettling loss to River Falls, South Korea appeared headed toward humiliation at the Olympics. For far too long now, Murray watched her lines execute sloppily. In practice, she continually had to stop and scold them for mistiming drills they had practiced for years. In lengthy discussions with her staff, Murray concluded that the coaches had exhausted their arsenal of motivational tactics and it was up to the players to figure out the root of their malaise. The team was equally exasperated and believed Murray should be offering more specific instructions. There was clearly a philosophical divide at the worst possible time, and each day it spidered like a cracked car windshield, edging closer to shattering completely.

Issues plaguing team chemistry had long been simmering. More than three years into her contract, Murray took sporadic Korean lessons but still spoke very little of her team's native language. As a result, Susie Jo, the team's assistant captain, and assistant coach Kim Do-yun relayed instructions to the Korean-speaking players during games and practices to overcome the verbal barriers. It was a tedious delivery method to say the least.

A majority of the players thought the team and head coach should have fostered a closer relationship, which wouldn't have left them feeling isolated just one month before they stepped onto the biggest stage of their lives. That premise remained one of Murray's greatest conundrums: the daily balance between being confidante and coach.

"I feel like she puts up a wall against the players," lamented sixteen-year-old Kim Hee-won, who never understood why coaches and players sat separately during meals.

Though Heewon did not expect Murray to fraternize with players socially like girlfriends at a school lunch table, her tendency to keep a strict distance even away from the rink led many to feel as if they could not approach her with questions or suggestions about hockey. That sentiment only worsened when Murray changed lines before games without explanation. Without that direct level of communication, some players felt like they were being punished or that younger players were favored and getting more ice time. Most of the veterans knew that a secondary goal of the coaching staff was to put the teenagers on the radar of NCAA Division I colleges in hopes of obtaining scholarship offers for them. They were not exactly resentful; by playing college hockey in the US, the teens could continue to mature after the Olympics and build a sturdy foundation for the future. But some of the older players had given a decade already to the national team and did not want to be simply pushed aside. "The fact that the coach didn't open up to the team felt like she did not have faith in us," grieved Choi Ji-yeon.

Minor clashes only further alienated the players. One of Murray's tenets was transforming their diets, changing pregame meals from chocolate bars to more salubrious options like fruits and proteins. That was a sound decision, but when the team traveled to training camps or tournaments, they did not like that all of their meals were prearranged and never included Korean food—usually just American staples like grilled chicken or pasta and salad. Rebelling against what some viewed as infantile treatment, players often snuck out to Subway sandwich shops after dinner. At Taereung, when they knew no coaches were around, they texted each other to say that the coast was clear to raid the building's vending machines. In retaliation against authority, the players could be quite immature at times, wearing their gear backwards or goofing off during practice while Murray tried to give instructions.

While the occasional cheat meal would not collapse the team's foundation, the way dieting was handled represented a bigger disconnect between how Murray believed Olympic-level athletes should prepare for competition, and how the South Koreans held on to routines they had basically grown up with. Before the imports arrived, the top four lines hardly changed from year to year. In the US, jostling lines can affect chemistry, but it could also be an effective motivational tool. In South Korea, it was perceived as a threat. Before the St. Scholastica game, Murray stated her goal by the end of the training camp was to get her players comfortable with being uncomfortable. "They don't know how far they can push themselves," Murray stated. "When they start to feel uncomfortable, they stop."

Grace Lee played for years at the highest levels of junior hockey and understood the methodology behind Murray's tactics. She was used to an environment where every practice affected your standing on the team and sometimes superfluous skating drills were necessary for conditioning one's body so it did not fail you come a championship game. "I just feel like at some points some of the things said against Sarah were more of like a thing that would happen in the States, so it's not necessarily her fault," Grace explained, adding that for complaining in America, kids get bag skated—drilled in sprints up and down the ice. "I think it just shows how different Korean culture is to US culture."

While it is true that the South Koreans should have adjusted to and expected a different level of training once PyeongChang appeared on the horizon, transforming from a democracy to an oligarchy was jarring and predictably not well received. Randi Griffin once described this as the gift and the curse of gaining an automatic berth for the Olympics.

"I think there's no doubt that something was lost," Randi analyzed. "I suppose this is the case in many different scenarios, in different sports, in different countries, where a sports program or a sports culture for women transitions from being this kind of grassroots thing that is just maintained by this passionate group of individuals who do this thing because they love it—like true amateurism—and then when it gets transformed into an elite sports culture where suddenly the players are treated like animals, and you have people coming in and making tons of money and making careers out of this, the players lose control over the culture of the team, over the team operations.

"I think this team used to be a family first. It was a group of friends who loved hockey first. They decided how they were going to do things. They decided the culture of the team. They decided what they were going to have for pregame meal."

What complicated matters further was that neither side seemed willing to confront the divide. The players never rebelled openly for fear of jeopardizing their standing on the team, and without having received pushback, Murray did not think there was a fissure. Officials from KIHA were too focused on the men's team to detect any discord. But within such a volatile environment, an issue as innocuous as dinner menus could snowball into a much larger problem.

When Murray was hired, the team was still not allowed to use the cafeteria at Taereung. With a majority of the roster coming directly from school, Han Soo-jin ordered take-out meals from nearby restaurants. Every few weeks, the players treated themselves to fried chicken, a meal not associated with cholesterol and gluttony like it is in America. During one of Murray's first days on the job, she saw a delivery person handing Soojin a massive order of fried chicken and Coca-Cola for twenty people and thought it was emblematic of the kind of team culture she had to erase. "I think she had a bad first impression of me," theorized Soojin, the captain from September 2013 until February 2015.

A few months later, the locker room was moved from the third floor of Taereung to the second floor to be closer to the coaches' offices. When this message was miscommunicated, Soojin was blamed for the mishap and stripped of her captaincy. "She had told me nothing about it, so I thought that maybe that's how they notify people about things in the West," Soojin said. "Thinking about that moment still makes me furious and tear up."

Abandoning Soojin, perhaps the most respected player on the team besides Shin So-jung, did not land well. Over the years, these experiences of hurt feelings only multiplied, and by January 2018, the South Koreans were playing the worst hockey of their lives.

The team had a chance to breathe the night before their final training camp matchup, which was against Shattuck-St. Mary's, the school that for years funneled players onto the US and Canadian Olympic rosters. Not too far from the Shattuck campus, Ruth Murray invited the players for dinner at her house, a gorgeous lakefront setting with high ceilings and a furnished den replete with Ping-Pong and pool tables and wide-screen televisions. It was the kind of environment that forced relaxation and one in which Sarah Murray could finally let down her guard and not be the coach, but a colleague able to fool around with her dogs and show the players pictures from her brother's wedding album.

In the Murrays' spacious living room, Heewon gave piggyback rides, while other teammates chased each other with pool sticks and devoured plates of corn bread, pulled pork and mac and cheese. Susie video chatted with a friend in South Korea to show her Murray's smallest brown dog, Tofu, while Cho Mihwan danced around in her socks, listening to K-pop music on her phone. Downstairs, Sojung won a match of Ping-Pong and as her prize, licked two of her fingers and smacked them against her defeated opponent's wrist, the kind of trophy an adolescent claims after being victorious during a recess competition. After her hard-fought victory, Sojung sprawled out on a red leather couch and was soon joined by Lee Min-ji, who rested her head against the opposite arm and laid her legs on Sojung's, giving off the appearance of sisters relaxing at home after a long day. There was no talk of collapses or whose roles might get cut. The joy these players took in the company of one another was clearly one of their biggest strengths and proved time and time again to be able to get them through the valleys of their training.

In the team's final meeting before playing Shattuck, Murray canceled a long-anticipated trip to the Mall of America, and instead they huddled inside their hotel's stuffy conference room. Murray demanded the players finally become accountable for their lackadaisical play. Each member was called to write a message on a dry-erase board, a promise of how they'd carry themselves until the Olympics. One player wrote a popular Korean idiom that translated to, "Team play, not individual. Clean up your own poo." At last, the marker was passed to Randi, the deepest thinker on the team, but also one of its shyest.

Randi, who writes right-handed, approached the board with a red wool beanie pulled down and nearly covering her eyes. She rolled up her sleeves, kneeled and started scribbling. At first, her body covered up her message and some players began whispering in anticipation. Soon, as the letters formed across the board from left to right, it became clear that she was writing in *hangul*, the Korean alphabet. The room broke out into pandemonium.

"I always thought of Randi as somebody that's thoughtful and mature, but not so talkative and emotional," Park Chae-lin said. "When she started writing in Korean—and she was really good at it—it was really fascinating."

Randi's message was not thoroughly inspirational ("Fast changes, fast shots"), but her effort to relate to her South Korean teammates clearly resonated. Wearing a long-sleeved warm-up shirt from her days at Harvard, Randi displayed the impeccable timing that Katey Stone, her college coach, remembered as a defining quality.

"They genuinely appreciated when the imports would try, because we were constantly asking them to try," Randi acknowledged. "It's uncomfortable for a lot of them to speak English, but it's just the reality that their poor English is still better than our poor Korean. But when we would try and be willing to look a little stupid in the attempt to do things their way, they just appreciated that."

With renewed spirit, South Korea took the ice against Shattuck on January 10, exactly one month before their first Olympic game. Despite their mostly younger ages, the Shattuck stars dwarfed most of the South Korean team in size. They were a unit groomed to play hockey, receiving the best training and equipment and attending camps around the world basically since they were old enough to skate.

Allowing early goals had been a recurring problem during the US schedule, and it often led to a demoralizing spiral. Sojung was seldom beaten in one-on-one situations, her reflexes and read on a player's eyes flawless. But defensive breakdowns and players drifting out of position often led to deflections and cheap goals. South Korea was rarely able to climb out of such holes.

The game began ominously with Shattuck scoring just minutes into the first period. This time, though, South Korea did not wilt. After tying the game 1–1, Randi continued her outspokenness from the day before. Dragging her stick low to the ice and swooping after pucks like a hawk hunting prey, she became a perpetual disrupter to Shattuck's offense. After one turnover, she yelled for the puck as she sped down ice, received a pass and scored the go-ahead goal, quickly erasing Shattuck's early lead. Teammates celebrated by wrapping their arms around Randi, her number 37 on the back of her jersey disappearing amid the scrum. Originally, she wore number 4 and her nameplate used her first name in place of her surname, as it is formatted in Korean. But before the training camp, she asked to change the back of her jersey to read "HeeSoo"—her mother's Korean name, and her number to 37, the year her grandmother was born. When Randi received her first number 37 jersey, she emailed her grandmother to tell her the meaning behind it. Her grandmother then called Randi's mother and cried.

In college, when teammates found out that Randi's middle name was HeeSoo, they began calling her that as a joke. Not long after the discovery, they asked her if they should stop, understanding that it bordered on being insensitive. Randi did not really mind. Although at the time she was not strongly connected to her heritage, she was proud of her Korean middle name. "It was also just maybe a way to remind people, like I am Asian and it's not just a joke," Randi said.

After two periods, Shattuck led South Korea 3–2. Murray didn't give an impassioned speech during the break, she just praised her players for their effort thus far. But time was also ticking. This was South Korea's last game before the Olympics. "We've been working four years for this," Murray reminded them. The team entered the third period with gusto, charging the net like revolutionaries storming the front lines of a battle. As each shot sailed just wide or nicked the post, the bench grew louder, unshaken by their misfortune. Throughout the period, players banged their sticks and jumped on each other's backs in excitement as South Korea kept pressuring the Shattuck zone.

Another fault throughout the tour and particularly during the River Falls loss was the team's lack of simply putting the puck on net. It's not the soundest strategy in hockey—it is almost like closing your eyes and hoping for the best—but sometimes, a deflection can bounce off a player or a skate and angle the puck into an unexpected opening in the goal. In another unforeseen cultural quirk, Murray learned that some of her players thought it was selfish to just shoot the puck without direction.

Marissa Brandt was now an assistant captain, her role on the team increasing on the ice in addition to her maternal duties off it. She played the point on power plays, but sometimes struggled with confidence in her shot. With a few minutes remaining against Shattuck and South Korea still trailing by one goal, they once again controlled the action in their opponent's zone. Eventually, the puck landed at Marissa's stick near the blue line. Sensing her team was on the edge of returning home winless, without hesitation, Marissa fired a wrist shot toward the traffic in front of the net. The puck first struck a Shattuck defender in the shoulder and then careened toward the post, where it clinked off the inside of the steel piping and came to rest inside the net. Marissa had tied the game to force a sudden-death overtime.

*Marissa Brandt (left) and Grace Lee (right) made crucial plays when the national team reached their nadir during pre-Olympic training. Also pictured, Choi Yu-jung.*

When Eliza Lee was pregnant with her second daughter, she and her husband Albert learned early on that there were complications. Scans had shown that the child had severe clubfoot, a defect that could mean she might never walk properly, greatly affecting the quality of life for the child and its parents. Physicians even presented the Lees with the option of terminating the pregnancy. Albert and Eliza could not fathom such an absurd suggestion. They promised to find whatever methods available to help their daughter live the most normal life possible.

Grace Lee was born on January 13, 2000. As a toddler, she took longer than most children to crawl and even longer to walk. Her fragile legs were often wrapped in thick casts from surgeries, and she wore special shoes with the intent of repositioning her inward-facing foot bones. Just taking a few steps caused stinging pain. One suggestion the Lees had heard was that skating could further buoy the feet by strengthening the legs, but this prospect seemed dangerous. None of the Lees skated, and the idea of putting their daughter on ice, repeatedly falling as she learned how to navigate a slippery surface, frightened them. Grace tried figure skating but cried at the pressure the skates put on her ankle. She fell so much at first, it's surprising imprints were not left on the ice. Eliza cringed with each tumble, worried that her daughter's foot had worsened as a result. Children teasing Grace by calling her "chicken legs" did not help matters.

A colleague suggested Grace try hockey skates with more support. Again the Lees were terrified of the thought of slashing sticks and flying pucks and checks against the boards and the impact that all might play on Grace's physical condition. But Grace wanted to learn the sport. Throughout her life, Grace has always won these arguments with her parents. "If she wanted it, that was the end of it," said Eliza, who still clung tightly to railings or her seat rests when watching Grace play. "She would just convince us one way or another that she was going to do it."

The pain from playing hockey was hard to bear at times, but once Grace gained her confidence on ice, it never left her. "Both of us never expressed these worries toward Grace," Eliza admitted. "Her condition of her legs and feet were always on our mind and she's been teased before at school and with some friends. But I think she was in fourth grade coming home on a car ride after practice and said, 'You know, Mom, I have the skinniest legs in the locker room but I skate pretty well.' I said,

'Yeah, keep hanging on to that and you can do whatever.' So it all worked out."

Grace quickly developed into a star, which landed her at Shattuck and made her a possible candidate to enter the US national team player pool. Grace was set to enter her senior year in 2017, and then head off to Yale to begin her college hockey career. But she could not pass up the opportunity to represent South Korea at the Olympics once Murray offered her a tryout. Eliza and Albert still worried. They asked Grace to think about the 2022 Olympics, when she'd have graduated from college. Grace scoffed at the suggestion. Okay, why don't you take a few weeks to think about it, her parents begged. A few days later, Grace told them her decision was made. She was going to South Korea.

Eliza naturally worried about sending her daughter to live alone in Seoul. Grace still had regular visits with her orthopedic surgeon and Eliza wondered if intense Olympic training could cause irreparable harm. After meeting Murray for the first time and with the coach able to fully express her intention to see Grace prosper, Eliza's mind was at peace. "I felt Sarah, not with her words but through her actions and through her care, says that they're her team, the players are hers, she will take care of them," Eliza expounded. "It was very reassuring."

At first, Grace's feet, which had already undergone five surgeries, began to weaken under the intense training. At least two hours of skating and two hours of weight training, six days per week, was more than she had ever completed. Grace returned to Colorado, where her physician revealed her legs couldn't handle the exertion she was putting them through. The team's trainers and coaches convened to create a specialized workout plan for Grace that subdued some of the throbbing soreness, but it became something she just had to tolerate throughout her tenure with the national team.

"Sometimes after games I have a lot of pain," Grace said. "The most pain is when I'm forced to walk a lot or run. Growing up when I had surgery, they kind of had to reorientate my foot so it's centered, so I lost most of my mobility. Instead of having the mobility where people's toes hit and then their heel, my foot just comes down as a whole, so it's a lot of pressure on my ankles."

In addition to the physical hurdles, Grace was in the uncomfortable position of being added with less than a year before Pyeong-Chang. Although the team had grown to accept the imports, such a late new addition was worrisome. There were now twenty-four players on South Korea's active roster, meaning someone was going to get cut before the Olympics. "I remember texting a friend right before and just freaking out," remembered Grace, who landed in South Korea on July 4, 2017. "I was coming onto a team that had been together for years. Obviously, I would hate if someone came into my team last minute right before the Olympics. There was that worry that I was kind of disrupting everything."

"We felt a little awkward with each other," added Chaelin, who is one year older than Grace. "It's not like I disliked her for that reason. But for some of the other players it felt a little unfair."

While Grace had not gone through the rigors that Chaelin and older players like Sojung and Soojin had, she was a needed addition to the South Korean roster. The same determination Grace had shown in overcoming physical obstacles manifested itself on the ice. An alpha among a team speckled with reserved personalities, Grace, despite being one of the youngest players, quickly emerged as a vocal leader, telling players where to position themselves before face-offs or leading discussions about strategy during time-outs. She was not afraid to take matters into her own hands. She played how Lee Yeon-jeong assumed all Americans played hockey. Which, in proper doses, wasn't necessarily a bad element to add to this team.

The overtime period against Shattuck was played in a three-on-three format, as opposed to having the standard five skaters on each side. This created a more open rink, allowing for better goal opportunities to materialize. Inexperienced in this scenario,

South Korea spent the first minute wandering around the ice, out of position, as Sojung saved them from defeat. When Grace's shift came, she immediately changed the tempo.

As high schoolers are wont to do, when South Korea played Shattuck during their September 2017 trip to the US, Grace tried to showboat in front of her friends and teammates. Three months later and well-aware her team desperately needed a victory, after another overtime save by Sojung, Grace surged down the ice and received an outlet pass. She was one-on-one with a Shattuck defender, with Chaelin trailing near center ice. As Grace crossed the blue line and entered the Shattuck zone, she screamed for Chaelin: "Come on! Come on!" As soon as Chaelin sped across the blue line, Grace ripped a slap shot past her defender and onto net. The force of the shot sent the puck ricocheting off the chest of Shattuck's goaltender and landed in front of Chaelin, now just feet from the goal. With Shattuck's netminder unable to turn her body in time to Chaelin charging from her left side, she sent the puck into the net, winning the game, and immediately skated into Grace's waiting arms. With 3:21 left in overtime, South Korea had won their first game in months, 4–3.

After the victory, the team truly started to believe they could win at the Olympics. Some went a step further and thought there was a chance they could advance out of their group and reach the medal round. They had said this before to the media to keep up appearances, but now it rang true to them. The team's jubilation carried over to a steak dinner later that night, where all of the tension and stress of the past few months dissipated as quickly as the melted butter on their steaming baked potatoes. Tomorrow, Doyun would be able to spend time with his newborn child for the first time in weeks. The entire team was going to be back with their families, beaming with self-assurance. Beating Shattuck was the height of confidence.

It was also the last night they shared before their team was changed forever.

*South Korea's women's national hockey team at the Taereung training facility.*

# PART TWO

# CHAPTER FOURTEEN

# The Slap Shot Heard
# Round the World

Early in the morning of January 12, Sarah Murray was asleep in her parents' house when she was awakened by a phone call from Kim Do-yun, who had just arrived back in South Korea.

"We have a big problem," Doyun said.

The rest of Doyun's message sent an untoward flu-like chill through Murray's body. Moments later, her phone began ringing incessantly; first from NBC, then the CBC in Canada and other media outlets from around the world, asking if it was true—had South Korea actually agreed to invite North Korea to join their Olympic women's hockey team?

Murray was scheduled to have one week off at home before returning to begin the final stretch of training on the road to PyeongChang. The morning after beating Shattuck-St. Mary's, Murray and Rebecca Ruegsegger Baker gathered at 3:00 a.m. in front of the GrandStay Residential Suites Hotel in Faribault to send the team back to South Korea. As a heavy snow fell around them, Murray and Ruegsegger Baker waved goodbye until the outline of the team bus's high beams evaporated into the predawn dark.

The national team had been so mired in their slump that they hardly paid attention to any news outside of hockey. Two weeks earlier on December 31, while the players were slurping good luck soup in New Haven, Kim Jong-un broadcast a New Year's Day speech on North Korean state-run television that rocked the political climate around the world. Sitting in a gray Western-style suit as opposed to his traditional black Mao-inspired out-fit, Kim offered to send North Korean athletes to the Winter Olympics, which were starting in a mere five weeks. He proposed that the North and South immediately begin discussions for arrangements—the two sides had not yet officially spoken since South Korean President Moon Jae-in took office in May 2017, and hadn't had high-level dialogue in over two years. "I am willing to send a delegation and take necessary measures, and I believe that the authorities of the North and South can urgently meet to discuss the matter," Kim declared. "We sincerely hope that the South will successfully host the Olympics."[1]

Kim, with his slicked-back black hair resembling the tip of a Sharpie marker, also slyly requested an easing of military tension between the two sides.

For her book on South Korean culture, author Euny Hong interviewed Lee Charm, the head of the Korean Tourism Organization from 2009 to 2013, who once described North Korean leadership as thus: "The North Korean regime is not crazy. They are very calculating. They don't observe any rules; they use extortion. Basically, they're a criminal organization, but not crazy."[2] Just months earlier, North Korea detonated a purported hydrogen bomb, adding to their string of successful intercontinental ballistic missile test launches already under their belt.

In response to Kim's unexpected overture, President Moon, under immense pressure to quell the North's aggression, hastily accepted and suggested that South Korea could end its joint military exercises with the United States. "I appreciate and welcome the North's positive response to our proposal that the PyeongChang Olympics should be used as a turning point in improving South-North relations and promoting peace," he told reporters.

South Korean leaders had tried to field joint Olympics teams as far back as 1964 to no avail. President Moon previously worried that North Korea seemed more likely to be an agitator than collaborator for the 2018 Games, particularly given the country's history of responding like a petulant child when a spotlight was shone on the South. Before the 1988 Summer Olympics, North Korea, supported by communist allies China and the Soviet Union, demanded that they be allowed to cohost events, requests that went ignored. With a goal to scare off visitors, ten months before the opening ceremony on November 29, 1987, two North Korean agents posing as Japanese tourists planted a bomb on a Korean Air flight from Abu Dhabi to Seoul, killing all 115 on board. In 2002, when South Korea cohosted the World Cup with Japan, North Korean boats unloaded fire on a South Korean ship one day before the tournament final, creating a skirmish that killed sailors on both sides.

While President Moon had grandiose dreams for North Korea's Olympic participation, no one quite exactly knew where these extra athletes, if approved, would be added. The obvious option was the one raised just a few months earlier—the women's hockey team. But Murray and her players were so focused on their own problems in Connecticut and Minnesota that they barely recognized they had suddenly become a target of worldwide interest.

One week after Kim Jong-un's speech, on January 9, the team had their final training session at the Shattuck weight room, bouncing around eleven different stations set up to perform a variety of core exercises as K-pop beats boomed from a stereo. Murray sat down, took out her laptop and suddenly read a breaking news alert that after a meeting at the border village of Panmunjom, North Korea was indeed sending athletes to PyeongChang. No details were given on what sports were to be affected, but Murray nervously passed around her laptop to the coaching staff. Doyun tried to alleviate the tension, saying North Korea could probably only send a few competitors in an individual sport like figure skating, as that seemed the easiest way to accommodate a few new entries. Still, Murray's level of concern was rising. She clung to the hope that her team wasn't going to be affected since officials at KIHA had promised to notify her in advance if any talks of a merger were to materialize again.

A few hours after the team left for the airport, Murray was buoyant during a lunch at The Cheese Cave in downtown Faribault as thick snowflakes coated the streets outside. The denouement of her final set of pre-Olympic matches concluded with a much-needed victory, and she had not been told by anyone from KIHA that the team was receiving new additions. "I'm kind of like, it's not going to happen," Murray said in between bites of a salad. "Logistically, it doesn't make sense. They don't know our systems; they haven't been with us the last four years. Our players have earned their spots. They've improved together and to have these guys come in, like, literally thirty days before the Olympics is totally unfair."

One of the more heartbreaking aspects of the South Korean women's national team's communication problems was that Murray rarely personally expressed how much the girls meant to her. In one of our first conversations, Murray mentioned how during the 2016 Summer Olympics, she excitedly called her parents, telling them how "we won gold today."

"My parents assumed I was talking about Canada, but I was talking about Korea," Murray said. "I do miss my family and living in North America quite often. But I know what I am doing is something truly special. How many people get an opportunity to do something like this? These girls have such a passion for the sport and are such underdogs. I love the idea of surprising people at the Olympics and showing that Koreans can play hockey."

Murray valiantly defended her players throughout the merger rumors dating back to the summer and continued to do so even after the storm had seemingly passed. A few months earlier, when South Korea played the University of Minnesota in an exhibition game at Minnesota's Ridder Arena, Greg Brandt leaned against a railing overlooking center ice and discussed the poignancy of seeing Murray's and Ruegsegger Baker's pride in the team. In spite of their conflicting backgrounds and approaches to hockey, there was something different about this player-coach relationship. It was easy to see why Marissa and other imports were drawn to representing South Korea, but why were the coaches so willing to give up the prime years of their adulthood to move across the world to twenty-four young women who more than likely were going to get swept out of the Olympics? Greg interjected: "It's because they love them."

During the summer of 2017, KIHA told Murray under strict orders not to talk to the media about a possible merger. But as she revealed a few months later, she was incensed that her team could be sacrificed in such a manner. The disrespectful undertones of the idea appalled her. "It just totally takes away from what our team's been doing," Murray said. "It is insulting."

After the South Korean team's flight landed at Incheon Airport, the players sorted through the flurry of texts and emails now available to read on their phones. No one had received any notification regarding additional news about a unified team and, relieved, they made their way to immigration and then the luggage pickup area. With seemingly no need to stress, Danelle Im tucked her phone away and was patiently waiting near the carousel for her bags when Park Jong-ah and Han Soo-jin approached her. In searching the internet for updates about their team, Jongah and Soojin came across the news that while they were in the air, South Korea had proposed the formation of a joint women's hockey team to include North Korean players.

"People were pissed," Danelle recalled.

Some players chose to believe the reports were not true. Those still with skepticism collected their belongings and headed to Customs and then approached the sliding glass doors leading to the airport's exit. Upon passing through, a group of reporters awaiting the team began shouting questions, asking their feelings about playing with North Koreans. "I was denying it inside my head, like it can't actually happen," Park Chae-lin said. "It was only when I was in the airport and saw journalists with cameras that I realized it was happening for real."

North Korea, the country that Han Do-hee and her teammates forever looked at as a nuisance, buffoons instead of an actual danger, had finally gone through with one of their threats. "I got a feeling that this wasn't a joke anymore," added Cho Mi-hwan. "It felt as if our team would lose everything we had built until now if we were to form this unified team."

Officials at KIHA first heard about the merger from the Ministry of Culture, Sports and Tourism when the team was leaving Los Angeles, where they caught a connecting flight to South Korea. As expected, KIHA president Chung Mong-won stayed silent on the matter, likely not wanting to jeopardize his longstanding relationship with South Korean government leaders. "I feel like Chung couldn't have put up a fight against the government; that would have been absolute career suicide," Randi Griffin analyzed, "and he didn't care that much about us, anyway."

Soojin attempted to rally the team together as they combatted a maelstrom of confusion and hurt. Internally, though, she was full of rage. Soojin, who turned thirty in September 2017 and was the team's oldest player, once described hockey as an addiction, and like a chain smoker, she could never kick her habit. To get her fix, Soojin took a break from college and moved to Sapporo, Japan, where she could find better individual training for hockey. After running through the $1,750 in savings she brought with her for living expenses, Soojin took out almost $14,000 in loans to pay her rent overseas. She eventually procured a job in a Korean restaurant, rolling hundreds of dumplings per day and washing dishes for three years in a steam-filled kitchen to pay off the debt. When she finally completed her studies at Yonsei University, the entire team was there to attend her graduation concert, where she performed in a majestic one-shoulder yellow gown.

In comparison, the imports on the men's team made over $200,000 annually. They were afforded better ice times, unlike the women who trained late at night at Taereung, which already was a subprime facility with bad lighting and dirty nets, and where pucks got lost sliding under creases along the boards. The imports staying there had rooms that regularly were infested with bugs. Before the women's team was guaranteed a spot in the Olympics, not only were they not allowed to eat at Taereung, but they weren't even provided practice jerseys or other training clothes, having to bring their own from home. Veterans later learned that during the early years of the national team, some KIHA members pocketed money intended for gear and meals. "People at KIHA always tell us, 'You guys are the only women's team in the world that receives money.'" Soojin said. "They always say along the lines of, 'Didn't things get a lot better than before?' It's true that things did get a lot better than before, but why do they have to always compare the present to the past? Are they not thinking of improving beyond the current state? They say that it's become a lot more comfortable for us to train. So if we go up to them and say, 'We're having problems in this, or we're lacking that,' then they're only going to think that we're impertinent."

Without any help from KIHA or the South Korean government, like always, the team only had each other. The following day, Danelle's brother Justin threw a birthday party for his younger sister at Masa Tacos, a popular restaurant in Gangnam. Almost half the team attended and serenaded Danelle with cake and presents, including a stylish black leather jacket. But even as they celebrated, players could not hold back from discussing the incoming North Koreans and how it saddened them. It felt as if this night could be one of the last times they'd experience such cohesion together.

COURTESY OF THE SOUTH KOREAN WOMEN'S HOCKEY TEAM

*The team gathered for Danelle Im's birthday the day after North Koreans were officially added to their roster.*

Shortly after Doyun called Murray with the shocking news, she scampered to find an immediate flight back to South Korea. During her cross-continental trip, cramped in a tiny seat, Murray felt nauseous. After collecting her luggage and wheeling it on a dolly past immigration, Murray walked toward the automatic sliding door exit. Once the glass panels parted, a sea of flashing lights went off and hordes of media members began rushing toward Murray. South Korean media are notoriously aggressive and here they pushed and elbowed for prime position, creating a scene that harkened to old newsreel videos that showed The Beatles arriving at airports around the world. Tired of being inundated with questions, KIHA notified reporters when Murray was arriving, passing the buck to her. Without much knowledge of the situation or having any time to rehearse answers about the sudden worldwide interest in her team, Murray instinctively became extremely protective of her players. Backed up against a wall with dozens of cameras and microphones shoved in her face, Murray, wearing a black Team Korea warm-up jacket, went on the offensive and wholeheartedly vouched for her group. They had no desire to become a political statement and just wanted to play hockey. The head coach made clear she would not be pressured into playing anyone, despite now being expected to integrate a group of new players in two weeks, a process she estimated normally took three to four years. Murray didn't expect any of the North Koreans to be talented enough to penetrate the team's three top lines, anyway. Everything had to be earned.

When Chaelin saw Murray's quotes on the news, she was grateful that her coach had stood up for the team. It was one of the first times she could sense a common ground with her, and it came at a time the team needed it most.

"Sarah constantly reminded us, nothing changes for us," Danelle said. "She was just like us, how we were feeling. All of this was so new to her, too. She had just as little control over it as we did, the players. She definitely defended us."

"Even before this happened, she used to always tell us don't worry about the things that you can't control, but be your best and be faithful to the things that you're responsible for," Susie Jo added. "That's how we were going to approach it."

Without any prior notice, South Korea's women's national hockey team was suddenly thrust into history's most ambitious geopolitical saga. As much as the team sought to reclaim their destiny, government officials and men in positions of power continually pried away the last remaining semblances of control that the players were clinging to. On January 20, the IOC officially approved the participation of North Korean athletes on what was now being called the Unified women's hockey team. In the Olympics, twenty-two players dress for each game, with each team allowed to carry one inactive reserve. But under these special circumstances, twelve North Koreans were to be added to the Korean team roster, expanding their locker room to thirty-five, after initial estimates only had three to six new members coming on. That was not all. For each game, at least three North Korean players were required to dress in uniform. Murray originally would only have to sit one of her players per game, but with the new mandates, at least four South Koreans had to watch each game from the stands.

In the IOC's official declaration, the organization praised the IIHF and the governments of North Korea and South Korea for demonstrating "how Olympic sport always promotes the Olympic spirit of understanding and mutual respect." Nowhere in the three-page document was the South Korean women's national team thanked for their implied cooperation.

The IOC was not the only body ignoring the plight of Murray's players. Sports Minister Do Jong-hwan, who first suggested the idea of a unified team in the summer of 2017, claimed the additional dozen players would have no effect on performance and even help with their added numbers. Minister Do explained that in hockey, substitutions occur every two minutes (when in reality the intervals are closer to forty-five seconds) and theorized that more players allowed for more time to rest in between shifts. When Greg Brandt heard this back in Minnesota, he boiled over in anger. "The naivety of the officials that were making these decisions," he fumed. "Hockey, like you can throw anybody out there—they didn't even understand the game!"

Robin Brandt had an equally valid concern with the rash decision. "The only thing I thought about that is they aren't doing it to the men's team," she noted.

Robin was onto something. As much as the government claimed the women's hockey team was chosen for schematic reasons, the decision had centuries of personal, economic and Korean cultural roots attached—the selected athletes were so easily sacrificed because they were female.

The backhanded statements did not stop. An official on the president's staff told South Korean reporters, "I'm 100 percent sure nobody would have paid attention to them if it wasn't for the proposal." South Korean Prime Minister Lee Nak-yeon added that the women's team should bear the brunt of the merger, since, "Speaking honestly, the women's ice hockey team is not going to win a medal during the Olympics, is it?"[3]

"We were disappointed when the minister said we were going to lose, anyway," Chaelin admitted. "We were really hurt by it. Even though we knew we weren't the best team out there, we had been working hard for the last four years."

When the South Korean team left the US, beating Sweden or Switzerland was still a long shot proposition, but it no longer felt like a pipe dream to the players. Political interests were one foe, though, that seemed impossible to topple.

"We felt completely used," said Marissa Brandt, familiar with that feeling from her high school days when colleges took advantage of her to recruit her sister. "Like we didn't matter."

Somewhat surprisingly, the ignorant comments by government leaders created an unexpected backlash from South Korean citizens. One petition submitted to the Blue House—the South Korean presidential office and equivalent of the White House—garnered over fifty thousand signatures in support of South Korea's women's national team players. Internet users furiously defended the young women, offended by the government's strong-arm tactics. One poll posted on the website of the South Korean newspaper *JoongAng Ilbo* showed 96 percent of more than five thousand voters disagreed with the government's actions. Gallup Korea conducted a poll that showed President Moon's approval rating dropped to 67 percent, its lowest mark in over four months, with particular ire coming from younger generations of South Koreans. Some media outlets speculated that IIHF president René Fasel only took interest in a unified team to boost interest in the Olympic hockey tournament after stars from the NHL opted not to participate in PyeongChang, the first time professionals were absent since 1994.

In the ensuing days, President Moon's approval rating plummeted to under 60 percent. Perhaps even more distressing figures to the Blue House were that additional polls found only four of ten South Koreans believed unification of the peninsula was necessary.[4] "We thought the public would understand and support the forming of a unified team," a Blue House official later told South Korean media. "We failed to gauge their feelings accurately."[5]

With tensions rising, President Moon visited the South Korean women's team at the Jincheon training center, a facility that recently replaced Taereung as the team's home base. Dressed in a white hockey jersey, President Moon, with his charismatic smile and round wire-framed glasses, told the athletes that the unified team "will be a great opportunity to thaw the South-North Korea relationship that is frozen solid,"[6] and echoed his prime minister's insouciant sentiments by saying the new team was going to also bring attention to "a less-preferred sport."[7]

"If we unify our team with the North's, it won't necessarily improve our team's strength very much," President Moon said in closing. "It will even require extra efforts to build up teamwork with the North Korean players. But if the two Koreas unify their teams and play a great match together, that itself will be long remembered as a historic moment."[8]

At the end of his visit, President Moon took photographs with the men's and women's hockey teams. In a majority of the photos, the men's faces feature full smiles and raised right fists, a Korean tradition to symbolize the nation's fighting spirit. Mihwan, Dohee and many others on the women's team showed no emotion, their eyes staring blankly ahead, looking as if they'd rather be anywhere else than at this staged pageant. When the photographer asked everyone to say, "One, two, three, fighting!" the women's team members mumbled the phrase, if they spoke at all. "It was hurtful that the decision was already made, so we weren't in the mood to be happy just because he came for us," Chaelin sneered.

"We couldn't smile," Mihwan added. "He said that it would help improve inter-Korean relations, and although it may sound egotistic, I thought, 'Why does it have to be us? Why now?' We didn't want to get all the attention because of the Unified team. Instead, we wanted to get attention for the results we accomplished through our blood, sweat and tears.

"At that time, I felt betrayed by the Republic of Korea."

# CHAPTER FIFTEEN

# Suffering or in Joy, to the Love of Country

Park Jong-ah was furious after reading the dismissive comments emanating from South Korean authority figures. It wasn't the kind of anger she seethed with when the girls in Canada called her racial slurs, or when Japan put up scores against South Korea more commonly seen in football games. This attack implied that not only was Jongah's life's work insignificant, but so was that of her teammates. Every validating moment, from scoring the decisive shoot-out goal against China to winning World Championship tournaments in the name of South Korea, was deemed worthless in the eyes of government officials that had never even played hockey. That Jongah wore her country's flag on everything from her backpack to her helmet and gloves did not seem to matter.

After President Moon Jae-in collected his photo opportunity at Jincheon, performing damage control for his tumbling approval ratings, the women's national team met with Sports Minister Do Jong-hwan. The former poet's unpoetic missives regarding the women's hockey team's chances of winning at the

Olympics were fresh in Jongah's mind. Previously, he sent his vice minister to Jincheon to try and cool tensions, but the players screamed him out of the facility. When Minister Do entered the meeting room, Jongah's first instinct was to unleash a similar tirade of vulgarities that would have made a sailor blush. "I almost tore into them," she admitted. "Saying what he did was an insult to the national team players."

Like President Moon, Minister Do knew that his comments did not chart well with the public. He was now willing to face the firing squad, but hoped to soothe emotions with a promise to create a semiprofessional team to be housed in a new $46-million-dollar arena being built in Suwon, a city just outside of Seoul. However, there was a major flaw with that proposal. It was the same problem that plagued Shin So-jung and Lee Kyou-sun when they first joined the national team at the turn of the century—who would they play? Creating a semipro team was admirable in theory, but there was no mention of forming a full-fledged league. It was like offering to build a child a glamorous new seesaw and then telling them they'd have to ride it alone.

Not satiated by this morsel, Choi Yu-jung spoke up first. Yujung's family moved from the southern city of Busan to Seoul for her hockey dream. Yujung, recognizable by her pursed lips and puffy cheeks, was once described by Danelle Im as very *chakhae* (good-natured). Before the Olympics, she had to interrupt her second to last year of high school for training, which put in jeopardy her standing as the top student in her class—a talisman that would have made her a shoo-in for almost any university in the country. Yujung was still undecided if she'd leave hockey once she began college and did not think it was fair that such a decision had to be made in the first place. She told the minister there needed to be teams at the middle school, high school and university levels to truly grow the sport.

Next, Park Chae-lin described how hearing the South Korean national anthem before a game was one of the moments she was proudest of in her life—

> With this spirit and this mind, give all loyalty, in suffering or in joy, to the love of country.

"He said he understood and he knew about all the things I was explaining," Chaelin recalled. "He tried to explain why he had to make this decision. He was responding the same thing to everybody, though. It wasn't completely satisfying."

One by one the players spoke up, explaining to Minister Do about the thousands of hours they spent making dumplings and washing dishes, the friendships they lost and the abuse they endured for South Korea. They mentioned how unfair it was to ruin the fabric of the team a few weeks before the grandest moment of their lives. All the minister could say to each emotional outpouring was that he understood, but what is done is done. "He didn't give us any certainty about the future, but instead simply said that he'd put in his efforts," Han Soo-jin relayed. "We were worried that our team was going to be abandoned and the promises unfulfilled after the unified team. We thought, 'Aren't they going to use and abandon us?'"

Jongah would not let that happen. After Kyousun retired in the spring of 2017, Jongah was surprisingly named the team's new captain after World Championships by Sarah Murray. She was clearly the most talented forward, but having just turned twenty-one, was greatly deficient in the kind of veteran leadership that Kyousun and Soojin before her had exuded. Early on, Jongah could be somewhat of a diva, taking advantage of her status to force matters in her favor for menial issues, like picking roommates for road trips before everyone else. But being the captain on such a diverse team like South Korea was about more than privilege and shaking the referee's hand before the game. "I wasn't ready," Jongah admitted months after first having the *C* sewn on the left shoulder of her uniform. "I realized there was a lot more I had to do than expected."

Jongah looked older than her age, and her strong eyes made people feel like she could release fury at any moment. Jongah calmed herself and stared down Minister Do, reiterating the need for more hockey programs for girls throughout the country. A single semiprofessional team was not enough. Her colleagues would grin and bear the situation they were forced into, despite feeling as if this whole charade was bullshit. They agreed to become guinea pigs for the greater good of the people they loved to represent, but they would not be forgotten. In the same fashion that young Korean women took to the streets to protest Park Geun-hye, Jongah stood up to authority and did not let Minister Do forget that South Korea owed the women's hockey team and they'd collect after the Olympics. Their time was coming.

"Because she's a playful person, I wondered if she was too immature to become a leader," said Park Ye-eun, her childhood friend from Gangneung. "But Jongah is also very determined in her beliefs. She's a very trustworthy person. She has her own color. She has very strong opinions, which are all great traits for a leader."

Randi Griffin, Marissa Brandt and Grace Lee were not yet back with the team, having stayed for an extra week in the United States after the January training camp ended. When they returned to South Korea with their own doubts about what was transpiring, their teammates couldn't stop talking about the leonine strength that Jongah showed to Minister Do, who finally agreed that more concessions were coming. The players still were filled with anger, but Jongah's words made them feel as if they were not going to fall apart.

"She realized that by standing for something and being willing to put it out there, people actually started following her," Randi deciphered. "She definitely earned her *C*."

*Named captain before she turned twenty-one, Park Jong-ah (left) had large skates to fill when Lee Kyou-sun retired in early 2017.*

Shortly after women's hockey in South Korea landed on the front page of the *New York Times* and became the top story on CNN, the BBC and news stations around the globe, KIHA muzzled players from speaking to the media. Perhaps to its credit, KIHA kept the team in a bubble in Jincheon, and the majority of players shockingly had no idea they had become the most important story in the world. In between meetings with the president and sports minister, preparing for the arrival of the North Koreans and finding time to actually practice for the Olympics, there was little time available to tinker on their phones or talk with family members back home—relatives who themselves were suddenly being bombarded by friends, neighbors and strangers asking about their daughters becoming teammates with actual, by God, North Koreans.

Since the majority of the world never encountered citizens from the "hermit kingdom," speculation became rampant about what might happen once the two teams were combined. One commentator for South Korean television station SBS assumed that North Korean players would mesh well with Murray's detailed personality and prefer this order over a more charismatic coach.[1] Rumors abounded that in previous tournaments, North Korean players could not swap badges, pins or other items routinely exchanged at events, or even bring back souvenirs of chocolate or apples because authorities confiscated them at home. Hwangbo Young told Korean media, "This is going to backfire horribly."

In order to pay for the cost of bringing in athletes from North Korea, the IOC footed about $50,000, with South Korea spending an estimated $2.6 million for 418 North Korean nonathletes to attend the Games.[2] In addition, a special government fund was created to pay for expenses like tickets for the 229 North Korean cheerleaders who were being brought as well, which totaled almost $900,000.[3] The cost of tickets for the cheerleaders alone surpassed what had been spent on stipends for players on the women's national team over two and a half years.

While the South Korean government spared no expense in making sure North Korea had a comfortable stay at the Olympics, public criticism over the invite continued to rise. Far right activists protested outside of Seoul Station, a main transit hub in the capital city, where they confronted police and burned images of Kim Jong-un, the North Korean flag and the unified Korea flag. In response, prounification supporters became equally vocal, even threatening Lee Min-ji when she decided to voice her opinion on the merger.

Although she traveled to Minnesota in January, Minji had been informed before the trip that she was likely going to be cut to trim the roster down to the mandated twenty-three players for the Olympics (the arrival of Grace Lee earlier that summer put South Korea's roster one above the tournament limit). Murray told Minji that she could still come to the US in case there was an injury to another player, and Minji wanted to keep her teammates motivated—they did not know yet who was to be left behind, and she believed that her presence would ensure that everyone continued training at optimal levels to make the team.

Minji was basically born with a hockey stick by her side. Her father played on a professional team in South Korea when he was still in high school and also competed for the national team. Later, he became a coach, and Minji's older brother, Min-woo, played professionally for Anyang Halla. In over ten years representing South Korea, Minji was the unofficial chronicler of their daily minutiae, taking videos of bus ride sing-alongs or teammates sleeping in the airport. Few cared about the women's national team like Minji. All of the imports agreed they might not have been able to survive in South Korea if not for her warmth, like the times she'd invite them to meet her grandmother or take them out for burgers and chicken at Mom's Touch, the restaurant where her mother worked and treated them all like family.

Shortly after President Moon and Minister Do met with the team, Minji posted on Instagram a screen shot of Prime Minister Lee Nak-yeon talking on television about the women's team, along with a lengthy screed on the unfairness of the turn of events. "How can one think that the players would take this situation in a good mood, even when anyone can become such a sacrificed player?" Minji wrote. She had witnessed twelve North Koreans added by the government with the snap of a finger, while after giving half of her life to the national team, she still remained on the outside looking in.

With the women's hockey team now being covered by every news outlet in South Korea, the media quickly scooped up Minji's message, and it became a national story. Some citizens sharply attacked Minji on her Instagram page and through other social media sites for betraying her country. "It was a difficult time for me," sighed Minji, adding that she felt like a controversial celebrity being hounded by the paparazzi. "When I was on the news I was really scared. But I was able to say what I wanted to say, so I have no regrets."

Despite the controversy surrounding the team, excitement for the Olympics boomed and the women's hockey team suddenly became the hottest ticket in the country. All of their games sold out online, so secondary markets began scalping tickets for five times their face value.

Even more stoked for the games were politicians. Choi Moon-soon, the governor of the province of Gangwon, where the Olympics were being held, boasted that the women's hockey team might pave the way for North Korea's denuclearization.[4] Another high-ranking government official told Korean media, "I get all emotional just imagining the North and South Korean athletes working up a sweat as they strive to win and then taking off their helmets and greeting the crowd after the game is over."[5] Of course, whenever administrators described these political fantasies and referred to the team as a vehicle for peace, none of the players were ever mentioned by name. They likely did not even know their names. Their individual stories were meaningless to them.

What none of these bigwigs recognized either was that by stuffing a dozen North Korean players on the roster, not once, but twice, the South Korean members had to accept interlopers. First it was the wave of imports. Now it was a group of individuals whose lives they believed they had even less in common with.

On January 25, a bus carrying the North Korean hockey players crossed into South Korea at 9:21 in the morning. Roads were blocked off for miles to provide an uninterrupted ride, but that did not prevent a horde of news vans and helicopters documenting their path from above and alongside, creating a scene not unlike how American cameras infamously chased O. J. Simpson's white Bronco. After passing through a Customs, Immigration and Quarantine office in Paju, northwest of Seoul, it took about another three hours until the convoy arrived in Jincheon. Bundled up in navy parkas on a sun-filled, although briskly chilly and windy afternoon, the South Korean players lined up and stood waiting outside their training facility. Many were shivering cold in the 18-degree weather but were unable to put their hands in their pockets since they were holding small bouquets of yellow, blue and pink flowers that they had been instructed to give their new teammates upon their arrival. There was no excitement, no anticipation. "I was just thinking if they were going to come, then come quickly," Han Do-hee said.

After North Korea's white bus pulled into the Jincheon training center parking lot, the team filed off slowly, led by their coach, Pak Chol-ho, a forty-eight-year-old with short black hair and the glint of a mustache on an otherwise unscathed tan complexion. His presence was disconcerting to some of the media, hearing rumors that he was a strict disciplinarian and could potentially challenge Murray's authority. Coach Pak, who stood only a few inches taller than Murray, competed for the North Korean men's national team in the late 1990s and later coached the men's team. With such a pedigree, he did not seem like the type of proud competitor to just step aside for a twenty-nine-year-old female foreigner.

Once the entire delegation of North Koreans came off the bus, each wearing long parkas swirled in white, red and blue stripes and reading DPR KOREA in large red letters on the back, they lined up across from the South Korean team. For a brief moment they stared into each other's eyes, unsure of what to say, curious what the person standing in front of them was thinking. In the moments before the North Koreans arrived, Susie Jo worried that there'd be conflict between the two teams, and it did almost look as if they were two gangs ready to engage in battle. Finally, Sojung stepped forward with her flowers, followed by her teammates, and quietly they bowed and offered greetings of "Nice to meet you" or "Welcome." Still, players like Dohee were nervous, even scared in the presence of North Koreans after previous icy interactions at World Championship tournaments.

Palpably tense, the two sides stood across from each other for a few more moments. "It was just so weird and formal and everyone knew we were going to be on the nightly news and we have to put on this show, and there was all this planning of who was going to give them the flowers," griped Randi. "It felt so fake."

Perhaps the only player not overcome with uncertainty was Grace. While back with her family in Colorado, Grace saw that unified team rumors were heating up again and texted Randi and Marissa, gauging their opinions. Her two older teammates were still wary to believe the news, but Grace was confident that a merger was going to happen. Throughout the week she sent them updates, increasing her conviction, but not theirs. On her plane ride back to South Korea, Grace was the only import not struck by fear. She couldn't wait to see Marissa and Randi again to tell them that she was right all along. "Both of them texted me and were like, it's not happening, no, you're wrong," Grace remembered. "I'm like, when we go back to Korea you'll see. I was pretty happy to be right."

Now, face-to-face with the North Koreans, Grace became awestruck. "When they first got off the bus, my first reaction was like, 'Oh, my God, they're from North Korea,' which is something not a regular person gets to see every day," Grace said. "That was really cool."

To break the tension, journalists requested that the two teams take a picture. They bunched together uncomfortably like in an elementary school class photo and were told to shout, "We are one!" It was a moment of propaganda sent around the world, but at the time the players did not think much about it. "Before we introduced ourselves to each other, I was angry," said Eom Su-yeon, who was rarely not flashing her dimples. "Not at the players, but at the government and the people who organized this. The North Koreans, I knew they weren't bad people. I thought some probably didn't want to come here, either."

Still unsure what to make of each other, the teams finally entered the training facility. It was time to get down to the real business at hand, at least in the minds of the South Korean players, if not anyone else in the country. Murray had arranged the locker room to ensure two South Korean player stalls sandwiched every one of the North Koreans'. The two sides began making informal introductions, resembling a speed-dating session. As Murray began taking note of the new additions, she realized there was an abundance of forwards—nine in total—and only two defenders and one goaltender. Murray had repeated her desire for defensive players to South Korean Olympic officials. In particular, she liked Kim Nong-gum and Won Chol-sun, a defender who stayed on the ice after stopping a slap shot with her face during the April game at the World Championships. Neither was among the selected group.

That was not the only glitch. Susie knew she was now going to have to translate Murray's messages to twelve more teammates whom she assumed spoke no English, which could lead to twelve more sets of questions. Then Susie discovered the North Koreans didn't even use the same hockey terms as the South Koreans. The locker room now not only had two teams, but essentially three languages.

The South Koreans used mostly English terms for hockey vocabulary. While the North Koreans used Korean words, they were very direct in their meaning and not formed in a traditional hockey parlance. For example, if a North Korean wanted to say "pass," they'd say something along the lines of "contact me," which a South Korean could understand, but not in its context. As frustration mounted, Lee Ji-yoon, the team manager, along with the assistance of some South Korean players, rushed to print sheets of paper and created a makeshift dictionary with more than seventy entries, with the North Korean term for a word next to the English-style hockey word the South Koreans used, written in both English and Korean. Since it was more difficult for the North Koreans to learn a new English vocabulary, many of the South Korean players stuck individual notes on their lockers to study North Korean colloquialisms. Susie also simplified phrases, telling the North Koreans "five versus four" for a power play.

"In the beginning it felt like a burden because I was busy with my own responsibilities," Susie said. "When we first met, we were very divided and I didn't feel any kind of sympathy or friendship. But after a while, watching the North Koreans trying to learn South Korean terms, I felt more of an urge to help them out. I started realizing the North Korean team is there because of their government, as well. Who knows if they are there if they want to be? I realized the North Korean players, they're also kind, innocent and warm."

Throughout the day, members of the South Korean team realized they needed to take the lead to create chemistry. Dohee began making the occasional joke to lighten up the mood and the imports, reminded of the generosity of Minji, YeEun, Susie, Sojung and Ko Hye-in early on, felt the need to reciprocate. "I could definitely relate," Marissa said. "I tried to put myself in their shoes. They're coming into a team, the language is quite different. I was like, okay, make them feel welcome like the South Koreans did for you. Look where you're at now, look at the relationships you've built. Try and instill that."

Earlier in the afternoon, Marissa had noted during the arrival ceremony that one North Korean player stood out from the group, because she was the only one who seemed unabashedly overtaken by joy. Later, Marissa learned her name was Kim Un-jong, she was the same age as her, twenty-five, and that she first began playing hockey at an outdoor rink near Taesongsan mountain in Pyongyang. "She was the most smiley," Marissa said. "I was like, ooh, I like her."

That evening, when Marissa arrived early to a meeting with Grace, Un Jong was already there, sitting down, still flashing a radiant, huge grin. Marissa couldn't resist any longer and pointed, then waved to Un Jong to come over and sit next to her, which she gladly did.

"This was the first day so everyone was nervous, kind of shy, kind of timid, but this girl was so happy to be here and she couldn't stop smiling," Grace confirmed.

After the final meeting, the South Koreans were excused but the North Koreans were told to remain for further lessons on the team's playbook. After Marissa took in Un Jong, Grace asked Hyein, her roommate at Jincheon, to similarly engage other North Korean players. When Hyein wavered, Grace grabbed her hand and forced her to stay behind and introduce themselves to their new colleagues. "Just because I know how it kind of feels coming onto the team late," Grace said. "I knew some people weren't happy about my arrival, so I knew some people weren't happy with the North Koreans' arrival, too. I guess it was just trying to make them feel like it was fine."

For almost twelve hours, South Korean news media waited outside the training center for the first day's orientation to end. They talked about how earlier in the afternoon, many of the faces that stepped off the North Korean bus showed no emotion. Now, there was a buoyancy in the North Korean players' steps as they funneled back outside to head to the separate residency in Jincheon where they stayed for the next two weeks. As their bus pulled away, one videographer caught Un Jong smiling through the bus window, waving at the camera.

Over the next four days, two North Korean players—Jin Ok and Choe Un-gyong—had birthdays. The team celebrated with cakes and even wiped vanilla icing on the birthday girls' faces, then sang "Happy Birthday" as Ok and Un Gyong blew out their candles. The South Korean government and Olympic officials aggressively pushed out photos of the moment, a sign that the miracle of sport and peace was happening and that they were justified all along in forcing this never before seen mix of sports and politics.

"This is exactly what the Olympic Games and Olympic spirit are about," proclaimed Thomas Bach, president of the IOC. "You can see at the beginning that there may have been some skepticism among each other. These players arrived, and they got to know each other. They were training together, and a couple of days later, they were celebrating birthday[s] in such a way. If someone asks you, 'What's the Olympic spirit?' This is it."[6]

COURTESY OF MARISSA BRANDT

*Imports like Marissa Brandt (left), Danelle Im (second to left) and Grace Lee (second to right) decided to make the North Koreans feel more welcome, similar to how some South Koreans integrated them into the team early on.*

# CHAPTER SIXTEEN

# Family

Shin So-jung had never been a fiery orator. She usually kept her feelings inside during uncomfortable situations, but when KIHA issued a gag order on the women's hockey team, Sojung decided she could not stay silent.

On January 19, the day before the merger was officially approved by the IOC, Sojung gave an interview to the *Chosun Ilbo*, one of South Korea's largest newspapers. Sojung was "perplexed" and "disappointed" in her government's willingness to form a unified team without their players' consent. Speaking for her teammates, Sojung described the locker room as "frustrated" and "demoralized."[1]

Some players were surprised to learn Sojung expressed herself in such an unfettered fashion, but even they did not know how the decision to add North Koreans to Sojung's hockey family stung on an extremely personal level.

Hockey may have been stitched into Sojung's soul, but after her father passed away she began crafting various detailed plans for a postplaying career. Sojung once told Randi Griffin her idea for opening a chain of North American restaurants; inspired by visiting a Chipotle Mexican fast-food establishment, Sojung planned to sell *bibimbap*, the popular Korean dish that contains a base of eggs and rice in a bowl, and can be varietized with a plethora of spices, meats and vegetables. While in college, Sojung often mentioned to Sarah Bujold, a friend on the women's hockey team, about her lifelong dream to become an actress. On the surface, this choice seemed the oddest and least logical next step after hockey. However, what Sojung never divulged was that working in motion pictures was actually a Shin family legacy, and that she was connected to what is perhaps one of the most fascinating stories ever told in the history of the Korean peninsula.

Sojung's grandmother's brother was Shin Sang-ok, South Korea's most famous director. His dramas regularly portrayed Korean women struggling to break free from their oppressive lives and were devoured by the farm workers, cooks and seamstresses who yearned to live out Shin's narratives, searching for two hours of escape from their war-torn surroundings. Originally from Chongjin in the North Hamgyong province of North Korea, Shin was dubbed the "prince of South Korean cinema." Along with filming the first on-screen kiss in South Korean film, he married his country's most famous actress, Choi Eunhee, whose long nose, full lips and twinkling eyes made her the center of attention even when photographed alongside the likes of Marilyn Monroe. They met at one of Choi's theater performances in the city of Daegu; Choi, twenty-seven, collapsed on stage and Shin picked her up, thrust her onto his shoulder and carried her to a local hospital.[2] After their wedding, the couple adopted two Korean children.

In 1978, Shin and Choi were involved in a series of bizarre events that sound as if they were plucked from the script of a Hollywood film. Choi was invited to visit Hong Kong, where she was kidnapped by North Korean agents. Shin went searching after Choi, only to be captured himself. These orders came directly from Kim Jong-il, the son of North Korea's "Supreme Leader," Kim Il-sung. Before succeeding his father as the ruler of North Korea, Kim Jong-il was the head of his nation's Department for Movies and Arts. Not only did he amass a library of twenty thousand motion pictures, but he published a book on film-making in 1973, called *On the Art of Cinema*. Depressed by the low-grade material being produced in his country—even though he hired 250 full-time employees at his national film studio in Pyongyang—Kim Jong-il demanded that Choi and Shin resurrect the North Korean film industry, pining to have his country's films regarded among the world's finest cinema showcased at Cannes and Venice.[3]

Choi was put up in a glamorous but well-guarded villa in Pyongyang that served exquisite meals of shrimp, ribs and Korean delicacies, while Shin was held separately under house arrest and then sent to a North Korean detention center for insubordination, where he was confined to a bug-infested solitary cell. Shin attempted to escape and then, after finding that was nearly impossible, he tried to commit suicide. Finally, feeling withered and defeated, Shin agreed to produce Kim Jong-il's films featuring Choi until 1986, when while in Vienna, he and Choi fled to the United States Embassy.[4] Shin briefly lived in Los Angeles and died in 2006, never getting the opportunity to meet his niece.

Sojung should have never made it to the Olympics, the NWHL or even college in Canada. She stood at a generous five feet five inches and had better odds of winning the lottery than developing into anything more than a recreational hockey player in South Korea. But her desire to make Korea proud never wilted, no matter how many roadblocks she encountered. That is why Sojung told the *Chosun Ilbo*, "All of us had to give up something in our lives, but we've been striving toward one goal—to play in the Olympics. We could bear it all because we're proud to represent our country. That's why we feel so devastated now."

South Korea betrayed its women's hockey team without knowing the pride felt each time they saw their country's name on a scoreboard. Choi Yu-jung almost cried when she saw workers removing all images of the South Korean flag from the Jincheon locker room to accommodate the North Koreans. This included the new jerseys the team planned to wear in the Olympics that featured a patch of the national flag. A few weeks earlier, when Park Chae-lin tried the garment on for the first time, she described the moment as surreal—it felt like she was finally an Olympian. Now, she felt as if she did not exist at all.

During their year living in Seoul before the Olympics, the imports also developed newfound patriotic feelings. Like Randi, Grace Lee requested that the back of her jersey include her Korean middle name, Jingyu. "Growing up, people would ask me what my middle name is, I'd be embarrassed to say it," Grace said. "I usually didn't want people to know. Now after this whole experience, it actually makes me feel more connected to Korea. I like being called it."

Marissa Brandt put her full birth name, Park Yoon-jung, on hers. Marissa also joined a campaign called "Letters to Angels" to raise adoption awareness within the country. For a promotional photo shoot, Marissa was asked to cradle a young orphaned girl named Hayul in her arms. She learned that the infant was the same age Marissa was when she was put up for adoption. Afterward, Marissa wrote a letter to the child that concluded by telling her: "I hope you feel loved and always stay true to your heritage."

Having reacquainted herself with her own Korean heritage, Marissa felt obligated to perform well at the Olympics not only for her birth country, but to ensure that women's hockey in South Korea did not fade away after she and the other imports left. "Hockey, it's like the first sure thing they have in their lives," Grace learned. "Without that, everyone's future is kind of scary."

While Sojung presciently knew there'd come a day when she could no longer lace up her skates, other veterans like Han Soo-jin were hockey lifers. But without continued support after the Olympics, she'd be living at home in her thirties with no prospects for the future. Recognizing this dilemma, some of the teenagers were already leaning toward quitting the sport after PyeongChang, despite having the talent to continue on and play NCAA Division I Hockey with the world's best skaters.

Kim Hee-won, already five feet six inches in high school with leg muscles like a linebacker, had all but decided by age sixteen to attend college in South Korea. One of Heewon's best friends, seventeen-year-old Eom Su-yeon, was the most enthusiastic about playing college hockey in America, but even she had doubts of how beneficial that would be when she returned home and entered job interviews with employers that had no idea about university names like St. Cloud or Minnesota-Duluth. "I often wonder, should I attend a university known for hockey, or one Koreans know more about?" Suyeon said.

Attending college in South Korea would certainly be more comforting. Despite the presence of a Sojung or Grace sprinkled throughout North America, Korean hockey players were not always treated with the same levels of respect abroad. During a practice before South Korea played the University of Minnesota in September 2017, a local fan walked down toward the bench and asked Sarah Murray what group she was with. When Murray responded passionately that she coached South Korea and how diligently the team had been training over the last three years to reach a point where they felt they belonged on the ice with a storied program like Minnesota, the six-time national champions, the man's only response was to knock her down from her high. "Oh, that will be a bloodbath tomorrow," he guffawed and walked away. A few minutes later, as the South Koreans finished skating and headed back to their locker room, they squeezed past an impatient squad of teenage boys that wanted them out of the rink so they could begin their recreational league game. As Susie Jo and others politely walked by, saying, "Excuse me," the coach for one of the boys' teams, an obese, unkempt figure, chirped to his players mockingly, "Make way for the DHL—the Dickhead Hockey League."

Occasionally after their games in the US, the host school held a dinner, which often turned into uncomfortable, patronizing meals that the South Koreans couldn't wait to be finished with. They'd encounter American college students who were somehow astonished that some players spoke English and then were peppered with elementary inquiries like if they'd ever eaten a cheeseburger. Not only would Suyeon or Heewon put themselves in line for better jobs staying at home in South Korea, but they wouldn't be trivialized with such asinine questions or gifts of toy sheriff badges.

While being a Korean hockey player in America had its share of cringe-inducing moments, it was in the US where the players often demonstrated why it was worthwhile for the South Korean government to fully invest in women's hockey. Desirae and Steve Rembeck, a young Caucasian couple from the Twin Cities, brought their two sons to watch South Korea play Minnesota. Seven-year-old Simon MinHwan Rembeck was adopted at twenty-two months, while his younger brother, five-year-old Archer Jaewon Rembeck, arrived when he was thirty-five months old. Desirae Rembeck had read articles about the importance of children seeing themselves in various influential figures, like how Michelle Kwan was inspired by watching the Olympic gold medal performance of Kristi Yamaguchi. Cognizant of this effect, Desirae took her sons to Minnesota Twins baseball games after they signed South Korean slugger Byung-ho Park in

2016, and to the women's hockey game. The Rembeck boys did not know anything about Jung Si-yun or Lee Eun-ji, but once inside the arena they begged their parents for miniature South Korean flags and ran after the players for autographs. When the Rembecks returned home, they stored these mementos in a special trunk alongside the baby clothes the boys wore when they arrived in the US and other reminders of their birth country.

Similar to how the Rembecks felt drawn to support South Korea's women's hockey team, Molly McCormick brought thirty students from the school where she worked as a teacher. The Sejong Academy opened in 2014 as a Korean immersion charter school, intended to target adoptees from South Korea. For weeks after the game the children showed off their pictures, pucks and autographs they received from players. "It was an experience they will never forget," said McCormick, who learned about the team while visiting Seoul, where she met Danelle Im at a church service.

Theresa Utecht, the mother of children adopted from South Korea, was compelled to attend the game in River Falls and present the players with souvenir Olympic pins that she had accumulated over decades, as a thank-you to their country and their service to it. After South Korea beat Shattuck-St. Mary's in January, Minnesota residents who had driven from hours away, hearing rumors that their native South Korea was competing in a hockey game in Faribault, hovered near the exit from the ice among a bustle of Korean American students from the school. Waving South Korean flags, these admirers hung over the glass, hoping to shake hands with the players. Michelle Yunjung You traveled from Mankato with her seven-year-old hockey-playing daughter, Christine Soojung Kim; after the game against Minnesota State-Mankato the week before, Sojung handed her a goalie's stick. On the way home, You's daughter told her mom that she hoped to play for the South Korean national team one day, too.

Rachael Miyung Joo wrote in her book, *Transnational Sport: Gender, Media, and Global Korea*, that Korean American immigrants regularly feel marginalized and invisible in the US, and viewings of Korean athletes competing abroad "enable Korean Americans to articulate their relationships to Koreanness and what it means to be Korean/American in the United States."[5] To You and others, the idea of South Korean women engaged in hockey at first seemed an idea so dissonant, yet these sons and daughters of the Korean diaspora were able to find a connection to home watching the way Sojung commanded the net and seeing the joy in Heewon's plump-cheeked smile.

COURTESY OF CHOI EUN-YOUNG

*Korean students at St. Cloud State University felt a semblance of home meeting their women's national hockey team.*

One of the most poignant examples of the South Korean hockey team's influence occurred in St. Cloud, Minnesota. Although it is only an hour drive north of Minneapolis via Interstate 94, St. Cloud paints a stark contrast to the bustle of the Twin Cities. After leaving the metropolis, the stretch of highway to St. Cloud is marked by the odor of manure and farmland. Because of its less than diverse population, the city mockingly became known as "White Cloud." One way the school attempted to change its demographics was by appealing to international students looking to improve their English skills with a relatively low-cost education option.

About one hundred members of St. Cloud's Korean student population descended upon the Herb Brooks National Hockey Center for their school's exhibition game against their home country. Thirty minutes before the puck was dropped, what had previously been a quiet arena save for a few family members of St. Cloud players scattered about the stands, suddenly became disrupted by the banging of Korean *sogo* drums and yells of "go Korea, go, go, go," emanating from coeds with their faces marked with red-and-blue stripes resembling war paint.

The contingent screamed the first time South Korea knocked the puck out of their zone and yelled even more euphorically when Heewon scored a goal that evened the game, 1–1. The sound of the blaring red goal horn caused many of the students to put their hands over their ears and laugh, but even without knowing the names of players or the details of how the sport was played, that did not dampen the atmosphere. The assembled Korean students felt more in tune with their surroundings than ever, buying cheese curds from the concession stand and waving homemade signs that displayed in two languages the phrase "Fighting Korea." South Korea lost a back-and-forth game, 4–3, but that did not matter either as the players received a standing ovation from a collection of fans finally finding a slice of Korean pride 6,000 miles away from home in White Cloud.

After the game, St. Cloud staff made accommodations for an impromptu meet-and-greet session. One of the Korean students began following Heewon on social media; months later, she wrote to inform her that ever since that game in September, she had become obsessed with hockey and had traveled around the US to watch the sport. Choi Eun-young, a junior from Incheon majoring in radiologic technology, never knew her country had a women's hockey team, but now she proudly hung on her dorm room wall a flag of South Korea signed by the entire team. Lee Jung-hyeok, a sophomore from Suwon studying biomedical science, was shocked at the young age of so many of the players. Displayed in Lee's dorm is a signed T-shirt featuring smiley faces courtesy of Chaelin and Susie.

*The team poses for a photo with a family from Mankato, Minnesota. The homemade sign in the background reads, "We root for the dreams of all the players on Team Korea."*

"I used to be a person who gave up easily," Lee said, "but then after seeing them, that they were much smaller and younger than the opponent and still not giving up the match, made me think about myself again."

Lee was not alone in finding a luminous quality to the team. Ko Hye-in transferred schools six times and moved to Seoul by herself in the sixth grade to play for the national team. Hyein grew up in Jeonju, three hours south of the capital, and was too rambunctious to stick to one sport. Dance, ballet and soccer all came and went. One day, shortly after Hyein had moved on to speed skating, she snooped in her training facility's basement and, like stumbling upon El Dorado, discovered a rink outfitted for hockey and found her calling.

At first Hyein commuted by bus to practices in Seoul, trips that could take up to five hours each way if there was traffic.

Hyein's mother eventually rented an apartment in the capital city under her name so her daughter no longer needed to suffer through lethargic bus rides and visited every few days with home-cooked meals. Hyein's cousins lived nearby, but like Jongah, Hyein found living alone scarier than dreamlike. The only perk was that her apartment had an oven, which not only helped pass the time, but bonded her closer to her teammates.

"One thing I got into living alone was cooking," Hyein said. "In Korean culture, people don't use ovens as much. I was really excited when I got mine because the idea of baking a cake for my friends seemed really special."

Hyein labored for hours mixing eggs and flour and whipping up icings whenever there was a birthday on the team. Often, she'd bake cakes for no special reason at all. It is not surprising that Hyein was so inventive—in high school she earned several patents, including creating an ergonomic wheelchair designed so the user did not strain their back and could instead exert force in exercise. In college, Hyein studied nanotechnology at one of the nation's top universities, but she was willing to risk all of her academic achievements for hockey.

"I always wonder why are you playing hockey here, what do you get out of it?" Danelle said. "It's because they really love hockey. That's what I think about when I think of this team. They love hockey. That's it."

Of all the players, Choi Ji-yeon was perhaps the most fanatical about hockey and everything it brought into her life. Someone like Park Ye-eun cultivated outside interests and could become enthralled for hours visiting art museums and studying architecture, but for Jiyeon, whose favorite article of clothing was an Edmonton Oilers T-shirt of NHL star Connor McDavid, hockey was all that mattered. Despite knowing that her career would never extend beyond South Korea, Jiyeon was arguably the team's most determined player, always asking Danelle to stay after practice and run extra laps with her, or entering a state of almost "blacking out" on emotion as Murray described it, whenever Jiyeon tried to atone for making a mistake during a game. That is why in November 2017, when it looked like she might have to leave hockey behind, Jiyeon became tortured. But her hockey sisters would not let her go.

South Korea traveled to the industrial city of Miskolc for exhibition games against France, Denmark and host Hungary. Two of the three participants had reached the final qualification round for the 2018 Olympics, and the round-robin tournament should have provided a good barometer for where South Korea stood as a team just three months from the opening ceremony. Instead, the trip ended up showing where they stood then and forever as a family.

After posting a disappointing 0–3 record, the coaches were meeting in Murray's room on the last night in Miskolc, when Susie knocked on the door. As the team's go-to translator, Susie never had trouble getting to the point. But as Murray answered the door, she saw Susie shaking in the hallway. Confused and concerned, Murray pressed Susie on what was wrong.

"Jiyeon's dad has passed away," Susie said.

Kim Do-yun, whose own father died when he was around Jiyeon's age, bolted out of the room. When Doyun arrived at Jiyeon's door, her teammates were already there, huddled around her on the edge of her bed, including Sojung, who also lost her dad when she was nineteen. They held Jiyeon's hand as she remembered when her father bought her first equipment and taught her how to play the game; then when he became her personal coach, training Jiyeon to the point where she qualified for the national team when she was only twelve.

Jiyeon lived with her father and older brother and suddenly she began fretting over how she would pay her bills and her college expenses and where she would live. Jiyeon did not come from a very wealthy background. She was supposed to be one of the original attendees of OHA, but if she went to Canada, that disqualified her for the small stipend of a few hundred dollars a month from the national team. Because these funds were important to her family, Jiyeon declined the opportunity. She had to make the same crushing decision after impressing scouts at a special IIHF camp held for players from developing hockey countries. Jiyeon received interest to play NCAA Division I college hockey for the University of Maine and Minnesota State-Mankato, but instead, to keep her stipend, accepted a full scholarship to attend Chongshin University in Seoul. Like every other college in the country, Chongshin had no women's hockey team.

With Jiyeon's father unexpectedly gone and no contingency plan in place for how to make ends meet, Jiyeon's teammates pooled thousands of dollars together from saved stipend checks. They did not leave Jiyeon's side in the days after her father's death, enveloping her in their arms from the moment they found out the tragic news until they flew back home. "I was almost a little worried we were a little too present," Randi said. "Sometimes she looked a little overwhelmed and needed to be alone but the team was like, no, we are not going anywhere. You can't get rid of us, Jiyeon. We are here for you."

On the flight back to South Korea, Susie received an upgrade to first class and gave her seat to Jiyeon in the hopes that she could rest before going straight to the funeral. Naturally, the entire team attended to pay their respects and keep a cushion underneath their reeling sister. Lee Yeon-jeong first met Jiyeon in elementary school, and when they started playing hockey together, Jiyeon's father drove them to practice. Even as a child, before they stepped out of the car, he always asked Yeonjeong to take care of his daughter, and so when Jiyeon needed her most, she fulfilled Jiyeon's father's wishes.

"We see each other more than our actual family members," Susie explained. "We're there for each other through difficult times, through happy times. Even if we have time on the weekend to hang out with friends, we want to see each other. We feel the most comfortable when we're around each other and feel like a family. When Jiyeon's father passed away, it felt as if our own fathers passed away because we feel so close to Jiyeon. We didn't really know what to say to her. The only thing we could do at that point is to be there for her. That just seemed the most natural thing to do."

A few months later, when Jiyeon had moved in with her grandparents and remained part of the national team, she sat in a café in Seoul, answering most questions while looking down at her mango smoothie, overcome by shyness. When asked to reflect on what her teammates meant during the period after her father died, she paused to speak and then, becoming emotional, Jiyeon looked up with her winsome black eyes and said succinctly, "I was reminded once again my team is like my family."

A majority of the national team did not seem like they fit into South Korean society's standards for women their age. The heavy influence of Korean pop culture forces many young women to feel like they need to attain the features of beautiful models, with perfectly shaped eyelids, spotless smooth faces and cherry-red lips. Physical beauty is prioritized in a manner that borders on the insane. In Seoul, makeup shops seemingly take up more real estate than McDonald's and Starbucks combined in American cities. High school teenagers often receive plastic surgery as a graduation gift. Estimates range that one-fifth to one-third of women in Seoul have had beauty enhancement procedures, including having their jawbones sawed down to make a rounder-looking face. Euny Hong mentioned in her book that in the Apgujeong section of the city, a one-square-mile area has four hundred plastic surgery clinics.[6] Subway stations throughout the country are covered in immense billboards advertising plastic surgery, and tourists from around the world pay for vacation packages based around beauty enhancement procedures. Online ratings of hotels near Apgujeong are often dependent on how many customers are seen in the lobby with bandages.

Nicole Kaminski, a goaltender from Georgetown, Ontario, often discussed the cultural intricacies of beauty in South Korea with YeEun, Park Jong-ah and Kim Se-lin at OHA. "They would talk about how girls would get surgery to change their eye shape, apparently a very popular trend in Korea, which I was shocked by, and the three Koreans seemed to feel the same way," Kaminski said.

The women's national hockey team was one of the few enclaves where South Korean girls did not have to feel pressured by such standards. They could show, as Soojin once described it, a "wild and rough side on the ice" and maintain feminine qualities off it.

"I didn't like to look girly," said Lee Min-ji. "Even on the team if someone wears pink we'd say, 'Oh, she's wearing pink,' like a joke."

For someone like Han Do-hee, who didn't like wearing dresses and kept her hair short in a pixie cut, Korean society could make her feel like an outsider. She wasn't suitable material for the buttoned-down corporate environment of a *chaebol*. In hockey, though, she was the center of attention, the team's comedian and motivator, an iconoclast with a motorcycle and kickboxing training. Playing behind Sojung, Dohee was never going to become the starting goaltender, and although she used hand-me-down equipment until she was twenty, she never thought about quitting. The sport was more than a passion; it gave her something she could find nowhere else in life.

"For a lot of girls on that team, I think of girls like Soojin and Dohee, this family was like everything for them," Randi opined. "I especially think that someone like Dohee, for example, she does not fit into Korean culture. She is not a typical Korean girl. She wants to be a tomboy and she wants to wear suits and baseball hats and act crazy. There's no world in which she can do that and be loved and respected except this little hockey team. She tries to act that way working for a *chaebol*, like no way. But she has this little world where she can be herself and she's valued exactly how she is and I think that is everything to someone like her and that's what keeps them coming back."

Dohee didn't mind her label as the roster's class clown, and she found value in what her personality brought to others. "I don't think it's a bad thing as long as the girls are happy and enjoying themselves," Dohee reasoned.

Dohee could indeed make anyone laugh at any moment, but as Marissa learned, she was also extremely hard on herself. Whenever she received the opportunity to start in net, if Dohee allowed a goal, she'd bawl, crying after games, and nothing Marissa or anyone else tried to tell her seemed comforting enough. Like almost every clown, there was a layer of sadness inside Dohee that she only felt comfortable sharing amid the trusted circle of her teammates. "I think I was still able to do well during difficult times because I was able to lean on Hyein, Susie and Mihwan," Dohee said.

"Dohee is really funny and she's really good at changing the mood and the atmosphere," Hyein asserted. "I know she often does this to hide her darker sides. Sometimes she jokes about things like why do I have to live like this? She's saying those things because she compares her life to other people's lives, those people following a very obvious path in life. They graduate high school, go to college and get a job. She didn't go to university so that's why she has a lot of doubt about herself. I wish she would understand that everyone lives a different life.

"I think she's perfect."

Hockey gave Dohee purpose. When discussing her future with her teammates, Dohee dreamed of being a hockey coach not only to provide younger generations—particularly girls—with resources that she didn't have, but to let them know that they could feel the same warmth and acceptance inside the boards of a rink.

"I've belonged to this team for thirteen years," Dohee proclaimed proudly. "They're as important as my family. This team, it's my everything."

*Han Do-hee (top center) found special meaning among the camaraderie of her teammates. From L to R: Park Chae-lin, Park Jong-ah, Susie Jo, Park Ye-eun.*

Not President Moon Jae-in or Sports Minister Do Jong-hwan, nor even KIHA president Chung Mong-won knew that the bonds of the team resonated so profoundly. They also did not know about the ruptured ligaments in Cho Mi-hwan's knees or the dislocated shoulders that she played with. Or Susie's chronic back pain and how the veins in her legs popped during weight training, bruising her thighs for weeks. Yet she continued on, like Yeonjeong did after tearing ligaments in her knees, even delaying surgery just to represent South Korea in the Olympics. Yeonjeong made this decision after watching Hyein push through year-round training with torn ligaments in her ankle that she never fully recovered from, all for her country.

"I think my life changed entirely due to hockey," said Mihwan, who was never interested when her family suggested more secure career paths, such as becoming a diplomat or military officer. "I didn't follow the track of being an ordinary girl. Hockey allowed me to experience exceptional things, meet many people, and throughout all of this my personality changed a lot. I guess I could say that I've come to embody my teammates' various personalities. If Cho Mi-hwan was a book, around 80 percent of that would be about ice hockey.

"The most important thing that happened to me as a result is that I now have a new family. I wouldn't have been able to play ice hockey until now if my teammates weren't there, and after all, they are the reason why I am playing. I've believed that we would be able to create miracles as a team."

The decision to create the first unified Olympic team of North Korean and South Korean athletes was made out of convenience, the government claimed, but was a plan rooted in disrespect. It also just happened to be placed upon the shoulders of twenty-three young women absolutely made for the moment. They had two weeks to achieve the impossible and were the only unit in the world equipped with the fortitude, love and emotional strength to do so.

"It's cliché to say, every team says they're a family," Grace said, "but not like this. This is something else."

# CHAPTER SEVENTEEN

# Comrades

Shortly after the North Koreans arrived on January 25, the thirty-five players and five coaches sheltered themselves around two-person desks in a glass-paneled meeting room at Jincheon. Inside, they combined years' worth of lessons in language and hockey in an attempt to learn not only their new teammates' tendencies, but those of their opponents.

Camping outside, international media became frenzied in finding out every morsel possible about this rare assemblage of North Americans and North and South Koreans. There were rumors of the players sharing meals of *tteokbokki* and giggling like schoolgirls (only partly true) and a claim that the South Koreans tried to smuggle cell phones to the North Korean players to stay in touch with them at night (not true at all). Then there was the story of the mysterious appearance of two alleged North Korean spies planted inside to keep tabs on the proceedings. Despite sounding like the most outlandish of all the gossip, it was also the most accurate.

For over a week, these two men lived with the North Korean players in a separate dormitory away from the rest of the athletes. They looked to be in their late thirties to midforties, with lean, athletic frames, and were unusually tall for Koreans, standing at nearly six feet. The duo were present at team meals, but not meetings. The only times they seemed to speak were near Pak Chol-ho or to cut off South Korean journalists trying to ask Coach Pak questions after practices. Not even the South Korean government knew their identity. Ko Hye-in was suspicious of the duo's South Korean accents, which indicated they were highly educated and likely North Korean government officials. On February 3, the *Wall Street Journal* and South Korean media reported on the presence of the mystery men, and within days they vanished from the Unified team's delegation.

Such a tense environment made forging sincere connections between the two sides almost impossible, a stark difference to the depiction being presented to the world in statements and photos released by the Blue House and IOC. In their first week together, there was a pervasive Big Brother atmosphere surrounding the Unified team, not only due to the presence of possible spies, but also South Korean government officials orchestrating every aspect of their daily lives. Park Chae-lin was sternly told by these officials not to say "North Korea," because it was deemed offensive. Instead, she was told to refer to it as "the northern side." Players were also ordered not to take photographs together, because hacked or leaked unapproved images could allegedly get the North Koreans in trouble. Only staged photographs were permitted, like the ones at Jin Ok and Choe Un-gyong's birthday parties, events that were actually the ideas of the officials at Jincheon, not the players.

As a result, when both sides did engage in conversation, the South Koreans could not discern if what they were being told was authentic or propaganda. One day, Hyein listened to the North Koreans praising Kim Jong-un for their hockey gear, even though they arrived with old-model wooden sticks that were outdated in the 1990s. Another topic of discussion was ice cream. The North Korean players extolled the ice cream shops in Pyongyang, which thanks to their "Great Leader," featured three robust flavors. "We were joking they'll all defect if we take them to Baskin-Robbins," Randi Griffin quipped.

*The two Koreas rarely interacted before games against each other.*

COURTESY OF SIMON CROSSE

    This reminded Hyein of a popular South Korean television show, *Now On My Way to Meet You*, featuring North Korean defectors discussing their lives under communist rule. Hyein remembered that almost every guest mentioned not being able to trust your neighbors. An overheard comment that was negative toward the state even made in jest could lead to prison or worse, while the snitching party was rewarded for their servitude.

    "I had an assumption they were afraid to say anything else because of the government," Hyein recounted. "We had asked these type of questions out of curiosity. It was supposed to be a simple question, but it would lead to something much more serious. Whenever that happened I'd try to change the topic quickly."

This inability to interact without anodyne banter particularly frustrated Hyein. She did not like meeting someone new and sensing awkwardness. This is why she purposely reached out to the imports when they first arrived in Seoul. Behind her scientific mind and extensive vocabulary, Hyein could actually be quite droll.

One of the first times Marissa Brandt remembered laughing around the team was when Hyein was shaving her armpits and noticed she missed one hair, then looked at Marissa and dryly commented, "Oh, look who got away from me."

Hyein's comedic stylings did not go over as well with her audience from North Korea. "Their jokes were very serious," Hyein said. "Cynical. Their intonation is different from ours. If we'd laugh, we'd laugh together, then after I'd be thinking, 'Why exactly did we laugh?'"

Hyein became so unnerved by the Stasi-like surveillance at Jincheon that she eventually developed a sixth sense to know whenever North Koreans were about to enter a room. If a television was on in the vicinity, an official turned it off before the North Koreans could arrive, lest they consume any information that was not state-sanctioned. Hyein hated seeing the North Koreans watched over and controlled so carefully. The South Koreans had accepted them in hopes of gaining a level of the cohesion and vitality that had made their unit so strong. Instead, it seemed as if they could only connect superficially.

For the imports, being able to communicate with the North Korean players seemed even more of a lost cause. While Marissa Brandt could make Kim Un-jong feel welcome by sitting next to her, she was likely never going to tap into her innermost feelings like she had with Park Ye-eun. Only vaguely able to pick up a few words in Korean, Randi began asking Hyein and others what conversations were really like. "The way they described it to me," Randi said, "it seemed kind of like if you are meeting with some people that speak your language, but they come from an isolated cult and they have very strange accents and very strange ways of saying things, and bizarre beliefs about the world."

*Ko Hye-in (third from left) wondered if she and her South Korean teammates could ever form strong bonds with the North Korean players.*

In the new expanded locker room at Jincheon, Hyein sat next to Un Gyong, who was also born in 1994. Hyein had noticed that Un Gyong, too, desperately wanted to get to know her better, but she sensed she was afraid to speak too candidly. Then one afternoon, Hyein saw Un Gyong purposely leave her watch in Hyein's locker.

"Hey, you left your watch here," Hyein said.

"Don't call me 'Hey,'" Un Gyong responded. "Call me 'Comrade.'"

It was Un Gyong's attempt at relating to Hyein's wry humor, and although the joke fell a bit flat, the South Koreans appreciated attempts like these to inject some sort of personality away from the watchful eyes of the emotionless-looking men tracing their steps. Grace and Marissa taught Un Jong how to say certain body parts in English and they'd laugh whenever she'd point at her arm instead of her head, flashing her trademark smile regardless of a right or wrong answer. Kim Se-lin began chatting up Ryo Song-hui, twenty-four, and Hwang Sol-gyong, twenty-one, and both liked to feign disbelief in Selin only being seventeen. She looked much older, they told her, a positive trait in North Korea. These were not Eddie Murphy *Delirious* levels of uproarious humor, but served well as icebreakers. "When we saw them laugh, it made me realize they're not just stern people," Selin said.

Selin soon picked up that Song Hui and Sol Gyong were just as nervous and curious about this whole enigmatic scenario. Han Do-hee found popular North Korean songs on YouTube and played them in the locker room to loosen the atmosphere. Another North Korean player who latched onto Marissa's warmth was Kim Un-hyang, who was just eight days older than her. Each morning when Un Hyang saw Marissa, she'd greet her with a hug. It became routine that at some point in the day, Un Hyang asked Marissa for her phone. It wasn't to call Pyongyang or to gain access to the internet—the way she handled the device, Marissa could tell that Un Hyang did not even really know how to use the phone—but she'd physically communicate that she wanted to see Marissa's album of photos. Almost in a trance, Un Hyang stared at the pictures of Marissa with her American friends from back home—the times in college at Gustavus with Courtney Boucher or at her wedding. Un Hyang wanted nothing more than to get closer to Marissa, and the few minutes each day flipping through these pictures allowed her a glimpse into her life, and even perhaps a vision of what a different existence would look like outside of North Korea.

There was no moment of epiphany where the team fused overnight. Similar to the South Koreans' relationship with the imports, it took time before a level of comfort set in. With only a few weeks together, the tight bonds that had made the South Korean national team a family were never likely to form as strongly with the North Koreans. That did not mean that the South Koreans could not care for the North Koreans or make them part of their lives. The more they realized their shared aims, the more the South Koreans became protective of the North Koreans, which helped foster team chemistry.

With many of the national teams in other sports based at Jincheon before the Olympics, hundreds of athletes were milling about. During lunch, the South Korean players began noticing that when the North Koreans entered the cafeteria to sit and eat with them, other residents, including imports on the men's national team, would gawk and stare, even recording video on their phones to send to their bros back home or to post on social media, even though officials at Jincheon explicitly told all athletes not to do so. "I didn't like that," said Danelle Im, a Pollyanna who almost never voiced her displeasure with anything or anyone. "That didn't seem right to me. I didn't think they should be looked at that way. It objectified them."

"You could notice people were staring at them," added Choi Yu-jung. "One of the North Korean players asked, 'Why is everyone staring?' The North Korean players knew why they were being stared at; she didn't say that in the form of a question but more of a comment. That's when I felt bad."

Just like how the South Koreans didn't like being characterized as puppets or undeserving, the North Koreans did not want to be seen like circus animals or some unhuman sideshow attraction. They wanted to be treated with respect, just what

YeEun and her teammates had fought for throughout their entire careers.

"It's our greatest trait of our team—our unity, closeness and
being a family," said YeEun, the team's serene twenty-one-
year-old defender. "It's not common on a national level to be
so close to each other because players are competitive and you
want to stand out from your team. We're always thinking about
each other and how to help out each other. Sometimes I wonder if that's unprofessional because we should be focusing on
our hockey skills instead of caring for others, but I do think it's
a positive trait of ours. In that sense, I do think we're the only
team that could have handled this."

# CHAPTER EIGHTEEN
## One Step at a Time

A police caravan escorted the Unified team toward Seonhak International Ice Rink in Incheon just after 3:30 in the afternoon on February 4. They were to play a tune-up match against Sweden that evening, just five days before the start of the Olympics. One week earlier, the three thousand tickets for the event sold out within minutes and KIHA became inundated with hundreds of credential requests from news outlets around the globe. A few weeks later, KIHA's head of public relations started attending therapy to decompress from the accumulated stress of handling media for a team that few cared about for years, one that overnight became the epicenter of the international news cycle.

The majority of the players, from sixteen-year-old Kim Heewon to twenty-nine-year-old Randi Griffin, still had no idea that reporters from Australia, Ireland, or anyone outside of Korea even knew about the Unified team. Looking out their windows as their bus approached Seonhak, Heewon and Randi saw protestors shouting into megaphones, cursing Kim Jong-un. The conservative demonstrators, a majority of them elderly men, also tore up North Korean flags and proudly waved flags of South Korea and the United States, whom they believed were allies in the fight against tyrannical commies. A few feet away, hundreds of college students peacefully carried white flags with the light blue image of the unified Korean peninsula that matched the sky above. They also unfurled large banners calling for a formal end to the Korean War. Since there was no peace treaty signed in 1953—only an armistice—the two Koreas have technically been at war for the last six and a half decades. Watching these two mobs demonstrate while rows of police stood in between dressed in fluorescent yellow jackets, Heewon and Randi gained their first inkling that they had suddenly become part of the biggest story in the world.

"We had been completely secluded out at Jincheon training center," Randi said. "In a lot of ways it didn't really feel real until we went to that game. It was just like reality hitting us— *This is actually a big deal to people.* We realized this is what we got ourselves into."

When the arena doors opened an hour before face-off, a standing-room only crowd rushed in through the entrance with the urgency of Black Friday bargain hunters, not wanting to miss the first glimpse of the Unified team. Some patrons dressed up, costumed as tigers, an animal comparable in meaning in South Korea to the American bald eagle. Others draped the railings with prounification messages. None of the protestors against the Unified team seemed to have tickets, but dozens of police officers, both in uniform and in plain clothes, traversed the concourse on alert for any signs of mischief.

The players' parents huddled into a section across from the home team's bench, equipped with South Korean flags and wearing their daughters' old jerseys; it almost seemed like an act of defiance, one last symbolic rebuff against the forced merger. The team now sported blue uniforms with the light blue Korean peninsula outline and the word KOREA in bold capital letters across the front. The new sweaters were hastily manufactured by the Finnish company Tackla, since the previous Nike iterations reportedly caused a conflict with North Korean sanctions.

When the teams entered the ice for warm-ups, the sold-out crowd began fanatically waving unification flags and banging thunderstick noisemakers. Amid a sea of camera flashes there were deafening screams of "Fighting!" which is a common Korean slogan of support. The few empty seats visible were such because some ticketholders were still waiting in miles of traffic stretched outside Seonhak. Groups unfurled huge banners of the Korean peninsula that took up whole sections, while cheer squad leaders with their faces painted red and blue held white scarves that read "One Korea Yes!" As this buzz of energy continued on throughout the pregame skate, the Swedish players stopped their drills, leaned along the boards and soaked in the surreal scene.

Minutes before the puck was dropped, Kim Un-hyang gave Marissa a fist bump. The two teams then lined up on opposite blue lines and took off their helmets for an instrumental version of "Arirang," a Korean folk song that dates back hundreds of years. The ballad is so revered on the peninsula that it has been compared to being as essential to Koreans as eating rice. Even North Koreans play it during newscasts, and its melody is known to elicit tears. "It's synonymous in many ways with what it means to be Korean—which of course is very complicated," Hilary Finchum-Sung, an ethnomusicologist at Seoul National University, told the *New York Times*'s Andrew Keh in a 2018 story he wrote about the song's history.[1]

The crowd's mood changed from fervent to solemn as they quietly sang along to Korea's unofficial national anthem. Hearing the notes of "Arirang" that she memorized as a child, and looking up into the rafters at the thousands in attendance, Park Chae-lin, the nineteen-year-old South Korean forward who often visited karaoke rooms alone to sing somber songs, became

overwhelmed with emotion. "That's when I realized we're finally here," said Chaelin.

Ten days after they met, the Unified team was ready to take
the ice together.

*A sold-out crowd in Incheon watched the Unified team's first game, an exhibition versus
Sweden on February 4.*

With the pungency of fish and other Korean-flavored snacks
permeating the atmosphere, Sweden held a 3–1 lead after the
first period. Korea's lone goal came on a precise snipe from Park
Jong-ah, who whipped the puck over the left shoulder of Swedish goalie Minatsu Murase.

Over the course of the game it became clear that the North
Koreans were not fully integrated into Sarah Murray's systems
and were arguably hurting Korea's performance. Forward Jong
Su-hyon repeatedly stationed herself at the blue line or close to
center ice, cherry-picking and waiting for breakaway opportunities that never materialized, while the rest of her team was
attempting to stifle Sweden's attack deep in the Korean zone.
At other times, right winger Ryo Song-hui drifted out of place
toward the center of the ice on breakaways and almost inadver-
tently intercepted passes intended for Susie Jo.

Although the game turned lethargic after the first period, the crowd remained full of brio with constant chants in support of the team, shouts of "We are one!" and other bursts of encouragement. Many patrons, never before having watched live hockey, found pleasure in the little nuances, like Eom Su-yeon's head fakes to set up a slap shot, or watching the bigger Swedish players push down the head of Choi Ji-yeon along the boards as she fought for control of the puck. With Korea unable to formulate sustained offense, Sweden coasted for much of the final two periods, seemingly playing at three-quarters of their potential. Perhaps the loudest cheer of the night came after Sweden closed out a 3–1 victory and the Unified team lined up and tapped their sticks against the ice to thank the crowd for their support.

Ignoring the lack of chemistry and disparity in talent between the two squads, many South Korean fans were given hope from the exhibition. "This is the first time that I'm seeing hockey," said Jung Soo-yoon, a twenty-nine-year-old from Seoul attending with an organized cheering squad called Young Generation. "I'm really nervous and excited. We're having really great expectations for the North and South Korea united ice hockey team. It's a symbol of peace. We hope that this PyeongChang Winter Olympics will give us a chance to renew relationships. The problem in Korea is all up to this."

To accommodate the burgeoning interest in the Unified team, a postgame press conference was held in the basement rink of Seonhak. For the South Korean journalists covering their first hockey game, KIHA workers dispersed hand warmers and hastily duct-taped a grey carpet over the ice, which only seemed to increase slippage. Shortly after the hundreds of media finally reached their seats safely, Pak Chol-ho, Murray, Jongah and Suhyon arrived to the dais wearing long white parkas.

Murray opened by stating that the North Korean players were quick learners, hard workers and great students. When Suhyon was handed the microphone, the twenty-one-year-old from North Korea was greeted with hundreds of flashes blinding

her, overcome with a level of attention that she had never encountered before in her life. With her long black hair tied in a
ponytail, Suhyon frequently looked up as if she had memorized
her speech and spoke in clichés about aiming for good results
and hoping for support from around the world. Coach Pak and
Suhyon were then escorted away without answering questions,
followed soon after by Murray and Jongah as the team took off
for the Olympic Village in Gangneung, where the spotlight
was about to expand to a degree they could not have imagined.

Before the Unified team's first Olympic practice at the Kwandong Hockey Center, two lines of fifteen police officers on each
side formed a human barricade for the players to pass through,
shielding them from mobs of media shouting questions in various languages and pushing closer for photographs. Over the next
week, the women's hockey team was covered with the intensity of a baseball team heading into the World Series or movie
stars socializing at the Oscars, with every action dissected for
mass discussion.

On their first morning in the Athletes Village, shortly after
Marissa Brandt found Hannah and they shared their first moments as Olympians, photographers captured Marissa and Grace
Lee wearing their white parkas with a patch of the unified Korea
logo on the left chest. This design included a microscopic blue
dot that would cause a gargantuan uproar. The pencil-point-
sized mark, located just east of the peninsula, represented the
Dokdo islets, as they are called in Korean. However, the land
is also claimed by Japan, which refers to the area as Takeshima.

Korean records reference the islands as far back as the sixth
century, but that has never placated Japan, which claims they
have held sovereignty over Takeshima since the early twentieth
century; South Korea's response is that such an argument is void
since it stems from the period of Japan's forced annexation of
Korea. After World War II and Japan's surrender, South Korea

declared Dokdo as theirs and for more than sixty years has employed about forty-five police to patrol the area. In 2012, two South Korean residents lived on the rocky, almost uninhabitable island ready to defend against anyone who infringed upon what they believed was their nation's rightful property.[2]

Later in the day, outlets began reporting that the two Koreas agreed to march during the opening ceremony on February 9, carrying the unified flag that included Dokdo. Japan's chief cabinet secretary, Yoshihide Suga, called the usage of such a version "unacceptable" and its presence in the Olympics as "extremely regrettable."[3] One month earlier, Japan opened a permanent exhibition in Tokyo highlighting Japan's right to Takeshima.[4] This occurred only twenty-three years after South Korea created an entire museum dedicated to the history of Dokdo, in Seoul.

For the next few days, eagle-eyed journalists zoomed in on every outfit the team wore in practices and in public, to search for the blue dot that suddenly was now absent from patches. To escape the constant trailing of cameras, two days before their opening game, Murray organized a trip to Gyeongpo Beach on the coast of Gangneung. Bundled up in their heavy jackets as winds blowing in from the turquoise blue waters of the East Sea whipped into their faces, the players ran across the sands like toddlers on a playground. Kim Do-yun, one of Murray's assistant coaches, conspired with Coach Pak to throw her into the white, foamy waves. Soon after, some of the North Koreans pretended to push Han Do-hee into the sea.

Later, as Dohee tried to keep her shortly cropped hair parted just how she liked it against the force of heavy gusts, players from North Korea snuck up from behind her and ran their hands across her head each time she had just perfected her styling. Away from the intrusion of Olympic officials, Jiyeon snapped dozens of pictures with her new teammates, and Kim Un-jong and Kim Un-hyang goaded Marissa into standing on the edge of the sand and yelling across the oceanic horizon, telling her that doing so was a North Korean tradition that brought good luck.

After the beach, the team went to a boardwalk café and sat on the rooftop, where seagulls glided across the impeccable blue skies. As Marissa was drinking her coffee, Un Jong pointed at the birds and said, *"galmaegi,"* the Korean word for seagull. That evening, when the team was eating dinner, Un Jong slyly bounced around, picking off slices of meat from the plates of unsuspecting teammates. When Marissa caught Un Jong, she called out, *"Galmaegi! Galmaegi!"* which became Un Jong's new nickname.

"You want to be around her all the time even though I can't talk to her," Marissa said. "She has these little dimples and this smile that couldn't get any bigger. It's so contagious. She could make anybody love her."

After providing the world a breather from fears of war, the Unified team finally received a respite of their own, devoid of orders and onlookers that were sapping away their desire to play hockey.

"We were outside of any kind of confined borders," Danelle Im relayed. "It was a freeing day. We finally got to know the North Koreans."

Danelle, perhaps more than any other player, was in need of the break. As had occurred during her college career, in recent months Danelle became stuck in Neutral, held on the third and fourth lines with less and less playing time. The arrival of the twelve North Koreans put her role further in jeopardy.

Watching Danelle struggle was disheartening to her teammates. Not only had she been the rock for Randi, Marissa and Grace during their tumultuous beginnings on the team, but she was the import who tried the hardest to fit in, carrying around a notebook to write down Korean words to improve her language skills and always making efforts to converse outside of English. Danelle was the prototypical girl next door, a person so authentically kind it made you question your own temperament.

At the Olympics, Danelle was roommates with the gregarious Choi Yu-jung. Sensing Danelle's stress, when the team arrived back from the beach, Yujung wrote her a letter with her limited English knowledge.

> I'm your new roommate. it's such a big proud that I can use my room with great hockey player. We have two days before our game so hope we have you good luck. May the odds be ever in your favor. Love Yujung.

*The Unified team visited Gyeongpo Beach in Gangneung to escape the media circus surrounding their every step.*

On February 9, the Unified team slid on matching outfits—long white jackets, navy blue wool hats, black tracksuits and black-and-red sneakers—then boarded buses to PyeongChang for the opening ceremony of the 2018 Winter Olympics. For the South Korean players, despite the recent government interference that thrust them into a political showcase, the night still represented the culmination of years of sacrifice. Bouncing around like kids on a sugar rush, seventeen-year-old Suyeon and thirty-year-old Han Soo-jin cracked jokes with colleagues from North Korea, and took turns in having them try on novelty plastic sunglasses shaped like the Olympic rings.

Before the first team of Olympic athletes from North and South Korea was revealed to the world, some players remembered the cold dinners they ate outside Taereung when they weren't allowed to dine inside, and the cursing outbursts from older teammates annoyed by their presence. Jiyeon and Shin Sojung thought about their fathers, who always supported their rare interest in hockey, and whom they hoped were watching from a celestial seat in the sky. Others were reminded of Lee Min-ji giving half of her life to the team yet not being there, a victim of cruel circumstance. Making Minji's absence even more painful was that during the Sweden exhibition, forward Lee Eun-ji tore a ligament in her ankle, which forced her to miss the Olympics; before the merger, Eunji's spot would have gone to Minji. They also were thinking of Lee Kyou-sun, who that morning had to relinquish her place in the opening ceremony to a South Korean Olympic official who wanted to insert himself into the historic moment.

Finally, the public address announcer called on the athletes from Korea, and Coach Pak suggested to Murray that they hold hands in a sign of unity. During the opening ceremony's parade of nations, tradition dictates that the host country marches into the stadium last. Carrying the unified Korean flag were two athletes, one from each side of the peninsula, including twenty-two-year-old women's hockey player Hwang Chung-gum from North Korea. As Chung Gum swung the majestic giant flag from side to side, Caroline Park threw her arm around Sojung, while Randi, a Korean American from Apex, North Carolina, walked nearby Choe Jong-hui, her teammate from Chongjin, North Korea. Looking into an expanse of fluorescent pink, purple and blue lights flashing around the stadium, Yujung and Lee Yeon-jeong waved to no one in particular, soaking in the adulation that resonated through the frigid mountain air. As the delegation completed their lap, in their private box seats South Korean President Moon Jae-in and his wife waved at the players and then shook hands with Kim Yo-jong, the sister of Kim Jong-un. Another North Korean dignitary in the section was ninety-year-old Kim Yong-nam, the second most powerful person in his country. After bickering with the South for nearly seventy years, he wiped away tears watching women's hockey players from both sides of the peninsula march as one team.

Stunned by the sight of thirty-five thousand fans in awe of her team's presence, Grace, whose feet had been punished by years of surgeries, felt as if she was floating. "It's a feeling words can never express," Grace said. "Being the host country and seeing thousands of people supporting you, it's something special and something that I'll never forget. I fell in love with Korea right then and there."

Next, it was time for the Olympic torch to enter the stadium. First, the flame passed through a cavalry of several famous South Korean professional athletes, before being handed off to two relative unknowns representing something worth more than their predecessors' millions of winnings ever could. The previous night, Jongah was dumbfounded when she was informed by Olympic officials that she was needed in PyeongChang upon special request. She wolfed down her dinner and waited for Suhyon, who also had been invited to attend this top secret meeting. Jongah waited for an hour, unaware that Suhyon did not receive clearance from her handlers to leave the North Korean party. Suhyon had to inform Coach Pak, who then had to inform a government official to get proper approval. By the time the order made its way through the bureaucratic chain of command, it was too late and the messengers in PyeongChang canceled the appointment.

The next morning, Jongah and Suhyon were sent a video—a rehearsal of two athletes climbing to the top of the Olympic Stadium with the Olympic torch, which since ancient Greece represented honor, divinity and inspiration. Every other aspect of the ceremony had been rehearsed hundreds of times. Jongah and Suhyon had one shot to get it right. Hours later, wearing matching gold-and-white jumpsuits, they stood at the bottom of a staircase that was designed to only hold one person and was intentionally created to form a slope that curved like a tidal wave, to signify the challenging hardships Olympic athletes must conquer.

With Jongah wearing an earpiece to receive directions on when to begin their ascent, the lights dimmed and a spotlight shone on their backs, creating the sense that they were the only two people in the stadium. Suhyon turned to Jongah on her left, smiled and whispered, "Let's do a good job." The two twenty-one-year-olds then put one hand each on the torch and began their voyage to soothe seven decades of pain caused by the separation of North and South Korea, seven decades that cemented in the minds of everyone watching that this was not possible. Jogging up the first of 120 steps, Suhyon started out slightly ahead, forcing Jongah to catch up from behind. This was a bit nerve-racking, as actually traipsing up the staircase proved much more difficult than Jongah imagined. "As soon as I started going up it was even steeper and higher," Jongah said. "I was scared that I would fall. It was tiring, as well. There were so many steps."

Jongah and Suhyon finally achieved harmony as a captivated audience watched their trek to the cauldron. Awaiting them at the summit was Kim Yu-na, the South Korean national icon royally outfitted in a sparkling white dress. Understanding the gravitas of the moment, Jongah tried to stay emotionless, but couldn't hide her grin the closer she neared her childhood idol. Finally, they reached the apex of their journey, and turned and waved to an audience full of teary eyes. Jongah and Suhyon calmly walked over to Kim Yu-na, and she took the torch that the hockey players had worked so ardently to bring to the uppermost reaches of the stadium and finally lit the cauldron, illuminating what many around the world including the Pope came to regard as the "Peace Games."

"I wish future generations will remember this day and record this day as a special day of the Winter Olympic Games when peace began," President Moon proclaimed.[5]

On a freezing night in the mountains of South Korea, just fifty miles from the Korean Demilitarized Zone, thirty-five young women warmed the hearts of millions of viewers who no longer saw Korea as two separate countries. The Korean peninsula that Jongah and Suhyon represented is only about the size of Utah in square mileage, but the symbolism that they projected, of this idea of one Korea, resonated through the most embittered souls. Jongah and Suhyon overcame yet another obstacle in their lives, a journey that only could have been completed together.

Months later, sitting in a Starbucks in Seoul, Jongah recounted that memorable night, when two young Koreans from the most disparate of backgrounds, seemingly sharing only a common love of hockey, found out that they were not so different after all. "Being able to carry the torch was a significant event on its own, a fascinating experience and an honor," Jongah said, "but the fact that I did it with a North Korean player who I'm on the Unified team with made it even more special to me."

Jongah's teammates actually did not see the torch climb until the next morning. After the Unified team completed their lap around the stadium, the South Koreans headed directly to their buses since their first game was the following day, information somehow not transmitted to Jongah. Following the conclusion of the opening ceremony, she hugged Suhyon goodbye, then looked for the rest of her colleagues. A bit scared, not unlike how she used to walk alone at home late at night from Taere-ung, Jongah worried how she would get back to Gangneung. The North Korean players had stayed behind to wait for Suhyon and spotted Jongah circling around, looking lost. Naturally, they invited Jongah on their bus and rode back home, together.

# CHAPTER NINETEEN
## A Spotlight Stolen

The Kwandong Hockey Center was built on the edge of Catholic Kwandong University, a small hillside campus in Gangneung City. To reach the arena's front gates, patrons walked down a forested slope covered in pine needles and made their way through a maze of statues featuring a combination of mythical Korean animals and religious iconography. On the night of February 10, 2018, over six thousand ticketholders emerged from the copses—literally coming out of the woodwork—for the Unified Korean hockey team's first game, whereby they entered into a realm of patriotism, politics and protest never before seen at an international sporting event.

On the main street running alongside the north end of the arena, mobs jostled for prime protesting positions in front of a 7-Eleven convenience store, a small fried chicken shop and a café. Idealistic twentysomethings yearning for peace volleyed messages for unification across the street toward groups of mostly senior citizens who were disparaging the women's hockey team as Kim Jong-un enablers, and calling for the de-

struction of North Korea. Hundreds of police dispatched to
the arena prevented any outbreaks of physical violence, but for
the Brandt family and other ticketholders attempting to snake
their way through this chaos, it was a discomfiting environment to say the least.

Ninety minutes before Kwandong's doors even opened, a few
thousand fans were already lined up at the security lanes. Instead of griping as they would in an airport, a majority bobbed
up and down in excitement, singing along as Top 40 hits like
"Despacito" played over outdoor speakers. To help pass the time,
many attendees were willingly interviewed by the hundreds of
international journalists sniffing about, telling the cameras such
things as how their parents were happy in heaven seeing the two
Koreas join together. Nearby, progressive groups handed out
hundreds of white-and-blue unification flags, while carrying
large placards promoting the "Peace Olympics." On a makeshift wooden staircase that led down to the arena's front gate, a
group of twelve-year-old girls had less political reasons for attending. They traveled from Seoul, where they played for the
Jubilee Ducks club team. Wearing red headbands with two South
Korean flags as antennae, Chun Se-hee, Jeon Si-huck, Cheaung
Bin-yu and Cheaung Ha-yoon sat on the steps and drew signs
of support for the women's hockey team. "Sarah Murray, she's
my favorite," said Sehee.

Once inside the arena, spectators buzzed with anticipation.
Rumors floated throughout the day that President Moon Jae-
in, Kim Yong-nam and Kim Yo-jong were going to attend, as
well as the "beauty squads" of North Korean cheerleaders. The
North had previously sent these troupes to international sporting events in South Korea—an estimated three hundred women
dressed in traditional Korean *hanbok* dresses were deployed to
the 2002 Asian Summer Games in Busan—and their presence
has always created a sort of phenomenon. Euny Hong wrote in
her book how Koreans often assume that the prettiest women

are from the North and that South Korean dramas perpetuate the idea that Southerners "feel very benevolently toward North Korean women."[1]

*Huge crowds lined up hours before face-off to watch the Unified team at the Olympics.*

At 8:30 p.m., forty minutes before the opening face-off, the first parade of cheerleaders entered Kwandong's lower bowl, drawing the attention of the entire arena to their sharp red jackets. Walking single-file, their matching red track pants swished with each step. With immaculately styled eyelashes and hair resembling 1950s pinup models—shoulder-length and curled at the tips, creating a fluffy, bouncy appearance—the women charmed every onlooker with plastered-on smiles and gentle waves. Completely smitten men whipped out their cell phones with the speed of Wyatt Earp drawing his Smith & Wesson from his holster.

Once seated, the cheerleaders put on red-and-white knit hats that made them look like Santa's helpers. The accessories matched their red fingerless gloves and immaculately clean white track jackets decorated with blue and red swirls. The only parts of their wardrobe that didn't quite complement their ensemble were grey socks and white sneakers; each pair of shoes had three light blue or pink stripes, resembling the iconic layout for Adidas. But they also contained a winged logo on the heel resembling a swan, suggesting they were knockoffs of some kind.

*Members of the North Korean cheerleading squad enter the Kwandong Hockey Center.*

Each cheerleader carried a plastic blue shopping bag full of accessories—pom-poms, noisemakers and even cardboard cutouts of the face of a handsome young Korean man. The masks—which covered their pink lipstick and meticulously rouged cheeks that made their pale skin glisten—were speculated to be of Kim Il-sung, the first "Supreme Leader" of North Korea and grandfather of Kim Jong-un. Once South Korean media picked up the story, the masks stayed neatly tucked away in the bags through the duration of the Olympics.

The cheerleaders took up four to five rows in several sections in the arena. In sync, they chanted *"Him-nae-ra"* (let's go) and sang Korean folk songs, their soft voices carrying throughout the stands. While performing, they held up unification flags and even sometimes forcefully chopped them in a downward motion to emphasize their cheers.

Despite the rushed manner in which the cheerleaders were invited to PyeongChang, they were clearly well rehearsed. Each member received orders from a principal group seated at center ice, in the prime position for television cameras and in front of where the dignitaries were scheduled to watch the game. The other clusters peered over to this central nervous system after each routine to decipher the next chant. The repertoire sometimes included a cute shimmying of the shoulders or even "the wave," but they never deviated from the script.

All the while, spectators gawped and filled their smartphones with snapshots, while North Korean handlers and Olympic volunteers shooed off anyone who got too close. This did not stop foreign photojournalists from ducking under railings and perching themselves on all sides of the cheerleaders, clicking away with shit-eating grins as they captured the abnormality of the situation. Occasionally, a cheerleader looked down nervously at a photographer slyly positioned lying down in a stairwell to get a better angle. It was hard not to feel compassion for the North Korean women being treated like creatures on display in a zoo. Whenever they had to use the restroom, a government official chaperoned a group out, like teachers take children to the bathroom on a school field trip. Even then privacy was impossible; some members of the press didn't hold back from taking photos in the lavatory. All the cheerleaders could do was keep smiling as they had been ordered to. A few days later, once news outlets discovered the location of the resort where the contingent of North Koreans was staying, reporters trained their cameras on the living rooms of the 108 condominium units being shared by the women, snooping for footage.[2]

When the Unified team hit the ice for warm-ups, there was notable electricity in the sold-out crowd, which was the largest assemblage any of the players had ever competed in front of. But something also felt amiss. Marissa Brandt could not ignore the cheerleaders and their robotic movements. "It really was kind of creepy," she remarked.

Even the Swiss were astonished by the scene. Goaltender Janine Alder, who competed at the 2014 Olympics in Sochi, Russia, couldn't stop looking up into the crowd. "It was quite impressive how organized the cheerleaders were and they were striving for perfection," Alder noted. "Staring in the stands, it gave me goose bumps. With the president there and all the politics—I don't know quite how to say it, but it was like you could touch the air."

Alder may have been enraptured by the atmosphere, but the ambience was not how Shin So-jung pictured her Olympic debut. Instead of a celebration of her team's efforts, the game evolved into a circus. Moments before the puck was dropped, the public address announcer read off the starting lineups. Just as Sojung's name was about to be announced as Korea's goaltender, President Moon and North Korea's political envoy made their way to their seats, sucking all the attention away from the ice.

With most of the fans still buzzing around the statesmen and cheerleaders in attendance, Grace Lee took the opening face-off and initiated Korea's Olympic history. Wearing white jerseys with red side panels and the light blue peninsula on the front, Korea proceeded cautiously in the opening minutes, feeling out the Swiss game plan. Then, at the 8:22 mark of the first period, Kim Hee-won stole the puck from Switzerland's Lara Stalder and rushed down the ice. Stalder knocked Heewon down from behind, drawing a penalty for an illegal hit, but Han Soo-jin lunged in to take control before play could be stopped. Picking up the puck near Switzerland's blue line, Soojin had an unobstructed path to the goal and from about fifteen feet out took a straight-on shot at Swiss starting goalie Florence Schelling. The wrister had enough zip to beat Schelling over her right blocker, and for a split second, Soojin lifted up her arms as if she scored. The puck, however, hit at the junction of the crossbar and the post on the upper-left corner of the goal, then deflected away from the net.

If Soojin's shot was just one inch lower to the right, the Unified team's Olympic experience could have changed dramatically. It was clear that the majority of the crowd had never been to a hockey game before. Prior to the Olympics, the South Korean website Naver ran an article explaining the basic rules of hockey as a primer to its audiences. The first time Korea sent the puck in Switzerland's zone, in unison the building let out a marveled "oooooh." Cheers were elicited each time Korea simply touched the puck. A goal by Soojin and a 1–0 lead on the defending Olympic bronze medalists would have caused the arena to burst at the seams.

Despite Stalder's penalty, Korea's power play unit did not create any advantages. Their attempt to break the defensive zone with long, stretch passes proved ineffective and Switzerland's speed and chemistry on defense prevented the Unified team's offensive attack from finding a rhythm; at one point, Randi Griffin was able to create some space, but with Jong Su-hyon on her left wing, still green to the unit, Randi's pass to set up an open slap shot for her teammate from North Korea was misread and sailed wide. Twice during the power play, Korea negligently handled the puck behind Sojung and Switzerland crashed the net, almost creating a turnover and easy goal. Unable to settle themselves throughout the duration of the power play, Switzerland's Alina Muller capitalized on Korea's unsteady legs. After a deflection in her zone, Muller gathered the puck and zipped down the ice. Three Korean players awaited her in front of Sojung, but Muller easily deked out Suhyon playing the puck instead of her opponent's upper body to read where she might go next. That opened up a wide gap and set up Muller for a clear rip, and she sent a wrist shot off Sojung's left glove for a short-handed goal and 1–0 lead, 10:23 into the first period.

With Korea rattled, Switzerland kept their foot on the accelerator. One minute later, Switzerland dissected the ice with three unobstructed passes, the last from Sara Benz, lifting the puck over Marissa's stick to Muller, who ripped a one-timer past Sojung for her second goal of the game. The awkward chants of "Cheer up" or "We are one" from the North Korean cheerleaders did not help. Korea gained another power play in the period, but their offense was tentative to shoot, and the line overpassed without fruitful results. Twelve seconds before the end of the period, Muller netted a hat trick, sending Switzerland into the locker room ahead, 3-0.

During the intermission, the K-pop group Dynamic Duo performed, boosting the spirits of the audience. Many fans screamed throughout the medley of hits, more entranced by the surprise concert than the forty minutes of hockey that remained. As opposed to the exhibition against Sweden six days earlier in Incheon, the atmosphere surrounding Korea's first Olympic game was marred by distraction. From the politicians walking in just as the players' names were announced to the crowd, to the mesmerizing synchronization of the cheerleaders from North Korea, the actual competition—the moment Sojung waited almost two decades for—was secondary. While the majority of fans in both Incheon and Gangneung were not that well-versed in hockey knowledge, the support during the Sweden exhibition felt more genuine. One week later, it was all about the spectacle, the images that the Korean government wanted to create, even as their hockey team was drowning under the pressure on the ice. Muller finished the night with four goals in total—tying an Olympic record—and added two assists as Switzerland cruised to an 8–0 victory.

Park Jong-ah said after the game that she was nervous and did not have experience playing in front of such a big crowd. The fact that the North Korean cheerleaders didn't necessarily seem like they were cheering for her team did not help. Because of the scripted routines, a lot of players could not hear the referee's whistles, instructions from the coaches on the bench and most importantly, their teammates on the ice.

"One time, in the middle of the period I was skating up with the puck, I dump it in, and I just remember everyone chanting, 'We are one! We are one!'" Grace added. "I thought to myself, I know this is political, but come on; we're playing a hockey game here."

After the game, the team headed toward their locker room, where they had to pass through the media mixed zone and answer questions from reporters. One woman from NBC stopped Randi, hoping to get a cliché sound byte to send back to audiences in America. Randi, however, was in no mood for such encomium.

"I could tell the lady interviewing me was getting mad," Randi said. "She seemed really frustrated with my attitude and my answers because I think she wanted me to be really positive and talk about how awesome the North Korean cheerleaders were. I was like, 'I don't know, they looked weird.' She was like, 'But isn't it inspiring they were here cheering for Korea?' I was like, 'I don't know if they want to be here. I don't know why they're here.' She was getting super exasperated. When she asked, 'What does it feel like to play in the Olympics?' I said, 'Well, honestly, that was really disappointing. We want to be taken seriously as a hockey team.'

"She seemed really annoyed by that answer. I think it was supposed to be like, 'Oh, we're just so happy to be here.' It was a little bit degrading to realize how much people didn't take us seriously. That was our chance to earn it and it felt like we blew it."

# CHAPTER TWENTY
## Unified No More

Randi Griffin had another reason to fume after the loss to Switzerland. Just as the players began making their way to the exit, Olympic officials rushed down to inform the coaching staff to keep them on the ice. President Moon Jae-in, IOC President Thomas Bach, Kim Yo-jong and other North Korean dignitaries were coming down to insert themselves into the moment once again. The Unified team stood near their bench seemingly forever, when all they wanted to do was shower, get changed and hide their heads.

"The team wasn't there to see these people," said Susie Jo, who would have to translate all of the speeches to the team in English and Korean. "We had just lost 8–0. It was honestly very difficult to keep a smile on my face. It's not like we could just frown or show disappointment in front of them, but we wanted to avoid the situation as a whole."

"I was in a bad mood," added Eom Su-yeon. "I was angry at myself and also sad. They told us to wait for the president because he was going to talk to us. I thought, 'I just want to go. Why can't he just come into the locker room?'"

Once the VIPs arrived, it became clear why the visit did not take place behind closed doors. Most of the crowd remained in the arena after the game, curious as to why the team stayed back. Once President Moon and others appeared, photojournalists rushed down towards the Korean bench and fans hung over railings trying to get a better view. One by one, each speaker congratulated the team on a job well done, words that went in one ear and out the other. Like addressing a batch of Little Leaguers, Bach told the players the most important thing was that they fought well and to be proud.[1]

Park Jong-ah, the team captain, was ashamed to stand there and essentially be patted on the head like a child. She did not move to Seoul alone in the eighth grade or withstand racial taunts in Canada to be denigrated further after just losing by eight goals on the sport's biggest stage. "If we had won, we'd be happy to stay there," Jongah conceded. "Even if President Moon came immediately after it would be one thing, but we had to wait a while. We were exhausted and embarrassed."

To Randi, what hurt the most about being kicked when already down was that the words expressed by President Moon, Bach and others gave off the sentiment that the final score was expected. The Koreans knew Switzerland was not invulnerable. If they could have kept the game to a two- or three-goal deficit, the performance would have made a strong statement to the international hockey community that Korea was in fact a serious team. "We all wanted to go to the locker room and sulk," Randi said. "Then when all the stuff happened at the end with Moon and Bach, the way they were acting was just so patronizing. We could tell from them and the way the media was talking to us after the game, not only were they completely unsurprised that we had lost 8–0, but they also expected us to be unsurprised and not care about it later."

Afterward, the Unified team was forced to line up and shake the hands of the assembled officials. As the South Korean members made their way down the line, they glared at each figure with the iciest of stares from eyes that were now swollen and red from tears of defeat and degradation, as if to indicate, *You did this to us.*

Despite the opening loss, the Unified team served its political purpose. Kim Yo-jong passed along a message from her brother to President Moon, inviting him to Pyongyang for the first meeting of leaders from both Koreas in more than a decade.

Korea entered the 2018 Olympics statistically as the youngest and smallest team in the tournament. Switzerland's roster held an advantage on average of three inches and eleven pounds over each player. The next game was not going to be any easier. Awaiting was Sweden, which was once ranked as high as number two in the world and is the only country other than the United States or Canada to play for an Olympic gold medal.

The morning after their first game, Angela Ruggiero, a member of the IOC's executive board and a gold medalist on the 1998 US Olympic hockey team, suggested that the Unified team win the Nobel Peace Prize. "As someone who competed in four Olympics and knows it isn't about you, your team, or your country," Ruggiero told reporters, "I saw the power of what it did last night."[2]

Before the Sweden contest, Ruggiero asked to visit the Unified Korean locker room, thinking she could pump them up with the kind of inspirational speech that unfortunately, many of the players were sick of hearing and being associated with at that point. In an attempt to motivate the tough crowd, Ruggiero suggested a cheer, led by the youngest of the team. The room stayed silent with everyone looking at the floor. Finally, Randi volunteered Kim Hee-won, who begrudgingly stood up and in a monotone voice mumbled, *"Hana, dul, set,"* (one, two, three) and the rest of the group let out a subdued moan.

"It was a bit awkward," Marissa said. "It's always harder when someone English-speaking comes in. The girls, they didn't really know what was happening. I think also at that point we know why we're here. Yeah, we're unified, we've heard all this stuff before kind of thing. Not to downgrade what she told us or her visiting us, I just think it was kind of, 'Hey, we get it at this point.'"

Sapped of all of their excitement, the Unified team trudged toward the tunnel, unsure of who or what they were playing for anymore. By the end of the first period, Sweden, using their physical advantages and experience to their benefit, bombarded Shin So-jung with twenty-two shots on goal and scored four times. The last goal came on a particularly excruciating sequence. With Korea mounting pressure in Sweden's zone, the Swedes deflected a shot and squirmed free for a two-on-one breakaway. Forward Lisa Johansson sent a pass in front of the net to Erica Uden Johansson. Sojung stopped her attempt with a deft right leg save, but North Korean Hwang Chung-gum, in trying to catch up to Uden Johansson, fruitlessly dove in, trying to swing at the puck, and fell into Sojung, sending the loose rebound into the net. Each time that Sweden lit the lamp, a club remix of the song "Düp Düp" by German singer Mickie Krause blasted through the arena, as fans dressed in Viking helmets danced along merrily. The North Korean cheerleaders tried to ignore the commotion with their own chants of "Show your strength" and "Let's go," which were hardly as inspiring.

During intermission, when South Korean dancers in short skirts and low-cut tops grooved to American hip-hop songs, the North Korean cheerleaders sat on their hands. Their existence seemed so shallow, every second of their stay at the Olympics choreographed, without a speck of individuality allowed. Once play resumed, Sweden began to pull away, building a 5–0 lead, and a majority of the crowd began mumbling to themselves.

Surprisingly, though, the cheerleaders remained engrossed in the action and slowly seemed to morph into vested fans. When Korea earned a power play with five minutes left in the second period, they stopped their predetermined chants and froze, gripped by the potential for a goal. Suyeon tore a slap shot on net and they stood in anticipation and gasped, then yelped in anguish as the puck sailed just wide of the post. After the power play rush ended, one cheerleader sighed, "Ohhh Korea," ruing an opportunity missed.

The few times Korea was able to mount pressure the rest of the game, the cheerleaders began sweating underneath their polyester track jackets, clutching their pom-poms and cupping their hands near their mouths, hoping for a goal. When Susie was knocked down by an elbow, some of the cheerleaders hopped out of their seats in indignation. Han Seo-hee, a former North Korean cheerleader who defected to the South, said in an interview during the Games that women were selected based on their ability to work collectively, height and age standards (early twenties, taller than five feet three inches) and if they came from "the right families."[3] Over two days, watching a team of young Korean women of similar ages pushing through against insurmountable odds, seemed to finally inspire emotions that were natural and not rehearsed. After the Olympics when the cheerleaders returned back to Pyongyang, they reportedly were to undergo "re-education" training to wipe out the imagery observed while across the border. Other reports speculated that many of the women were forced into performing sexual acts for North Korean leaders, as well. For about two hours inside a hockey rink on the grounds of a Catholic University, sitting next to American and South Korean citizens, they were able to not ponder such a fate.

The women's hockey tournament was broken into two groups of four nations; each country played every other team in their group once. Group A contained the US, Canada, Finland and the Olympic Athletes from Russia.*

---

\* This was the designation given to Russian athletes at the 2018 Winter Olympics, after Russia was found to have been involved in a widespread doping controversy stemming back decades.

All four of those teams, due to their higher world ranking and sustained success in the Olympics, automatically advanced to the single-elimination medal round. In Group B, where Korea was placed with Sweden, Switzerland and Japan, the top two teams moved on to play the third- and fourth-place finishers in Group A. The winners of those games moved on to the semifinals, while the losers were placed in a classification bracket with the two bottom teams from Group B to compete for fifth place.

Korea's first two Olympic games ended with the same disheartening 8–0 score. Sarah Murray had always told her team that even when they were down by wide margins, their performance was not reflective of the final tally if they competed hard. Players usually could find solace in that after a solid effort against Minnesota or Wisconsin, but it was hard to see a silver lining at the Olympics. Their second defeat officially eliminated Korea from being able to advance to the medal round.

"After these two losses I felt hopeless," forward Choi Yujung said.

SETH BERKMAN

*Grace Lee hugs her mother, Eliza, after a devastating 8–0 loss to Sweden.*

Once again, the North Korean players provided little help versus Sweden. Looking up at the scoreboard and seeing 8–0 for the second straight game, the memories of Jong Su-hyon and Jongah carrying the torch and the team frolicking on the beach were fading. They looked unified no more.

"I was resentful of the situation and the fact we had to put in three North Korean players each game," Jongah said. "I was resentful of the Unified team."

# CHAPTER TWENTY-ONE
## Make Korea Proud

No matter how far North and South drifted apart since the Korean War, few activities brought them closer together than rooting against Japan. Every victory on a baseball diamond, soccer pitch or speed skating rink felt like a sliver of revenge for colonial oppression. With the Unified team fissuring after two humiliating losses in the Olympics, a common desire to topple Korea's historical antagonist was the perfect binding force.

During the era of colonial rule, it was actually Japanese officials who introduced hockey to the peninsula. In 1928, the Chosun Hockey Federation was created—named after one of Korea's longest ruling dynasties—which later became known as the Korea Ice Hockey Association. Since KIHA first formed a women's national team in 1998, the Japanese have always been the model for success, winning at least silver in every Asian Winter Games tournament. Even the favored set play that Han Soo-jin and Park Jong-ah used to score against Wisconsin-River Falls, where Soojin trailed Jongah as she wrapped around the net, was ripped from Japan's playbook.

Kim Se-lin, one of the youngest players on the Unified team at seventeen, did not have the extensive history of competing against Japan like Soojin, but still recognized the importance of a match against their rivals. In history classes in school, whenever students were taught about colonization and the enslavement of comfort women, Selin noticed her teachers became uncharacteristically animated and politicized because Japan never sincerely apologized for their actions against Korean citizens before and during World War II. "I don't view Japanese people negatively," Selin explained, "I only view the country in a negative light."

At one point, when South Korea tried to schedule exhibition games against Japan in an effort to improve, the Japanese declined, believing there'd be no benefit for them to beat up on a team they considered below them. After Japan's hard-fought 3–0 victory at the 2017 Asian Winter Games, their head coach, Takeshi Yamanaka, told reporters that he was disappointed his team didn't score more. The Japanese players in a rare moment of public boastfulness predicted they were guaranteed to win their first Olympic game ever in 2018, since Korea was in their group. When word of these taunts reached the South Korean locker room, Shin So-jung and her teammates became livid.

A victory against their perpetual tormentors on home soil in the Olympics could catapult the team into the nation's consciousness forever. The North Koreans were equally motivated. In three meetings in the Asian Winter Games, Japan held a 3–0 record against the North, although in 2007, when the North Korean team was at its height in power, Japan barely escaped with a 3–2 win. Earlier in the Olympics, when the North Korean cheerleaders attended a figure skating competition, they rooted on all of the nations except for Japan.

Prior to the women's hockey game on February 14, Pak Chol-ho, the North Korean coach, gave his first pregame speech. Previously, Coach Pak seemed fine in playing a background role—in the press conference after the Sweden exhibition game, he casually lounged back in his chair while giving an uninspiring statement that discussed the strength of the Unified team. But in the locker room inside the Kwandong Hockey Center, just minutes from facing Japan, Coach Pak raised his voice and gave an impassioned rant that included a North Korean slur for the Japanese that roughly translated to "Japanese bastards."

"He said that we have to win, that we can't lose," Jongah recounted. "He used a word similar to *jjokbari* in South Korean. I don't remember what it is, but we all laughed," as they were not expecting such an outburst from the normally reserved Coach Pak.

With the Unified team refocused on a mutual target and their nerves loosened after Coach Pak's diatribe, they took the ice in front of a predominately pro-Korean crowd that was animated beyond the levels of the previous two Olympic games. As the techno song "Sandstorm" blared around the arena, the third consecutive sold-out crowd of six-thousand-plus fans did the wave, pumping energy throughout the stands. With many schools off for the upcoming Lunar New Year, large clusters of children were in attendance, their high-pitched shrieks only amplifying the noise.

The anticipatory mood was quickly muted after the opening face-off. Just over one minute into the first period, forward Haruka Toko waited with the puck behind the Korean net and then directed a pinpoint pass to forward Hanae Kubo, cutting across the center of the zone to one-time a shot off Sojung's right leg that deflected into the goal. Less than three minutes later with Japan on a power play, Japanese defender Shiori Koike fired a shot on net that Sojung saved, but the rebound landed right at the stick of forward Shoko Ono, who tapped in the deflection for a 2–0 advantage.

Sojung appeared slow in net, her reactions a second late, particularly when moving from left to right. Early in the second period, Korea had a chance to build some momentum on a power play, but did not get off one shot on goal. With their systems failing and Sojung struggling, the Unified team appeared to be headed toward another lopsided defeat.

With just over eleven minutes to play in the second period, Japan missed a wide-open opportunity as Sojung again could not slide to her right in time. A third goal by Japan seemed imminent. A time-out briefly stopped action, and Sarah Murray put in the line of Caroline Park, Randi Griffin and Kim Heewon, with Marissa Brandt and Selin on defense. After winning the face-off back in their zone, Korea spent thirty seconds unable to move the puck past their blue line. As the puck slithered around, Marissa took control near Korea's left face-off circle and decided to charge ahead on her own.

Crossing the blue line, she threw the puck against the right boards past a Japanese defender, where it rolled up to Randi. With Japan's Yurie Adachi hanging on to her right arm, Randi finally controlled the puck on her stick just shy of Japan's right circle. She then jammed herself free from Adachi just long enough to fling a shot on net. Although she put enough force into her swing, the blade of Randi's black stick did not strike the puck cleanly and so it fluttered along the ice toward the crease. Japanese goalie Akane Konishi mistimed the shot, expecting it to arrive with more velocity, and crouched down a split second too early, creating a triangular opening between her legs. The puck slipped through the five-hole and hit the inside of Konishi's right leg, then nestled into the right corner of the goal.

"I just didn't really have good body position to take a hard shot so my thought was just throw it to the net, because I knew Won and Marissa and Carol were all crashing," Randi recalled. "I actually didn't see it go in. I saw them celebrate first. I assumed one of them had poked it in. I didn't think there was any way that shot found its way in. When we were in the huddle and we were jumping up and down, I asked who scored and they said I did.

"I was really off balance and I felt my hands were super high on the stick. It was just a garbage goal. I remember I sat down and I was just joking about it with Danelle, like yeah, that was totally intentional. We were laughing basically about what a shitty goal it was."

The goal might have come on the worst shot Randi has ever taken in over two decades of playing hockey. But that did not matter to an arena full of thousands of Koreans who simultaneously stood and roared in delight. Elderly men attending the game with their granddaughters wiped away tears, as did members of the North Korean cheerleading squads. Coach Murray, notorious for hardly ever showing emotion on the bench in her customary black suit and white blouse, staying even-keeled through good times and bad, jumped and yelled watching the puck slide past the goal line, the smile on her face indelible. Greg Brandt, wearing one of his daughter's South Korea jerseys, let out a primordial yell of relief. Marissa, who was credited with the assist, had fallen into the net after the play was over. She remembered hearing the screams from the crowd and perking up to join Caroline, Selin and Heewon to jump on Randi, but was so caught up in emotion that she did not recall anything that happened afterward. "I literally blacked out during all of it," Marissa said.

Standing next to the Brandts in the second level of the arena were Randi's parents, Thomas and Elizabeth, with Randi's maternal grandparents—Peter Taidoo Kang and Margaret Hyosook Kang—for whom not only the goal, but the simple experience watching their granddaughter represent Korea resonated in several ways. Randi's grandmother had family members kidnapped by North Koreans, never to be seen again. Randi's grandfather worked in the South Korean government under President Park Chung-hee and knew close friends who were killed in terrorist attacks and assassinated by the North Korean regime. Worried about his family's safety, Peter Kang moved them to the United States in the early 1970s.

"For them, Korea is their home," Randi said of her grandparents, now residents of Chicago. "That's where they feel comfortable, and it was a huge sacrifice for them to come and live in this country where they don't speak the language and they don't have roots. Seeing me living there, seeing me represent the country, I think that was kind of coming full circle for their life choices. At the end of the day, everything was making a new start for the family, but there was also this sense of loss for leaving Korea. Seeing me being successful was a really big deal for them. I was just happy they're still alive for this so I could give them that."

The Olympics were also validating for Elizabeth Heesoo Kang Griffin. When Randi was first contacted by KIHA, she remembered her mom being somewhat amused by the preposterousness of the offer. All throughout her adolescence, Randi's mother tried to distance her children from their heritage, believing that their mixed background always made them white in the eyes of Koreans. When strangers asked about their ethnicity, she told Randi and her siblings to say they're American and their family is from Chicago.

"Her just kind of seeing that all of a sudden Korean people had something to gain from acknowledging my Koreanness—like now I can be Korean—I think to her the whole concept of it, me getting citizenship and everything was kind of funny," said Randi, who dyed her short black hair various shades of platinum white, blond and purple. "My mom I think feels complex feelings towards Korea. She has experienced racism from white people in the US, but she's also experienced racism from Korean people, and received a lot of backlash from people in the Korean community for leaving Korea, for marrying a white guy, for the fact that her Korean is broken now so when she speaks it she doesn't sound perfect. All of these things make her an outsider to Koreans, as well. I think in some ways that almost has given her a somewhat negative view on Korean culture. Before coming to Korea she was expressing a lot of anxiety to me over how Korean people were going to treat her in Korea and she almost didn't want to go."

After Randi's goal, Greg Brandt walked over and shook hands with Randi's parents. Television news cameras came flocking to their section, bombarding Elizabeth Griffin with questions on how it felt that her daughter was now suddenly a national hero. Elizabeth could not help but smile at this turn of events. Randi may have scored on a "garbage goal," but like South Korea itself, which was created from rubble and blossomed into a modern wonder, the meaning of the goal transformed into something beautiful. Before play resumed, referee Drahomira Fialova handed the puck over to Olympic officials that would send it to the Hockey Hall of Fame in Toronto, representing a moment that was not about politics, but created through determination. It all started with a heady pass from Marissa to Randi, the two players most unsure about their identity along this journey, now forever etched into Korean lore.

COURTESY OF THE SOUTH KOREAN WOMEN'S HOCKEY TEAM

*Randi Griffin (center) and Marissa Brandt (right) were responsible for Korea's first Olympic goal.*

★ ★ ★

The game versus Japan was being broadcast around the world
and live on several Korean television stations. One network,
SBS, contacted Lee Min-ji after her controversial Instagram
post. With Minji's knowledge of the South Korean players, SBS
asked her if she was interested in providing color commentary
for the Olympics.

During the first two contests, Minji provided insightful detail, able to identify a player simply by their skating stride. But
some viewers complained that she was not showing enough
emotion. Unlike in the US, South Korean sports commentators
are renowned for their favoritism while calling events. When
Randi scored 9:31 into the second period to cut Japan's lead to
2–1, Minji could no longer contain herself, leaping out of her
seat and shouting with unbridled joy.

"The team is a part of my life," Minji said. "I had a really hard
time when I wasn't selected for the Olympics. My dad told me
ice hockey wasn't your entire life. He was sad I was sad about
this. But I told him this is my entire life so it's hard for me to
give up. Still, I don't want my team to ever perform poorly if
I'm on the team or not. I always want the best for them."

With momentum now trending toward Korea, they continued bruising the Japanese zone. Less than a minute after Randi's
goal, Eom Su-yeon sent a crisp feed from center ice to Grace
Lee, who crossed over her defender and directed a pass to Choi
Yu-jung, whose shot was just blocked at the last moment by
Konishi. For the next ten minutes, Sojung was a wall in goal
and Korea's defensive intensity ramped up to unforeseen levels, led by Randi shadowing Japanese forwards throughout the
rink, giving them as much space to create with the puck as if
they were stuck in an elevator.

The cheers in the crowd were for the players' efforts and
nothing else.

"It felt like we had taken control of the game," Randi said.

"Not only had we not felt that way in those Olympics, but I think we hadn't felt that way since the World Championships last year. We actually were running the game and Japan was surprised, were back on their heels and weren't ready for that at all. Throughout the second I thought we were going to win the game the way momentum shifted."

Japan calmed themselves early in the third period, but Sojung's heady play warded off a power play and kept the deficit to one goal. With Japan's defense tightening, Korea could not find the seams to score an equalizer and the two sides treaded water for the first half of the third period. Then with 10:03 to play, Randi was called for an illegal hit penalty after she hip-checked an unsuspecting defender, sending Japan back on the power play. Sojung withstood a barrage of pressure from Japan for the first one hundred seconds of the two-minute advantage, but Korea could not clear the puck out of their zone. Standing at the blue line, Koike finally ripped a slap shot that somehow found its way through six players standing in front of the net, and the puck went through Sojung's legs for Japan's third goal of the afternoon.

Despite being down two goals, the Unified team did not quit. Sojung made several diving saves and Choi Ji-yeon repeatedly attempted to break through the Japanese zone with her steadfast determination. With 2:12 left, a time-out was called and Murray pulled Sojung to put an extra attacker on the ice. After an unsuccessful initial push, Grace tried to regroup the offense, pulling the puck back out to center ice. As Grace waited for her linemates to get back onside behind the blue line, Japan's Rui Ukita came charging and Grace lazily attempted to dump in a pass that Ukita stole, and then she cruised in untouched to score an empty net goal, effectively ending the game at 4–1.

After the final horn sounded, the Korean players skated over to congratulate Sojung, but there was a feeling of dejection for letting a golden opportunity slip by. Heartbroken, Grace was comforted by Soojin, who originally hated that a young, brash American teenager could be added to the team less than a year before the Olympics. With her arm around Grace, Soojin reminded her that they win and lose as a team. When Korea was finished shaking hands with the Japanese players, they formed a horizontal line and faced the fans behind their bench, who were still out in full force applauding their effort. Then, as the Korean players tapped their sticks on the ice in appreciation, a shower of stuffed bears and seals came raining from the stands and the cheers multiplied in volume. At that moment, it was the first time that a majority of the South Koreans felt respected as hockey players.

"People finally had interest in our team," Jongah noted. "I finally felt like I was part of the national team."

That was only the beginning of the adulation.

About thirty minutes later, after the players showered and received a postgame speech from the coaches, they headed up to the main level of Kwandong Hockey Center to see their families, as they had been doing after every game of the Olympics. This time, though, hundreds of supporters awaited their arrival.

Heewon was the first to emerge, walking up a back staircase to the long concourse hallway, where a group of young children wearing headbands with blue cat ears rushed over and begged for photographs. The kids were students of one of Heewon's relatives, who thought it'd be motivational for her classroom to see young Korean women represent their nation so proudly. Though the youngest player on the team at sixteen, Heewon had a tendency to march to her own beat, forgoing traditional Korean femininity for her own tomboyish style. She was an outlier among most girls her age, who tried to mimic the stylings of K-pop stars, and to the schoolchildren she seemed equally as cool in her own skin.

Throughout her life, Han Do-hee was rarely told that she was important, that being a hockey player could be inspiring. Once she appeared after the game, Dohee was encircled by young boys from the Goyang Twins roller hockey team, who wrapped their pudgy arms around her legs. Dohee struggled lifting up as many of them as she could at once. Nearby, teenagers gasped in the presence of seventeen-year-old Jung Si-yun, now suddenly adored by mobs of girls her age who didn't view her as different.

Not surprisingly, Sojung drew the largest crowds. After the Switzerland game, she had walked through the hallway unnoticed with a grey baseball cap covering her tearful eyes. Now she wore the same hat, but strangers instantly noticed her. The arms and legs of a pair of young women shook in anticipation of meeting her, their hands barely able to grip the black pens in their grasp. When a group of teenage boys crowded around her for a picture, they made sure to quickly style their hair, pushing their bangs tightly to the right, wanting to look their best for Sojung. After two volunteers finally secured her autograph on the back of their grey, orange and red jackets, they celebrated like groupies meeting a rock star, holding hands and jumping in a circle.

All the while Sojung's mother stood nearby, covered in one of her daughter's old Team Korea jackets, a long black parka with the South Korean flag on the sleeve. Two decades earlier, Seol Kyoungrang brought Sojung to her first hockey practices, but could not stay for fear she might see her only child get injured. As she grew older and they stayed together after Sojung's father died, almost every morning began with Seol making coffee for her daughter, basking in the few quiet moments of the day she was afforded with her. Though Seol knew her daughter had determination like few others, the rest of the hours in the day were often spent questioning where Sojung's life was headed.

Sojung, too, never knew if a moment of acceptance like this would occur, particularly while living halfway across the world and constantly debating in her mind if it was all worth it to leave her aging mother alone.

But now Sojung's mother looked on with delight. Seol finally realized Sojung was okay on her own. The decade of worries while raising a young woman as a single mother no longer consumed her. As Seol stood in the background with these thoughts pinballing in her mind, she was interrupted and thrust into the present new reality when fans asked to take pictures with her, as well.

When Park Chae-lin's mother spotted her daughter, she ran over and enveloped her in a hug. Wearing one of Chaelin's old white South Korean jerseys over a grey smock, she rubbed her hand along her daughter's brown ponytail, caressed her left cheek, and then planted a wet kiss on her right cheek, causing Chaelin to blush in front of her friends on the team. Chaelin's mother was once staunchly against her daughter playing hockey, but over time she and the other mothers, many of them housewives, saw their daughters maturing into women who were shattering the mold of the life young Korean woman were supposed to be leading.

SETH BERKMAN

*Park Chae-lin (left) receives a kiss from her mother after the game against Japan.*

Korean television crews queued up to interview Randi's grandparents. Rebecca Ruegsegger Baker's family snuck in among the mob to greet Sojung, who, like Brenda Berthiaume, came to regard her like family. Ruth Murray, who along with Sarah's two brothers traveled to South Korea, became emotional recounting the change in mood in the arena as the focus turned to the merits of the team and not the politicians in suits sitting in the stands.

Newfound stardom did not go to the heads of Korea's newest celebrities. Susie fulfilled every request for a photograph or signature by bowing her head, as if she should be the thankful one. When the players were able to break from their fans for a moment, Dohee teased Heewon's brother, pinching his cheeks like she would whenever she saw him hanging around his older sister's games. Lee Eun-ji cornered Chaelin, held up her phone and mimicked being an interviewer, asking her how it felt to be adored, to which Chaelin could only laugh in embarrassment.

"It was the first time we were going through any of this," Chaelin recognized. "So it would be a lie if I said I didn't feel good. I hadn't felt this way before. It's almost like when I watched TV and see all these famous athletes, I'd wonder what it would feel like if I were in that position. This time I finally felt like I was an athlete representing our country."

At 7:23 p.m., with the game against Japan over for more than an hour, scores of patrons still milled about. Some Olympic workers walked through the concourse with megaphones, asking people to make their way to the exits. No one budged. There was another game scheduled to start soon and long lines of crowds outside became restless, since they could not yet enter the arena. But since half of the audience seeking autographs were volunteers and other staff, there was no rush to empty out the halls. Eventually, the volunteers with megaphones gave up and joined the queue to meet Sojung.

Japan had won their first Olympic game, but their joy did

not compare to the feeling the Korean players were experiencing. When some of the Japanese players tried to meet their own friends and families, they could not believe the sight of all of the Korean fans. "This is crazy," observed Nana Fujimoto, a goalie for Japan.

More than two hours after the game ended, the crowd finally started dispersing. The following morning, not the North Korean cheerleaders or President Moon Jae-in were on the front page of national newspapers, but members of the Unified team, who had come to embody the slogan on the back of their warm-up shirts: "Make Korea Proud."

*Shin So-jung (center in baseball cap), is surrounded by fans clamoring for a photograph.*

# CHAPTER TWENTY-TWO
# Becca

The IOC had no problem bending its rules to serve as a platform for politics by adding North Korean athletes at the last moment before the PyeongChang Games. The Unified team, officials said, represented the true meaning of the Olympic spirit—a romanticized idea that did not include mention of the $13 billion spent to host the 2018 Winter Olympics or the allegations of bribery and corruption that have trailed almost every Olympic bid in modern history. The IOC, however, could not in its best conscience allow Shin So-jung to wear a custom-made goaltender's helmet that featured an image of her deceased father. That was going too far.

Goalie's helmets have long been a canvas for artistic expression, with animated images of eagles or flames often personifying the wearer's demeanor. Sojung was informed that due to Olympic rules, she could not feature a specific person's face and so she had to tape over the baseball-sized rendition of the man who first encouraged her to play hockey. "I was upset, but I knew that he could see it from up there," Sojung confided, looking to the sky. "I felt like I was with him during the games. At times I would be searching for God, but also talking to my dad, and during those moments I felt more confident and certain."

Inspired by her father and feeding off the emotion from Randi Griffin's goal, Sojung played some of the sharpest hockey in her career during the later stages of the game against Japan. That momentum carried on to Korea's next contest, where they again drew Switzerland and had a chance to atone for the 8–0 shellacking from eight days earlier. The Swiss finished atop Group B during round robin pool play, going 3–0, and advanced to the medal round along with Sweden to take on the four teams from Group A. In the quarterfinals, Switzerland held a 2–1 lead in the second period, but gave up five straight goals to an awakened Russian attack and lost, 6–2, sending them into the classification round, where the remaining teams jostled for fifth to eighth place.

Although many Korean players were dejected in having let Japan slip out of their grasp in the third period, the Switzerland rematch suddenly trumped that game in importance. They knew the Swiss were not eight goals better and were determined to prove it. Five minutes before face-off, the scoreboard inside Kwandong Hockey Center broadcast a live video feed from Korea's locker room. The camera zoomed in on Sojung, stretching her neck with an intense look of focus. Over the next two hours, Sojung gave the best performance of her life, snapping her glove with catlike rapidity for save after save.

The North Koreans had yet to contribute much to the Unified team's systems, but that was not the only handicap. Caroline Park incurred a high ankle sprain in Minnesota the month before, and estimated she was playing at only about 70 percent of her capacity. Like in college, Caroline did not gripe about her injuries, gritting her teeth and pushing through. In April 2017, after winning at World Championships, Caroline flew back to New York to have surgery on her right shoulder, which left a gruesome five-inch scar running down to her armpit. For the next year, Caroline took a mix of six pills per day to fight the pain saturating her upper body.

Behind her charming looks, Caroline meant business 24/7. While other teammates warmed up by kicking around a soccer ball, Caroline always sat in solitude with headphones on, glaring out at the ice as if picturing how she envisioned the upcoming sixty minutes of action to play out. Her intensity was so deep that when Caroline first joined, she approached Sarah Murray about the team's habit of dancing to loud K-pop music in the locker room; Caroline worried about showing up at the Olympics and having Team Canada walk by and observe this absence of focus.

Caroline was still able to log nineteen minutes and fifty-two seconds against Switzerland, but lacked the same flash that had made her such a dynamic scoring threat during Worlds the year before. Korea's offense was more crisp than in the first game, but still with so little time afforded to let their sets take shape against the experienced Swiss defense, much of the pressure ended up around Sojung's net. As the first period wound down, Susie Jo was called for a holding penalty and with the five-on-four advantage, Switzerland scored a power play goal with 3:25 remaining on a beautifully placed cross-ice pass that led to a one-timer by Sabrina Zollinger.

Korea came out firing in the second period, putting the first three shots on goal. But as the tournament wore on, it became evident that Korea was not yet refined to a point to sustain offensive pressure against bigger and more seasoned opponents. Despite these circumstances, Sojung kept the Unified team in striking distance with the hope her forwards could squeak an equalizer past Swiss goalie Janine Alder. Throughout the second period, The Junger's theatrics amplified in net, including making one full extension leaping save with her right blocker on a crisscross play similar to the one that led to Switzerland's first goal.

With over thirty saves already and less than two minutes before intermission, Sojung hoped to carry her team into the third period down just one goal. Throughout the game, Murray hardly played a fourth line, keeping her top skaters on for extended shifts to generate more pressure. But toward the end of the second period, Korea's bodies became tired, which allowed the Swiss more time to wait for openings in the defense to materialize. With 1:08 remaining, Switzerland finally notched their second score of the game, giving them an important two goals' worth of breathing space against a fatigued Korean side.

The 2–0 deficit did not discourage those in attendance. As Koreans became more accustomed to watching hockey over the first week of the Olympics, a new type of fan base was formed. The North Korean cheerleaders were absent from the Switzerland rematch, so extra tickets were gobbled up by curious locals intrigued by this team of unknowns that suddenly captivated the world's attention. The chants were as loud as ever, but felt more pure. Instead of choreographed cheers, it was groups of South Korean girls yelling "Ko-re-a!" throughout the afternoon. Early in the third period, a Swiss player broke free from the neutral zone and looked to be open alone against Sojung, but the lead pass sailed just long of her stick. One mother watching this tense moment unfold yelled, "Oh, my God!" and then waved away her nerves with her hand as Korea regained control of the puck. The crowd also noticeably included an abundance of elderly *ajummas*, who sat on the edge of their seats with their neatly permed hair and gasped in response to turnovers or checks, probably never imagining seeing young Korean women performing on a vaunted stage like the Olympics.

In all, Sojung stopped fifty-one of fifty-three shots, the most saves made in a game during the tournament. Korea lost, 2–0, but earned the respect of their competition, finally proving that they were on equal footing. During the postgame handshake line, Alder talked to Sojung for several minutes and then, before she skated off the ice, went over again to whisper into So-jung's ear. A student at St. Cloud State University, Alder played against the South Korean national team when they visited her school the previous September.

"I told her she's a fighter and she did such a great job," said Alder, twenty-two. "I can't imagine how hard it was to bring those players together. I really take off my hat to that team. So-jung, she faced so many shots and had so many big saves. Even during the game, how she saved some of those shots, I was just stunned."

Sojung likely would have never been able to stifle the defending bronze medalists if not for the arrival of Rebecca Ruegseg-ger Baker. When Murray invited her to volunteer during South Korea's 2015 training camp in Minnesota, the offer injected new vivacity into a career that had been cut far too short. In high school, Ruegsegger Baker won national titles starting in goal for Shattuck-St. Mary's and earned a scholarship to play for the University of Wisconsin. In 2007, she won a gold medal at the Under-18 World Championships defending the net for Team USA. As a regular invite to USA Hockey camps and festivals, Ruegsegger Baker appeared to be on a clear-cut path toward making the women's Olympic hockey team.

"She was just a workhorse," described American Olympian Jocelyne Lamoureux-Davidson, Ruegsegger Baker's teammate at Shattuck. "She scratched and clawed for any type of improvement on and off the ice."

In college, Ruegsegger Baker started twenty games as a fresh-man. The following season, she posted a 10–1 record, sharing time with future American Olympic goaltender Alex Rigsby, and Wisconsin won the national championship. However, she could not celebrate for long. Years of injuries, which began with hip pain during her sophomore year of high school, had begun stifling Ruegsegger Baker's development by the end of her fresh-man year of college. At first she thought she was experiencing the standard nicks that accompany high-level athletes and ignored the warning signs.

Ruegsegger Baker trained vigorously in the summer before her sophomore year, while attending physical therapy sessions. She was pushing herself so hard that she had difficulty walking after workouts. Searing pain persisted throughout the year, but she stayed on the ice as Wisconsin chased a national title. Ruegsegger Baker learned after her sophomore season that the pressure she exerted on her body tore muscles that required hip surgery. The recovery did not go as planned, with constant sharp pains piercing her abdomen and hips.

By the age of twenty-one, Ruegsegger Baker could not walk, stand or sit without assistance. She had tears in both hips and suddenly was inflicted with excruciating stomach pains, which she only discovered later stemmed from an allergy to wheat. Over the next five years, Ruegsegger Baker had seven more surgeries.

After each procedure, she rehabbed strenuously to reengage in the sport she first fell in love with at a rink in Arvada, Colorado, when she was three years old. While her spirit was in the right place, her body did not allow her to continue. "I tried multiple times to get back on the ice," Ruegsegger Baker said. "I'd get ready, and just walking from the locker room to the ice sheet I'd be in excruciating pain. I realized I just wanted to walk again and be able to do everyday things and not feel that."

Ruegsegger Baker transferred from Wisconsin to Bethel University, a Christian college located just outside St. Paul. While doing homework in her dorm, she had to kneel at her desk as her body recovered from almost a decade of overwhelming abuse. In classes, Ruegsegger Baker could only sit for a few minutes before having to stand up and walk around the room to keep her hip from flaring up. When sitting back down, she'd slouch her lower body to stretch out her hips, which occasionally drew an arched eyebrow from professors thinking she was bored by their lectures.

Ruegsegger Baker's last surgery came in 2014, but even while coaching the Unified team, she dealt with daily hip pain. Growing up, one of her favorite activities was running, basking in the sensation of her feet pounding the pavement while being able to explore the vitality of nature. In high school and college, she dreamed of competing in marathons when her hockey career was over. But as a result of her slate of injuries, Ruegsegger Baker couldn't jog for any duration longer than twenty minutes. When she studied game film with Sojung and Han Do-hee, she'd often lie on her stomach, because she still could not remain in a chair for more than thirty-minute intervals.

Ruegsegger Baker, a beneficent soul whose playing career ended prematurely, rediscovered her passion for hockey when Murray asked her to join her coaching staff. In PyeongChang, she was in the presence of former high school and college teammates playing for the American side she once seemed destined for, but was not resentful. Working with Dohee and Sojung provided a B-12 shot to not only her hockey appetite, but her life. Fully immersing herself in Seoul, Ruegsegger Baker searched far and wide for gluten-free noodles to cook Korean-style meals for her host family, and like Danelle Im, kept a notepad to mark down Korean words to use in conversation with her goalies.

Ruegsegger Baker's commitment to women's hockey in South Korea was so strong that even though KIHA did not want to pay for an extra coach, she bought her own airfare to attend international tournaments and training camps in Seoul during her first two years with the team. She did not tell the players about this arrangement, but after the Olympics, when Choi Ji-yeon learned of the lengths Ruegsegger Baker went to be a part of the team, a chill went through her veins. Dohee cried when she became aware of her situation. "I felt very sorry that she had to do that and oh so grateful," Dohee shared.

"She was a very passionate player," said Gordie Stafford,

Ruegsegger Baker's high school coach at Shattuck, where she won the coveted annual award for "Best All Around Girl."

"Hockey, any sport, anything in life, you can play from a place of fear or you can play from a place of love. You just talk to her and you know she just loves life."

After practices, Ruegsegger Baker and Sojung were almost always the last pair on the ice. Although it physically pained her to do so, Ruegsegger Baker would kneel on one leg to be at eye-level with Sojung and just ask about her day or if she had enough sleep before breaking into a lesson. After their training was complete, Ruegsegger Baker often skated around the ice by herself, cleaning up all of the pucks scattered around the surface. Sometimes, before she moved the goals out of the way for the Zambonis, she'd get in a crouched position in front of the net and quickly slide from left the right, practicing a motion she'd later teach to Sojung and still showing the kind of fluidness that had made her one of America's top young goaltenders a decade earlier. "I just love being out there on the ice," gushed Ruegsegger Baker, who has a resemblance to the actress Jennifer Garner. "It's one of my favorite places to be. Just to skate again, a lot of times I'll look around and say how blessed I am.

"I was heartbroken I couldn't play," she added. "It was my lifelong dream to be an Olympian. I needed to take some time away. For one year I didn't go into the rink at all. It was hard to just see that. But it brings me the same joy coaching them as when I was playing. They'd do certain things that really remind me of when I'd play and they bring tears to my eyes."

The Korean team returned to Ruegsegger Baker an essential part of her being, and in return she molded Sojung into one of the best goalies in the world. Before her arrival, Sojung or Dohee had never done video training, but the ability to break down film and see their weaknesses in action helped refine the weaker points of their game. Even when the South Korean team wasn't active, Ruegsegger Baker invited Sojung and Dohee to train in the US; in their spare time they went paddleboarding or visited the Mall of America. And when Sojung played in the NWHL, Ruegsegger Baker joined her in New York.

*Rebecca Ruegsegger Baker instructs Shin So-jung after a practice at AMSOIL Arena in Duluth, Minnesota.*

Because of her own health history and a developing kindred connection with her pupil, Ruegsegger Baker knew when So-jung was hurting and pushing herself too far. Before the Olympics, when Sojung felt distant from hockey and thought about quitting, Ruegsegger Baker helped her overcome her doubts.

"Even two to three years prior to the Olympics, I was going through some difficult times," Sojung admitted. "I didn't want to play as much. Whenever I was going through these difficulties I shared it with Becca. She was kind of like my mentor, but we were the same age so she was my friend, as well. We got along really well and it would have been really hard without her. Becca kept me strong, helped me survive during the hard times especially right before the Olympics. We would have these twenty to thirty minutes after practice together on the ice and these were our happiest moments. I'm very grateful to her but also sorry that she had to help me out so much.

"I'm also very thankful and sorry she had to pay her own way," Sojung continued. "I didn't know at the beginning but I found out later on. I can't ever forget her. It's because of my personality I don't express these things directly to her, but she's a very special person in my life. I get very sad knowing we have to say goodbye. I was my happiest with Becca."

# CHAPTER TWENTY-THREE
## The Miracle Off Ice

After a redeeming effort against Switzerland, a crowd infatuated with women's hockey saluted the Unified team for the second straight game at the Kwandong Hockey Center. Their games had become chic social events, a place to be seen like the sidewalks outside Seoul's most exclusive nightclubs; in attendance were actual famous K-pop stars, who wanted to meet the players. As the team skated around to acknowledge their new fans, the song "Helicopter" by British rock band Bloc Party played over the sound system with its repeated chorus: "Are you hoping for a miracle?"

There would be no "miracle on ice" for the Unified team, but their transformation from political patsies, to overwhelmed neophytes, now into a team earning the respect and adulation of an international audience was nearly miraculous in and of itself. After the music stopped, the public address announcer told the audience they had thirty minutes to clear the arena. Once again, hundreds of fans awaited the team's arrival after all of their postgame commitments were fulfilled. Police officers and medical staff who were supposed to be patrolling the facility were acting like crazed fans meeting their sports idols. Olympic volunteers brought flowers and good luck charms for the players and waited nervously, shuffling their legs for the opportunity to greet their newfound icons.

Through all of their individual journeys, the members of the Unified team left a lasting impression on many who crossed their paths. Back in Antigonish, Nova Scotia, Shin So-jung's college teammates from St. Francis Xavier University woke up before sunrise in the hopes of catching a glimpse of her during the opening ceremonies. The girls from OHA did the same for Park Jong-ah, Park Ye-eun and Kim Se-lin. In Minnesota, Courtney Boucher and college teammates of Marissa Brandt held breakfast viewing parties for Korea's games. Christina Kessler, Randi Griffin's roommate from Harvard, received an abundance of text messages from her family and friends who beamed when they saw Randi on the Olympic ice.

"She's the type of person you meet and you don't forget her," said Kessler.

COURTESY OF BRENDA BERTHIAUME

*Brenda Berthiaume (right) made sure to wake up early in Canada to watch Shin So-jung at the Olympics.*

Genevieve Knowles, Korea's third-string goaltender, was originally put in contact with the coaching staff after enrolling in a camp run by Jessica Koizumi, Murray's college teammate at Minnesota-Duluth. Koizumi also recruited Grace Lee to Yale before coaching at Vermont. Watching two of her disciples in the Olympics, Koizumi, whose mother is Korean, no longer felt like "the most white Asian person ever" as she described herself for much of her life. "The older I get, the prouder I am to be an Asian American," Koizumi affirmed. "Seeing the girls grow up and represent, it's like I wanted to be a part of it."

In January, Sarah Murray talked about how her mother, Ruth, and her two brothers were going to be in Gangneung. When asked if her father might attend, Sarah smiled and replied no—the Olympics were occurring right in the middle of the college hockey season. With wistful eyes, she added, though, that she was holding a modicum of hope that her dad might surprise her and fly over for one game.

Although Andy Murray did not make it to South Korea, he followed the team's every step with the same intensity that he had while coaching in the Stanley Cup playoffs. In practices and film sessions at Western Michigan, he cited the Unified team's gusto as motivation for a room full of future NHL players.

"My dad doesn't really express his emotions very much," Sarah said. "My mom's always kind of like the positive cheerleader, whereas my dad is a little bit more intense. I always say 'Love you' before I hang up the phone and he usually just hangs up.

"So she had to yell at him," Sarah continued, laughing. "'You have to say love you back.' So when he's in the office he'll be, like, whispering 'Love you,' and then hang up. He won't, like, tell me, but send me a text message or like an email saying, 'I'm so proud of you.'"

Now, Andy Murray could not stop publicly gushing about his daughter. Though he did not always communicate it, his happiest moments in hockey came from watching Sarah, from her days as a peewee player outsmarting all of the boys on the ice, to yelling at her college team's medical staff to let her play through a broken ankle. "All her life, she's been making me smile," he said during the Olympics.[1]

The morning of Korea's final Olympic game, the clear skies made way for an almost blinding sunshine that illuminated the groups of schoolchildren that had come in droves to watch the women's hockey team. As they patiently sat and ate sandwiches on the steps outside Kwandong Hockey Center, the protestors with ulterior motives were nowhere to be found, replaced by giggling and play-fighting children, and teachers and parents asking young girls to hold up their tickets while posing for pictures. Hundreds of fans unable to secure tickets before, lined up hours prior to the gates opening for the opportunity to purchase any seats that might be released last minute at the box office. Volunteers milled about, their jackets now covered in black marker from the panoply of autographs collected from the Unified team players over the last week.

While many of the new supporters were hoping for another shot against Japan, that rematch would not come to fruition. After a 7–2 Sweden loss to Finland in the quarterfinals, in the second classification round game, Japan defeated Sweden, 2–1, in overtime, when Ayaka Toko scored the game-winner on goaltender Sara Grahn. It was the first time a team from Asia defeated a European team in the Olympics. Japan advanced to play Switzerland for fifth place, which excited Sojung, who actually preferred another matchup with Sweden. Just like when Korea verified in their second meeting against the Swiss that an 8–0 loss was an aberration, she wanted to make amends for the blowout with the Swedes.

Against Japan, the once proud Swedes—the 2006 Olympic silver medalists—had played with an attitude of having nothing left to compete for, appearing wholly disinterested and slogging around the ice, taking careless penalties until they lost. Two days later when they faced Korea on February 20, Sweden gained an early 1–0 lead in the first period and, buoyed by this advantage, began coasting again. Within the first six and a half minutes of play, Sweden was called for three infractions. It seemed as if they committed penalties just to release pent-up anger in the midst of their worst Olympic performance ever.

If Sweden had taken Korea seriously, they would have scouted their opponents more in-depth and sniffed out Jongah and Han Soo-jin's bread-and-butter power play move—the maneuver they cribbed from Japan and used to score against Wisconsin-River Falls one month earlier. After that game, Randi thought they tried it too often and divulged that if any team ever watched video of South Korea, they'd know that Jongah and Soojin attempt that play all the time. But for the uninitiated, it was the perfect sneak attack.

On their third power play of the first period, 6:21 into the game, Soojin wrapped around the net and received a pass from Jongah, then sniped the puck past goaltender Minatsu Murase to tie the game, 1–1. As Soojin tackled Marissa in celebration, in the stands, a sea of unification flags fluttered in the air, making it look like a wave of snow flurries. Mothers grabbed their daughters' hands and bellowed in joy.

It was a wake-up call for Sweden to salvage their last ounce of pride. Korea was no longer a joke and had to be respected. After that goal, Sweden played with a level of energy missing from their earlier Olympic outings. Once a power of the sport, Sweden could sense these emerging countries nipping at their heels. Despite the absence of the North Korean cheerleaders, the crowd created a ruckus. Within this new narrative the tenor was different—the cheering was organic, the interest was authentic.

"That was really special to me," Grace said. "Towards the end, every time we shot there'd be a huge outburst and a lot of the political cheers were toned down. I definitely felt it was more about us and hockey than North Korea, South Korea and the world."

For the remainder of the first period, the two sides battled intensely, with Korea pushing to score a go-ahead goal, buoyed by the raucous home crowd. But a penalty with under two minutes remaining put Sweden on the power play, and with twenty-three seconds before intermission, Sojung couldn't stop the pressure from bursting through and allowed a second goal, sending Korea trailing, 2–1, heading into the locker room.

Sojung held strong for much of the second period, now facing a reinvigorated Swedish push. But as the period wore on, the weariness from playing five games in ten days and all of the emotional feelings that had tugged at them from the past month wore down the Korean side. Like a wobbly boxer grasping onto his opponent in the waning seconds of a round, hoping to be saved by the bell, if they could hold the game to a one-goal deficit, Korea could go into the second intermission riding the belief that with one period left in the Olympics they were in striking distance of taking down mighty Sweden. But at the 16:27 mark in the second period, another puck slipped past Sojung, increasing Sweden's lead to 3–1.

The Korean players' legs now weary, Sweden applied more pressure than they had all tournament to avoid another stunning upset, and Sojung allowed two more goals in the third period. With 2:59 remaining in Korea's Olympic voyage, Sojung was pulled from the game to allow Han Do-hee to enter. The substitution was hardly noticeable at first and probably glanced over by many in attendance still getting their bearings about ice hockey's rules. During the time-out when the substitution was made, Sojung skated over to the bench and was greeted by Kim Do-yun with a tap on the shoulder. She lifted her mask and sat down, finally gaining an opportunity to rest after giving her life to women's hockey in South Korea. The appreciation for Sojung's efforts did not go unrecognized for long.

Postgame handshakes were exchanged after the 6–1 Sweden win and then the Unified team took a lap around the ice to a rousing ovation. The Swedish players tapped their sticks to hail the moment. A catchphrase Murray had used throughout the Olympics and in talks with her team over the years was a mantra to never get "too high or too low" with their emotions.

But as the game ended, it was hard for her thoughts to not get the best of her now. Murray hugged Pak Chol-ho and began crying as four years of memories came flooding back into her conscience—of her mother cooking meals for her players the same way she had thousands of times for her when she was just a little girl growing up in Minnesota. Of the first day meeting little Eom Su-yeon and how she evolved into a mirror image of herself as a player. Of the struggles and worries if her words would ever get through. Of the politics of the last month and the maturation of two dozen women who had taught the world something about sacrifice and love. Murray told reporters after the game that politicians made the executive decision to make the Unified team, but the players and staff are the ones who made it work.[2]

"I think it's incredible for our team, just for how few players there are in Korea, how competitive we are," Murray said in a separate interview. "It's just astonishing. We're giving Sweden a run for their money. For us to be this competitive blows me away. It's pretty incredible. Just the chemistry. They're a good group. Like, really good. Usually you have a couple of egos on your team. They all care about each other."

As they had done before each game, for one last time the Unified team formed a circle and hit their sticks on the ice and shouted, "One team." In the background, "Hand in Hand," the theme song from the 1988 Seoul Olympics, played over the loudspeakers. Standing from his seat one last time, Greg Brandt hugged Albert Lee and Kim Hee-won's mother, celebrating the Korean team's journey.

*Lee Min-ji (right) covered Korea's Olympic games on television. From L to R: Choi Ji-yeon, Danelle Im, Susie Jo, Choi Yu-jung.*

A few days later, when Hannah Brandt and her teammates on the United States national team defeated Canada in the gold medal game, Greg admitted he felt relief more than any other emotion. The US victory held added significance. In March 2017, the team threatened to boycott their upcoming World Championship tournament if USA Hockey did not pay them livable wages and increase support for girls' hockey programs. Despite medaling in every Olympics and winning six of their last seven World Championships, the US women's team—much like their counterparts in South Korea—were treated like an afterthought. For two weeks, the Americans held firm in their stance and finally reached a deal that was heralded as a landmark moment in women's sports. Capturing Olympic gold only further solidified their movement.

But for Hilary Knight, the most visible star on Team USA and a leading voice in the fight for equitable support, what stood out most to her during that whimsical postgolden glow was the opportunity to forge closer relationships with members of the Unified team. Via Hannah, she already followed a few South Korean players on Instagram and once sent a handwritten note to Choi Ji-yeon for her birthday. In Gangneung, Knight finally met Jiyeon, and they spent their downtime in the Athletes Village, filming their budding friendship on social media. During

Korea's games, the US players congregated in Hannah's room to watch and support a group of women whom, despite their obvious difference in talent, the Americans had come to feel a kinship with.

"Honestly, it was probably one of the coolest experiences I take away from the Olympics," Knight said. "Getting to know all the girls, it really felt like a family. They're just awesome. They're so happy about playing hockey. It reminds me if I ever forget what that ever feels like and to be excited every single moment. They're honestly my favorite. What they did at the Olympics was outstanding.

"They're transcending sport and that becomes so magical and powerful to be a part of," Knight continued. "I have a tremendous amount of respect for all the women on that team, to not only have the competitive mind-set, but also to try and continue peace in the world and bring out the best in other countries."

COURTESY OF CHOI JI-YEON

*Choi Ji-yeon (right) hugs American Olympian Hilary Knight.*

The US won in a thrilling overtime classic when Jocelyne Lamoureux-Davidson, the high school teammate of Sarah Murray and Rebecca Ruegsegger Baker, scored the clinching shoot-out goal, giving the Americans their first Olympic championship since 1998. Lamoureux-Davidson felt the work of the Unified team was equally as important. The attention the Koreans brought to the sport at the beginning of the tournament was a perfect assist for the Americans, who capitalized on the spotlight and punctuated with authority the fact that women's hockey deserved a much larger stage. Days later, the IIHF announced that the 2022 Olympic women's hockey tournament was expanding to ten teams, signifying the growth of interest in the game. "I know there was controversy throwing players on their women's team, but also lessons I think the world could use a lot more of right now," Lamoureux-Davidson noted.

Knight and Lamoureux-Davidson were far from the only Olympic athletes who observed a spirit within the Korean players reminiscent of their younger selves, when they loved sport in a similar innocent fashion. Russian hockey star Ilya Kovalchuk, who once signed a $100 million NHL contract, wanted pictures with Jiyeon. His teammate on the gold medal-winning men's hockey team and a two-time Stanley Cup champion, Pavel Datsyuk, felt compelled to gift Soojin a signed, game-used stick.

Toward the end of the Olympics, the Unified team players could not walk anywhere without being stopped. Sojung, Susie Jo and other South Korean players received daily requests to appear on national television broadcasts. Randi, after worrying about how she would be received by Koreans when she first arrived three years earlier, was hounded like a movie star for pictures and autographs. The attention was even more overwhelming for Marissa, whose story became one of the most talked about narratives during the Olympics, as she appeared on CNN, CBS, NBC, ABC and all of the Korean television stations.

During the 1988 Summer Olympics in Seoul, one of the most popular storylines to emerge became the mass exportation of adopted South Korean children. The next time South Korea hosted the Olympics thirty years later, one of the most popular storylines became the South Korean adoptee who returned to her birth country and inspired hope across the globe.

To her family and all of Marissa's coaches and teammates at home, seeing her become recognized as her own star was a feeling better than winning gold.

"For me, one of the greater memories I have of being there with Marissa was just that she was kind of famous," Robin Brandt said, smiling like only a proud mother can. "We'd go out with her and people would stop and ask her for her autograph.

"I was like, 'This is how it feels, Hannah,'" Marissa said, laughing as she recalled teasing her sister. "Growing up here it was always like, 'Oh, you're Hannah Brandt's sister.' I'm like, 'Yes, my name's Marissa.' Like I've just always been her sister. But over there they're like, 'Oh, you're Yoon-jung Park's sister!'"

*Marissa wearing Hannah's Olympic gold medal.*

COURTESY OF MARISSA BRANDT

When the team skated off the ice after their final game, So-jung headed over to her bench and hugged her coaches. Naturally, the longest embrace was with Ruegsegger Baker, who told Sojung how proud she was and that she loved her.

Sojung circled the ice one more time, waving to an audience that had become smitten with her efforts. She left the rink with Grace and lifted up her mask to take in the atmosphere for a final moment and smiled with gleaming eyes at the thousands of Koreans who'd ignored her presence in the first Olympic game in favor of the president, but now finally knew who Shin So-jung was.

The rest of the players did not cry after another loss. Park Chae-lin's mother thanked Marissa for all of her work, for her willingness to come to Korea, to be a role model for her daughter. Elderly Korean *ajummas* turned into groupies, requesting to take photos with Sarah Murray and her mother Ruth, while holding flags of the US and South Korea together. Soojin's family could hardly contain their emotion, watching their daughter, the former pianist, now a popular athlete who had proved she was right all along in following her dream.

There was another game to be played in an hour and ticket holders bunched up outside, antsy to enter, but once again that did not matter to the fans who had traveled from throughout the country to thank the players for what they had done. The team really had no business challenging Japan and Switzerland or scoring against Sweden, which has 5,505 registered female hockey players compared to 319 in South Korea. Those countries were among the best in the world, having decades of top-level training under their belts. But the Unified team's hard work and belief in each other spurred them to not wilt until they finally proved they belonged.

When the crowd finally dissipated and the team collected their gear, the players could go off with their families or ride back on the team bus to the Olympic Village. Sojung's mother, Seol Kyoungrang, waited with Sojung's aunt so they could walk out of the arena together. After the first game, no one felt the sting of the loss more than Sojung. Following the Switzerland debacle, she quickly showered and then walked up to the concourse area. Upon locking on to the heavy sympathetic eyes of her mother, who hadn't watched her play since elementary school, Sojung broke down, feeling as if she had let down her parents, her teammates and an entire nation.

Outside, as the spectators for the next game finally began filing into the arena, Seol's eyes were now only brimming with pride, and she requested that her daughter take a photograph at the site of her greatest conquest. With late-afternoon sunbeams shining down over Gangneung, Seol snapped a picture of her daughter smiling, standing in front of the entrance of the Kwandong Hockey Center. Sojung then inserted herself in between her mother and aunt, put her arms around their waists and walked through the crowd, up to the pine needle–coated floor of the woods and before long, seemed to disappear into the ether. She had regained the Olympic dream that was taken away by the histrionics of policymakers and beauty squads. Sojung finally had her moment of acceptance and now was at peace to leave on her terms.

"I did feel sad about leaving this scene behind, so I cried at the rink when we were done with the game," Sojung said. "At that moment, I really felt like I accomplished everything and I felt relieved. I had been doing this for almost twenty years. I always thought I'd retire after the Olympics. In that moment walking through the woods, I felt very light. I felt really comfortable and I let down my burdens. I realized that I was done with this stage that I dreamt of and I can finally enjoy my time with my family without feeling stressed."

# CHAPTER TWENTY-FOUR

## A Foggy Road

In less than one month, the courage displayed by Korea's women's hockey players turned even the most hardened critics soft. At the beginning of the Olympics, *Washington Post* columnist Jerry Brewer was one of many to lambast the Unified team and its politics, describing the opening ceremony as "kumbaya at its most elegant," and mentioning that he began to fall asleep during Korea's first game against Switzerland due to the "uninspiring hockey."

"We're likely to look back at the Peace Olympics and consider it the Political Games," he continued, calling the women's hockey team "merely unification wallpaper."[1]

Two weeks later, Brewer was converted into believing that the Korean team provided a sterling kind of hope that the rest of world was desperate for amid the unstable international political climate of early 2018. "It succeeded because the athletes represented the best of us," he wrote. "It was only going to succeed if the athletes were authentic examples of those civil aspirations. It can't be forced. It can't be faked. That's the magic of sports; in the heat of competition, truths are revealed. By simply being themselves, the participants made the Peace Olympics turn into more than a naive theme."

Brewer concluded by writing that the most enduring image of the Olympics was when Park Jong-ah and Jong Su-hyon worked in collaboration during the opening ceremony to bring the torch to Kim Yu-na. "They didn't drop it, and that's the message: When you trust in humanity, the humans teach us about grace. Perhaps more of us will learn to run in sync without dropping the torch."[2]

Of all the summits and speeches and wars across the last century, it was women's hockey that was able to allow the world to view North Koreans on a human level. Audiences saw the likes of Suhyon emitting joy and a zest for life, normalizing her and her teammates beyond the tropes of being emotionless communist robots.

Over time, the South Korean players discovered that Suhyon and her North Korean teammates liked to make jokes and talk about boyfriends and eat Big Macs. They really liked eating Big Macs. For most Olympic athletes, once their competitions are completed it becomes time to indulge in the most bacchanalian of desires, bouncing from bars to clubs to party houses and breaking free from four years of regiment and sobriety. In the days after the Unified team finished their last Olympic game, the players shared burgers and McFlurries at the McDonald's located inside the Athletes Village. The South Korean women's hockey players, against the greatest of odds, had become one with women from North Korea. It was the result politicians dreamed of but knew in their hearts was unlikely to occur. Then, after achieving the nearly impossible in unifying on the ice, heartbreak struck again as the two sides were separated and forced to say goodbye all too abruptly.

In 1991, South Korean Kim Taek-soo was forced to partner with North Korean Kim Kwok-chul at that year's world table tennis championships, the first time athletes from two Koreas competed in an international sporting event. For forty-five days, they trained together and made the front page of all the newspapers in South Korea. They quickly became friends and in their rare moments away from the media, the Kims went out for beers.

"They called it the beginning step to reunification," Kim Taek-soo, now the coach of South Korea's table tennis teams, told the *New York Times*'s Juliet Macur in February 2018.[3]

When they first met, Kim Taek-soo was too young to realize the magnitude of his position. Eventually, though, he was forced to think about reunification and everything that encompassed. After the tournament, Kim Kwok-chul went back to North Korea. Kim Taek-soo tried desperately to find any information he could on his partner, but all sources turned up dry. Just like that, someone he had come to feel was like his brother had disappeared in an instant. They never saw each other again and Kim Kwok-chul seemingly vanished. Not even other North Korean table tennis players Kim Taek-soo encountered knew what became of Kim Kwok-chul.

Before the Olympics, Lee Yeon-jeong wanted nothing to do with her northern neighbors. "I thought of North Korea as always provoking South Korea and always asking for money," Yeonjeong said. "I assumed they were doing that because they were poor and spending all their money on military. Overall, I viewed them in a negative light."

As one of the players most affected by the rule of having three North Koreans dress for each game, Yeonjeong was only able to play two shifts for a total of 1:33 of ice time. Four of the five games she watched from the upper level of the Kwandong Hockey Center with the eight to nine North Koreans who also did not dress. Eventually, Yeonjeong became among the closest of all the South Koreans with the players from the North, along with Jung Si-yun, the seventeen-year-old who was sometimes left out by others on the roster, but now had a clique of twelve new friends who saw her as someone who epitomized cool.

"I felt very resentful toward the North Korean players at first," Yeonjeong disclosed. "I later realized it was not their fault. Siyun and I spent the most time with them. We'd play K-pop songs and teach them the lyrics and dances. Despite the preconceptions I had toward North Korea, in the end we were dealing one person to another person."

In one of their final nights together, members of the Unified team met in Yeonjeong's room. The North Koreans had become particularly fond of female K-pop group Red Velvet with their songs "Red Flavor" and "Ice Cream Cake," which featured lyrics like, "It's so tasty, come and chase me." Olympic officials told Yeonjeong and others not to play such music around the North Koreans, but together in her dorm, they did not have to worry any longer about such rules.

Later in the night, Han Do-hee put on a customized playlist that included the ballad "A Foggy Road" by Korean singer Ben, which contained the lyric, "Do you know how much I miss you?"

"The North Korean players started crying," Yeonjeong said, her sharp eyes turning solemn. "That's when I realized we wouldn't be able to keep in touch or see them again. Before we left, I wrote them each a letter saying don't forget me."

As the Olympics drew to a close, President Moon Jae-in, IOC President Thomas Bach and IIHF President René Fasel could not stop patting each other on the back for the strength projected by the Unified team. What none of these honchos considered when the merger was hatched one month earlier was the ramifications if the plan actually succeeded. "It wasn't something that could be accomplished just because the Korean government wanted it to happen," Susie Jo said.

Amid the unfairness of being thrown into a situation none of the players originally wanted—then being essentially told to shut up and roll with the punches—the Unified team somehow created genuine attachment and then experienced the cruelest emotions of loss, left feeling even more helpless than they did at the start of this whole experiment. The farewell infiltrated all the players' minds, but particularly stung Choi Ji-yeon. In the span of a few weeks, Jiyeon began referring to North Koreans Kim Hyang-mi and Hwang Chung-gum as her "older sisters." Just three months after her father died, Jiyeon had to say goodbye to more loved ones she never was going to see again.

That feeling of impending loss even plagued players who did not forge strong personal bonds. Danelle Im could only speak Korean at a beginner's level, but she sometimes gazed at Kim Un-jong, the girl with the precocious smile that drew in Marissa Brandt. Whenever she looked at Un Jong, Danelle saw her grandmother, with the same full lips, wide eyes and arching eyebrows, but most of all the gentle, loving mannerisms that she emitted. In those moments, Danelle wished that Un Jong could only live one tenth of the free life that her grandmother had when she moved to Canada.

"It makes me sad to think about that," Danelle said months later. "Sad to not know where they are or what they're doing right now. Sad for not being able to know what their life is like and what struggles they go through."

COURTESY OF LEE MEE-HYUN

*Rebecca Ruegsegger Baker greets North Korean goaltender Ri Pom at the Olympics closing ceremony.*

★ ★ ★

On the night of the closing ceremony, Marissa and Grace Lee milled about in the massive waiting area—white tents pitched outside the Olympic Stadium in PyeongChang—setting their radars to find Un Jong. When she finally came bounding through the masses smiling, she called out to Grace, "Jingyu!" referring to her Korean name. Even to Un Jong, there was no doubt that the imports were just as Korean as she was.

As they chatted and gossiped, Un Jong told Grace that she needed to visit her in Pyongyang and they'd go out and eat bowls of *naengmyeon*, the famous North Korean cold noodles. "How do you respond to that?" Grace asked with a hint of anger that she had to lie to Un Jong. "You have to tiptoe your way around what's going on in the world, so you're kind of like, 'Yeah, I'll come if I can.' You know maybe there's a 10 percent chance that you would even get to see them again."

That did not mean that Grace and Marissa didn't try to devise ways to cross the border. In the days before the Olympics ended, Marissa called her parents and asked if they knew of any way she could visit North Korea. "She told me, 'Dad, I have my Korean citizenship, I think I can go,'" Greg Brandt recalled. "I said, 'Nooo, I don't think so,' like, worried, but she was dead serious."

Marissa then started to think back to the 2017 World Championships. Because South Korea won their division, they were being promoted to the third highest grouping in April, ahead of North Korea. "This is bad to say," Marissa whispered, "but sometimes I wish we got knocked down back into the lower division so we would get to play them and I would get to see them.

"We don't look at them like North Koreans. They were our team."

Walking out into the stadium, the North Koreans wore the same red parkas that covered their backs on the first day the teams met in Jincheon, but now they strutted with their arms around their teammates from the South. Earlier in the day President Moon learned from Kim Yong-chol, a senior North Korean official attending the closing ceremony, that the North was ready to begin dialogue with the United States in fostering new relations between the two countries. For the Unified team, there were more important measures at hand. Han Soo-jin, fixing Un Jong's bangs, informed her that they were all going to meet back at McDonald's one last time after the closing ceremony.

"Ohh, a party!" Un Jong exclaimed.

COURTESY OF LEE MEE-HYUN

*Lee Eun-ji (left) and other players tried to keep as many mementos as possible from their time with the North Korean players.*

After one last round of fast food, Cho Mi-hwan and some of her teammates snuck into the North Korean dorm, where they stayed until the morning, not wanting to let go of the moment. The rest of the South Koreans woke up before sunrise to say their final goodbyes. Just after 7:30 a.m., waiting nervously inside the entrance to the Athletes Village where some of her teammates had been for over two hours, Dohee stood near the front door until she could see the North Koreans approaching. As the delegation became visible, Dohee ran inside to notify the rest of her team. The North Korean women were dressed warmly in wine-colored coats with black fur collars and matching hats, their eyes already welling up. The South Korean players originally arranged themselves in a horizontal line, not unlike when they stood when they first met each other, shivering with cold at Jincheon, but that quickly broke up. Two and three South Korean players at a time wrapped themselves in the arms of their North Korean sisters, their cheeks now apple red as tears streamed down their faces. Pak Chol-ho hugged Sarah Murray and offered an open invitation to visit Pyongyang.

Choi Yu-jung embraced Jin Ok, who only dressed for one game and did not log any minutes, but after each of Korea's contests, ran down to the locker room to tell Yujung that she played well. "There was something very comforting about her," noted Yujung, who eventually ran to a back corner to cry by herself, not wanting her reaction to be captured by all of the news cameras recording the scene. Susie Jo had to restrain herself from saying niceties like, "Let's keep in touch," or "I'll see you soon," knowing that they were heartfelt, but ultimately empty promises. Some players worried about the "re-education" the North Koreans were supposed to receive upon returning to Pyongyang. To make sure their memories did not fade, Marissa gave Un Jong a bracelet decorated with marble beads and a silver bar that her mother had gifted to her and that she always wore during games.

"I was like, you keep this and you can remember me forever," Marissa said. "In that moment I was like I want you to have this because you really made an impact on my life and I value our friendship and I really hope I can see you again. It just felt right."

Seeing Dohee's sadness was particularly striking to the North Koreans, having never met anyone before with her personality. Her jokes and antics pierced through the initial icy walls between the two sides. When the North Koreans arrived at Jincheon, Dohee learned that her grandfather originally hailed from North Korea and was relocated during the Korean War.

"First, my grandparents contacted my mom but not me directly," Dohee recounted. "After the North Korean players came to Korea, I called my grandpa and he told me to treat them nicely because they're good girls and I shouldn't be scared of them. At first it didn't feel like they were a part of our team. But after training, living together and competing together, it felt like they were not just a part of our team, but family."

*Han Do-hee (top) and Choi Ji-yeon (second right) with North Korean players Kim Hyang-mi, Jong Su-hyon and Hwang Chung-gum.*

As the North Koreans made their way outside, twenty-four-year-old forward Ryo Song-hui stood at the door shaking hands with Dohee, who was born in the same year, sniffling to try to hold in her emotion as best she could. When Song Hui stepped on board the bus that was to take her back across the thirty-eighth parallel, she grabbed Dohee's hand and held tightly. Slowly, the grasp loosened from five fingers to four to three to two, before North Korean officials finally closed the bus door and separated them. Not ready to say goodbye, with one final gasp Song Hui ran to a window and lifted it open to touch the hands of her South Korean teammates one more time, trying to contain her urge to run off the bus to stay behind with them. Similarly, the South Korean players' hands reached out and held tightly, as if they were trying to pull Song Hui and others back off the bus. Dohee put her hand through the window opening to gently wipe away Song Hui's tears, while Susie chose to stand farther back, feeling as if she would be unable to maintain her composure if she got too close.

When the bus finally pulled away, the rest of the bus's windows were slung open and the North Korean players waved farewell one last time, craning their necks as far back as they could to get one more glimpse of the South Korean players. Long after the white-and-maroon bus finally pulled away out of view, Dohee stood alone, waving northward, hoping it might turn around.

# CHAPTER TWENTY-FIVE

# Evolution

In the weeks that followed the 2018 Winter Olympics, North Korea, South Korea and the United States made rapid progress in their suddenly burgeoning rapprochement. During a meeting in Pyongyang between Korean officials, the North agreed to discuss the possibility of denuclearization with the Americans, setting the stage for US President Donald Trump to meet with Kim Jong-un. Meanwhile, North and South Korean sports officials continued working on inter-Korean exchanges, with major plans developing for the upcoming Asian Summer Games in August.

Thomas Bach, president of the IOC, admitted the Pyeong-Chang Games were on the brink of being canceled due to fears of North Korean aggression.[1] He also proclaimed that his organization opened the door for the political advancements stunning the world, just one of many peripheral figures milking the Unified team's popularity and taking credit for their labor. South Korean President Moon Jae-in reveled in approval rating boosts and René Fasel, head of the IIHF, asserted that he devised plans all the way back at the 2014 Olympics to create a Unified Korean women's hockey team. Bach later presented President Moon with the Olympic Order in Gold, the IOC's highest award to contributors of the Olympic movement. All of these men claimed that without them, none of the feel-good glow from the Olympics would have been possible.

These boasts barely registered among the actual individuals whose work paved the way for North and South Korea to come closer than ever before. Instead, there was a collective feeling of emptiness growing inside the players of South Korea's women's national hockey team. This originated not only from the loss of their North Korean cohorts, but of not knowing what was going to transpire next in their careers. They never wanted to be famous, only to be valued as hockey players.

By the time the Olympic flame was extinguished, some had lost their passion for the game, seeing how easily they were used. In reality, any chance the team had of winning was lost once the North Koreans came on board. Although they turned out to have charming personalities, the North Koreans' athletic skills were clearly lacking. None of the three players who dressed each game were comparable to Jung Si-yun, Cho Mi-hwan or Lee Yeon-jeong, the trio of South Koreans benched most often to appease the IOC's mandate.

"I am sure the defense wasn't as good without Mihwan," Ko Hye-in analyzed. "We formed our way of playing and our own rhythm for training four years together. Having North Korean players broke that. The government told us we weren't able to talk about any of this, which I felt was unfair. The government told us you have to accept this Unified team. If you do this, we'll give you a team in Suwon. It was basically forced upon us."

The concept of creating a semipro team in Suwon was indeed just window dressing. What women's hockey in South Korea truly needed was continued support—from the government, the IIHF, KIHA and Chung Mong-won. The men's team with their high-priced imports got smoked in the Olympics, going winless and finishing in last place out of twelve teams. But at least they had a cushy professional league and six-figure salaries to return home to.

Prior to South Korea being named the host of the 2018 Olympics, a majority of the women's team felt that KIHA never really cared about them to begin with. Even before the Games, they earned just over $50 a day—minus costs for health insurance—a stipend they only received if they trained at least fifteen days per month. One day less and there was no payment. "We all knew that KIHA prefers the men's team and that's always been one of our biggest complaints," said Park Chae-lin.

Han Do-hee noted she first recognized gender discrimination when she joined the women's national team at age twelve, "but nothing was going to come out of it if I complained." Ingrained with such a belief, Dohee and her colleagues begrudgingly toed the patriarchal company line.

With feelings of resentment bubbling and the ambiguity surrounding their lives increasing, Dohee, Chaelin and the rest of their teammates finally decided it was time take control of their destiny. They no longer were willing to subsist in the same manner they had prior to PyeongChang and did not want their futures dictated by anyone but themselves. By the end of the Olympics, they did not emerge so much as harbingers of peace, but rebels with a newfound voice for change.

In an attempt to have KIHA recognize their worth, on March 26, two weeks before leaving for World Championships in Asiago, Italy, the team crafted a letter, outlining their demands for the future of women's hockey in South Korea. If KIHA did not finally take the women's team seriously, they were going to boycott the tournament. Such an occurrence would have been a PR nightmare for KIHA just one month after the Olympics, with effects rippling all the way to the Blue House, which wanted to keep the pristine image of their benevolent hockey daughters who inspired so much hope around the world by working hand in hand with the North Koreans.

In March 2017, Park Jong-ah had watched intently as the US women's national team employed a similar maneuver when they threatened to boycott USA Hockey. "Even we have desire to fight for equal wages and gender equality," Jongah remarked then. "I don't know how to do that, but always think of equalities."

One year later, Jongah, now her team's captain, found her calling. During the last weekend of March, she ordered the team together at Danelle Im's brother's apartment in Seoul, where they stayed up all hours of the night authoring their decree. It was a daring action that carried a very Western influence. Over the years, the imports did more than just solidify lines and teach new tactics on the ice. As they became ingrained in the family of South Korea's women's hockey team, they emboldened their colleagues to aspire for progress in a way that was dissonant from Korean cultural norms.

"The boycott seemed like a very Western thing to do," said Han Soo-jin. "Foreigners are certainly more independent and direct in expressing their thoughts. So I think that's why we were more active."

While the hockey team's decision to stand up to KIHA was a necessary next step, there were unfortunate casualties. A common desire for much of the team was to not only continually improve and properly cultivate the sport, but to regain the democratic culture that defined the program before they became part of the Olympic machine. Sarah Murray deftly navigated the politics and turbulence that came with the Unified team saga, but the majority of players were unsure if she was fit to carry them to prolonged success on the ice. The struggles in the months leading up to the Olympics and the early eight-goal losses to Switzerland and Sweden did not alleviate those concerns.

A few weeks after World Championships, Murray was turning thirty. She often discussed her uncertainty of how long she could stay on as head coach. Murray genuinely loved the players and did not want to see the program die after the Games, but spending another several years in Seoul was a tricky proposition. Ironically, Murray also worried about KIHA's future commitment to the sport. In addition, her family and friends remained in the US and she felt some internal pressure to settle down. She saw all of her contemporaries buying houses and getting married and there was a sense that life was passing her by. Murray admitted that it was difficult to make friends in South Korea and maintain any sort of social life. She felt guilty when her aunt died and she could not be home to console her mother. But unlike in China, she had the team to keep her going. That was the only relationship she cared about.

"I wouldn't trade my life for anything," Murray said three weeks before the Olympics.

Perhaps sadder than the tears shed by the Unified team at their valediction were the unspoken words between Murray and her South Korean players. The team was too afraid to confront Murray about the aspects of her coaching style they found unproductive and Murray never openly relayed to them how important the team was to her. The tension carried on unabated and the relationship between both parties suffered as a result.

It was obvious that Murray, like so many of them, was waging an internal battle of defining her self-worth—long determined to escape the nepotism that had followed her career, to emerge out of the shadow of her father the NHL coach, and her brothers, one of whom played in the NHL. In South Korea, she found the most unusual of circumstances to distinguish herself and prove her viability, surrounded by a team fighting for something beyond hockey, pushing for a goal grander than any trophy they could ever raise. Like Murray, they wanted to be recognized on their own merits.

In some ways, what the Unified team achieved in uplifting audiences around the world was even more remarkable given the buried emotions in their locker room. Individually, Murray's maternal instinct to protect her players, Rebecca Ruegsegger Baker's gentle care, the determination of Eom Su-yeon and the steel will of Shin So-jung carried them through the most tumultuous waters an Olympic team has ever sailed into. It was clear that together they could achieve remarkable feats. But Murray's strength while leading the Unified team could not overcome issues that had been brewing for years. Within the letter to KIHA, the team requested a new coach, believing that a new phase could not occur with remnants of the old regime in place.

COURTESY OF DANELLE IM

*Before the 2018 Olympics, there were no girls or women's hockey teams at the high school, college or pro levels in South Korea.*

Murray's tenure was defined by her ongoing search for the proper mix in sternness—playing the role of coach—and being able to relate to her team on a personal level. It puzzled Murray that players did not ask her more intimate questions, like they did with the imports. There were moments in practice when she'd scrimmage with the younger players, untie her blond pony-tail and literally let her hair down, emitting candid glee skating alongside them. During the 2017 Asian Winter Games opening ceremony, she wished her players had marched in more reso-lute and almost militarized, like how the Japanese hockey team did, but could not help having her heart warmed by watching the teens hold hands and rest their heads on each other's shoul-ders as they walked around the stadium. In several interviews before the Olympics, Murray spent hours lauding her players. She ended each answer with either a blush or a giggle, whether it was talking about Lee Kyou-sun's kindness or Suyeon's feisty demeanor that did not back down to any opponent.

To Murray, almost as important as a good showing in the Olympics was to build up the teenage players like Suyeon and have them recruited by American colleges. If NCAA Division I programs weren't willing to look toward South Korea for talent, Murray was hell-bent on shoving highlight tapes in their faces until they recognized that Suyeon was as talented a defender as any seventeen-year-old in Minnesota. Murray fought in the same way for Kyousun, badgering KIHA officials until they agreed to hire her as a coach, making sure that she did not miss out on the Olympics. She often had a way of needling KIHA into submission whenever they tried to shoo her away. Right before Christmas, South Korea was scheduled to have an exhibition game against China in Seoul. When Murray learned a school of orphans was invited to attend, she pestered KIHA officials daily until they agreed to purchase skates so the children could go on the ice with the team after the game.

However, the support that Murray showed for the younger players was not always given to the veterans. While it was true that the teenagers were the future backbone of the program, the dedication of elders like Soojin probably should not have been overlooked. In late 2017, after Soojin complained about Mur-ray's coaching style, she said she was threatened with being cut.

KIHA called a meeting between Soojin and the coaching staff. Soojin explained that she never felt that she gained Murray's trust—even after being demoted from captain, she wanted to act as a bridge between the head coach and the players. "They told me that the team wouldn't function properly if I as one of the older and influential players on the team say negative things and complain," said Soojin, who often had the same kind of intense, hard stare that Murray's high school teammates shuddered at.

This episode troubled many of the players. While a level of authority has to be respected in any locker room, they felt that Soojin, the elder stateswoman on the roster, should have had as much say in the team's operation. That she could almost get tossed off, and then was muted by KIHA afterward, made the team feel that any challenge of authority could put them in danger of being left out of the Olympics.

The South Koreans were also bothered that Murray never learned Korean, which could have enabled her to relate with them on a more personal level. Aside from separating the coaches and players during meals, they wondered why she did not seem to ask simple questions about their lives outside of hockey. "I wish there was more interaction," Choi Yu-jung sighed. "We didn't communicate so much on a daily basis. We didn't get so much direct feedback from her. She would tell things to our Korean coach and the Korean coach told the team."

"When we asked her specific questions she'd say, 'Oh, I'll get back to you guys,' and she'd never get back to us about it," Hyein added. "We thought that she could never give us a straight answer."

That sentiment was compounded when forwards were promoted or demoted from lines with no explanation. Realistically, this gripe may have been a tad misguided. No matter their history or how they earned qualification, the South Koreans were now Olympic-level athletes. It's hard to imagine any coach on a premier level in any sport explaining each lineup move made. However, since the team and staff essentially lived together throughout the year, the silence that Murray kept on these changes only frustrated the players. The deft understanding of the game Murray showed throughout her career as a player did not always translate as smoothly on the bench.

*The South Korean national team's freedom to operate changed once they earned an Olympic berth.*

"I think the cultural difference had an impact," Danelle Im said. "Also communication. I don't think the players ever felt comfortable talking to Sarah. There was just that breakdown there. The age too, I'm sorry to say. In Korean culture, age works in such a hierarchal way."

"It's not like Sarah didn't have the will," YeEun added. "It was just her methods didn't work for us. As we wrote in the document to KIHA, it's not like we didn't like her as a person. I know that she was trying, we all know that, but looking at our accomplishments it wasn't enough."

Murray may not have been the best coach to lead the team on the ice, but she was the perfect coach to handle the merger and KIHA appreciated that. As the team reached a point of potential fracture, politics in South Korea were booming. If word of the strike came out, the government was assuredly going to become furious that their symbols of peace were pushing back against the patriarchy.

After laying out their concerns, the team ended their letter by stating,

Please understand that our request does not come from a place of malice or disrespect. We have taken this firm stance because we feel we have no other way to ensure our voices are heard. We are deeply committed to the national team program and to the future of women's hockey in South Korea. We look forward to hearing your response.
Sincerely,
The Korean Women's Ice Hockey National Team

Predictably, KIHA did not respond to the letter positively.

# CHAPTER TWENTY-SIX
# One Body

Before drafting their letter to KIHA, Randi Griffin and Shin So-jung met with executive director Yang Seung-jun to discuss possible outcomes for the team's future. Like an annoyed adult shooing away a child, Mr. Yang laughed at the idea that the players should have any input. Believing they had no other options, an anonymous poll was created in the team's group chat on the Korean messaging app Kakao. At the time, Caroline Park had returned to the United States to heal her injuries and continue her med school curriculum. Ko Hye-in, Choi Yu-jung and Genevieve Knowles also resumed their studies and Lee Yeon-jeong, still hobbling on depleted knees, sensed no future for older players like herself in the team's long-term plans and retired.

The rest of the collective voted unanimously to continue on with their planned course of action.

"I do feel bad for her," Park Jong-ah said of Sarah Murray afterward. "I know Sarah trusted us and put in a lot of effort. I know she invested a lot of time for us and we betrayed that.

However, we expressed our concerns and problems to her and there were no changes. So I think that was inevitable."

There was no turning back. A new Kakao account was created with the purpose to communicate with KIHA throughout their negotiations. The only snag was that no one knew what to set as the user name. Players often joked about the phrase "One Body," a nickname the media used for the team. The term never really resonated among the roster, though, and so they mockingly shouted it during workouts or to break up the monotony of practices. During one of the late-night meetings, someone suggested the group name be "One Body," which was followed by silence.

"Then everyone was like, 'Yeah, that's what it has to be,'" Randi Griffin recounted. "This is the moment we became one body."

The letter was not sent immediately. On March 26, the team was invited to a celebratory dinner in Suwon, a city about twenty miles south of Seoul. They were guests of honor as Mayor Yeom Tae-young announced plans to host the semipro women's team that was being created in honor of the Olympic effort. "This was the first unified Korean Olympic team in history and they have been leaders in all things, from helping the PyeongChang Olympics become the 'Peace Olympics' to the sprouting of peace through the upcoming inter-Korean and North Korea–US summits," Yeom told reporters.[1] After the mayor's speech, local children sent colorful paper planes into the air and a group photo was taken with the horde of politicians on hand. The women's hockey team smiles masked their nervousness and fear of the journey they were about to embark on, which could crash as quickly as the planes sputtering to the ground.

The planned strike had already caused some turmoil within their ranks. Over the course of the weekend, players began to waver, particularly the younger girls, perhaps not sensing the magnitude of their actions and just wanting to play at World

Championships. Danelle Im and Susie Jo wondered if they should approach Murray with their longstanding concerns one final time. But veterans like Han Soo-jin and Jongah knew their leverage evaporated if they backed down now. Through these impassioned debates, friendships that had persisted for decades began to fissure. Some players couldn't stop crying from the stress and torn feelings created by the situation. Led by Jongah's phlegmatic determination in the role of captain, the team persisted and held their stance.

After receiving the letter, Mr. Yang called a meeting at KIHA's offices near the Olympic Park that hosted the 1988 Summer Games. It was more of a belittling exercise than an exchange of ideas, as he spent a majority of the time yelling at them, labeling them stupid children and saying that KIHA leaders did not care if the team skipped World Championships. Many of the teenagers sobbed while Mr. Yang bombarded them with expletives. This display was particularly sickening to the imports.

"One of the things I learned that I didn't know going into it was how much of a deeper problem it was," Danelle realized. "It wasn't about Sarah anymore. Yes, she was the coach, but you saw the deeper underlying problems and politics."

Mr. Yang hoped to break the team through his tirade, but they did not cave. Beginning to fret, Mr. Yang called another meeting. This time, some of the teenagers brought their mothers along to block any further cursing outbursts. With a more respectful tone, Mr. Yang tried to convince the team to give in. After they did not relent, Mr. Yang was exhausted. He adjourned the meeting and declared, "Fine, it's done," and left the room. Many of the players began crying hysterically, believing the women's national team would cease to exist.

Soojin and Randi tried to soothe emotions, saying that Mr. Yang was testing their will. Two days later, KIHA called Soojin and told her that Murray was going to attend Worlds as the team's general manager, with Kim Do-yun as the interim head coach, to deflect questions from South Korean media covering the event. Doyun was expected to interview for college men's hockey coaching jobs after the tournament, so his authority behind the bench could be perceived as a send-off for his commitment to the program. Mr. Yang ended his phone call by telling Soojin, "If anyone talks to the media about this, you are all dead."

The team was willing to accept this concession and see what materialized after Worlds. But KIHA did not want to let them continue on without some sort of punishment. They canceled practices to skirt rules on payments, so the players did not hit their fifteen-day minimum. In response, Soojin laid out money to buy ice time at various rinks around Seoul. Players chipped in to defray the cost and ran their own sessions from midnight to 2:00 a.m., focused on capturing another world championship.

Revoking practices was not KIHA's only tactic for revenge, though. With Jincheon's facilities blocked off by KIHA, the imports had nowhere to stay. KIHA ignored their requests to help them with accommodations. Without stipend money coming in, Randi and Marissa began searching for affordable fleabag hostels in Seoul. When Soojin and the rest of the South Korean players found out, they pooled money once again to pay for the imports' hotel rooms.

"Reading the texts between the managers at KIHA and the import players made me think that they're acting nasty and cheap," Soojin fumed.

While the national team silently waged a battle against decades of hierarchal mistreatment, at the same time women throughout South Korea were finally speaking out against sexual assault in the workplace, where men have dominated powerful positions in business, politics and entertainment since the nation's inception. Long characterized as subservient and marred by the "comfort women" terror during Japanese colonialization, a new generation of South Korean women were fighting back against societal norms to change these perceptions. The protests against Park Geun-hye the year before showed the revolutionary spirit ready to burst within Park Ye-eun, Cho Mi-hwan and swaths of young Korean women not content with business as usual.

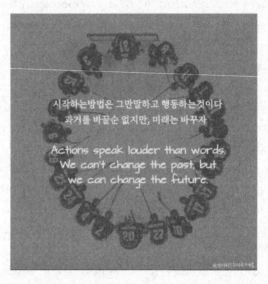

*The team used this message of solidarity across their social media pages during their stand-off with KIHA.*

"I think for all of my teammates, for the strike to happen there had to be this streak of rebelliousness inside of them that was not something that one generally associates with young Korean women," Randi said. "I think there was a lot of anger and frustration that had been bubbling beneath the surface for years. I think they needed just a little bit of leadership to push them over the edge and say your feelings are valid and sometimes it's okay to piss people off when you're right about something. I think it was a really empowering thing for them, for sure."

For KIHA, an organization engrained in *chaebol* culture and the dated mentality of Confucian order, the women's hockey team was the ultimate foil. Little did KIHA know that when they went fishing for imports, the women they brought over became a spark for change. Alongside them, the South Korean players, who all except for Soojin joined the national team before graduating high school, matured, becoming deeper thinkers unafraid to challenge authority. KIHA did not realize that and now had no idea how to confront this resistance. The South Korean women's national team did not forget their government's promises made at Jincheon. They sacrificed their moment for a greater cause and were not even thanked in return. It was time to collect what was owed.

Although Murray was devastated by the team's calls to replace her, she accepted traveling to Italy as general manager, saving KIHA from an embarrassing snafu. The week in Asiago was full of awkward moments; the players and Murray hardly talked. Forlornly, some members began to finally recognize the attachment she had with the team, which they were blind to before.

"I think for her to be able to say to KIHA, I'll step back so they can go to Worlds, shows how much she cares about us and how much she wants us to succeed—how much she wants Korea ice hockey to grow," said Grace Lee. "One of the things that sucks is obviously there were a lot of things that were not okay with the team throughout the year and throughout the past years, but just for me being there during the boycott and kind of observing the things that were said, some of them I understand in a way, but then some of the complaints that were risen against Sarah are just kind of what a US, Western hockey coach would do. It's not Sarah."

"When I think about how everything ended and how we went about everything we did, I do feel my own regrets, too," Danelle added. "I do really feel bad for her. It was nothing personal. It's easier to say that and obviously as a human being you take it personally. But 100 percent she gave her best. She wanted us to do well. She put a lot of work into it. She cared wholeheartedly about us first. I really appreciate what she's done for the program.

"For someone to come outside of Korea to coach this team, you've got the cultural thing, the language barrier, the age difference. You've got so many different things to work with, it would be so hard. There's so many pieces to that puzzle, you can't really ask for a perfect coach ever. I'll appreciate she did her best and you can't really ask more than that."

Yujung always planned to focus on her final year of high school once the Olympics were over and then decide if she wanted to return to the national team once she was accepted to college. With the departures of Caroline, Hyein and Yeonjeong days before the team left for Italy, Soojin called Yujung and tried to convince her to come back. Yujung remained unsure, until Soojin reminded her that this was her final opportunity to play together with Marissa, Danelle, Randi and Grace. Yujung dusted off her skates and rejoined the squad.

"The Unified team was a result of raising the image of the higher-ups," Park Chae-lin said. "We wondered what would it have been if it was just us, the team that had trained together for four years that competed in the Olympics?"

Without the pressure to fulfill political agendas, South Korea went 4–1 in the tournament and won silver. They actually tied for the best record, but just missed promotion because one of their victories came in overtime and thus was deemed of less quality by new IIHF rules that graded World Championship standings on a point system instead of goal differential (which South Korea had the best of). The element of their medals did not matter, though. Lee Eun-ji, fully recovered from her ankle injury, broke down crying in the locker room the first time she put her jersey back on. During those five games in a wooden-roofed, poorly lit rink in northern Italy, the South Koreans became the unit they always dreamed of. The team was theirs and when they achieved success, they knew it came solely from their toil.

In a game against Italy, the eventual gold medal winners, South Korea trailed 2–1 late in the third period. They were perilously close to falling out of medal contention until Randi scored with just under three minutes remaining. For the game's final sequence, Kim Hee-won threw her body after pucks, hungry to defeat the tournament favorites. With less than two minutes in regulation, Italy attempted to clear out of their zone when Soojin lunged in to intercept. Soojin dropped a no-look pass behind her to Choi Ji-yeon, who waited for Chaelin to cross the blue line, and then she swung the puck over to her at the point.

Patiently, Chaelin drifted along to the right side of the ice, outsmarting the overaggressive Italian defense, and fired a wrist shot top shelf for the go-ahead goal. One minute forty-seven seconds later, Rebecca Ruegsegger Baker emphatically pumped both of her fists on the bench and the entire team rushed off to mob Sojung in net. As the two sides skated to the blue lines to hear the winning team's national anthem played, the South Koreans scrunched up together like an accordion, their hands on each other's backs as they screamed the lyrics together as one body.

The autumn sky is void and vast, high and cloudless; the bright moon is our heart, undivided and true.[2]

"We were playing for us and we were playing only for us," Danelle said.

Marissa, Randi and Grace were scheduled to return to Seoul for two days before flying back to the US, while Danelle planned to stay a few more weeks with her brother. Finishing in second place at World Championships was arguably less prestigious than competing in the Olympics, and despite playing in front of empty arenas aside from a few family members that traveled to support them, the experience was exceedingly more memo-

rable for many of the imports. They did not want this feeling
to end there.

During the tournament, South Korean President Moon Jae-
in and North Korean leader Kim Jong-un finalized details and
agreed to meet at a historic peace summit scheduled for the end
of the month. No one on the team cared. All that mattered to
them was finding a way that they could stay together just a few
moments longer.

The night before the imports flew back to the States, the
South Koreans organized a going-away party. First, they met
at a barbecue restaurant in Seoul for dinner and then went to a
party room that the teens' moms rented out for the night just
for the players. There was a DJ, a dance floor, fluorescent lighting, homemade food and coolers full of booze. For some of the
younger players, it was the first time they tasted alcohol. With
each cautious sip, they joked that someone was drunk; when one
of the younger girls actually reached a point of inebriation, the
older players were there to help guide her through the maiden
voyage of dizziness and stomach churns with glasses of water or
a hand rubbing over her back. The players' moms who arranged
the party knew there'd come a point when their daughters grew
up and went out to drink, so they figured why not have the first
time be with the people they trusted them the most with, who
they knew would care for them like no other.

"How I see them interact with their daughters and their
friends and teammates, that's how I want to be with my kids if
I have some someday," Marissa said.

Throughout the night the team played beer pong and amid
thumping music, they stood in a circle, their arms clinging to
each other's shoulders as they screamed with delight just like
they had in Marissa's parents' den. Even Randi, who normally
ignored the pregame dance performances by the South Korean
girls, sang along and shuffled her feet off beat to K-pop tunes.

By the end of the festivities, the laughing and singing shifted toward a more somber mood, not unlike when the team said goodbye to the North Koreans. Their time together appeared to be over and so they sat weeping in each other's arms.

The next morning, Randi, Marissa, Grace and Rebecca Ruegsegger Baker left for Incheon International Airport. Greeting them there was Lee Min-ji; she attended the party but specifically wanted to say goodbye and thank-you to Ruegsegger Baker for her sacrifice to the team. Minji, now retired, had become a hockey coach like Ruegsegger Baker, with her goal to push for the creation of middle school and high school girls' teams, and for more female coaches in the sport.

*The imports all wanted to see the program flourish after their departures. From L to R: Randi Griffin, Danelle Im, Grace Lee, Marissa Brandt.*

Before Randi, Marissa and Grace boarded flights to their respective homes in Connecticut, Minnesota and Colorado, they discussed the empty feeling they all were experiencing. The imports worried about the future of the program, the still incipient careers of Heewon and the other teenagers. Randi and Marissa had already led full hockey lives even before the Olympics, but they felt like they were leaving the younger players out to dry. Grace could have entered the pool for candidacy on the US national team, but announced her intention to stay committed to South Korea. Marissa always wanted to play in the Asian Games, having missed the 2017 event because her citizenship was not completed in time. Together, Randi and Marissa began concocting ways to keep their Korean jerseys on, too, suggesting that if they played in recreational leagues at home and then returned to South Korea for international tournaments, that would allow them to hold down the fort until younger generations could develop. They felt like if they owed South Korea anything, it was for the national team to not be abandoned without being left with a solid foundation.

When the time came to head to their separate gates, Marissa's last words before leaving South Korea were to Randi, a message that their work was not yet done. "See you at Worlds next year," she said.

## CHAPTER TWENTY-SEVEN
# Nothing Else Matters

On April 27, 2018, shortly after 9:30 a.m., the golden doors of North Korea's Panmungak Hall swung open and out marched five young men with matching crew cuts, dark suits and blue ties. They aligned in a V-formation like birds peacefully migrating south and created a makeshift wall of protection around a man once considered by many to be the least peaceful person in the world.

Kim Jong-un was followed by more men in suits—twenty-three altogether—two military officials and his sister, Kim Yo-jong, sharply dressed in a gray jacket and matching skirt that hung just above her knees. At only thirty years old, Kim Yo-jong emitted a powerful radiance from her haunting eyes and pale facial features that made her a worldwide phenomenon since emerging from her brother's shadow and into the public eye during the Olympics as North Korea's designated messenger for peace.

The group quickly made their way down the thirty-four steps in front of Panmungak, located in the border village of Panmunjom, and arrived at a road that marked the end of North Korean territory and the beginning of South Korea. The party then suddenly veered off, leaving only Kim Jong-un remaining. Swinging his arms with a wide gait, Kim Jong-un smiled broadly and extended his right hand as he approached South Korean president Moon Jae-in, who had been awaiting his arrival at the military demarcation line that has separated the two countries since the end of Korean War combat in 1953. The leaders of the two Koreas spoke with their hands clasped for twenty-two seconds, before President Moon formally invited Kim Jong-un to become the first North Korean head of state to step foot onto South Korean soil since the war. After thousands of photos were snapped off in rapid succession, Kim Jong-un took President Moon's hand like a parent guiding a child, and led him a few feet forward into North Korea. This drew tension-releasing laughter from the assembled media on hand watching this surreal moment of history unfold.

At the beginning of the Korean War, President Moon's parents fled North Korea, and he was born in a refugee relocation center. His mother and father always dreamed of returning home. The iron curtain of communism never allowed them to. But here President Moon was, two months after the Olympics, peeking into his family's native land, chumming it up with a man who was supposed to be the gravest threat to his nation's well-being.

Kim Jong-un relayed a few more words to President Moon and sandwiched his right hand between both of Moon's hands, creating more applause. Moments later they walked down a red-carpeted parade route past spectators dressed in ceremonial *hanbok* outfits, and headed to the designated Peace House, ushering in new hope for Korean unification and world peace that was inconceivable just months earlier.

Four weeks after this milestone, KIHA formally responded to the women's hockey team's actions. Sarah Murray's contract was not renewed, Yang Seung-jun was dismissed from his position and the twenty-one players that signed the letter were "suspended" for six months. Outside of Mr. Yang's firing, the outcome was expected by much of the group. Never having been told what KIHA's plans were after the Olympics and World Championships anyway, players already had begun training on their own time.

In meetings with KIHA representatives later that summer, longtime employees acknowledged they should have identified the issues within the team sooner. But Chung Mong-won was upset that the status quo had been disrupted, and the consensus among KIHA was that the players made "a really stupid decision." KIHA figures noted how all of the country's hockey community and even athletes in other sports knew about the boycott threat, and how it seemed to leave South Korean sports open to a new reality, one where players could actually influence administrative decisions. The men inside KIHA describing this development viewed this as an unhealthy turn of events.

Shortly after word of the hockey team's actions reached other athletes, South Korea's women's national curling team gained the courage to fight back against their governing body. The curling team—which became known worldwide as "Team Kim" (because all five members shared the same surname) and the "Garlic Girls" (because they hailed from Uiseong County, known for its garlic production)—won silver at the 2018 Olympics and befriended many members of the women's hockey team.

The curlers alleged that they had long suffered unfair treatment by authority figures in the South Korean curling hierarchy, which included verbal abuse by staff, gag orders and the withholding of prize money. They also requested a new coach. Female Olympic athletes in other sports also followed in becoming brave enough to begin publicly speaking out about long-standing abuse and wrongful treatment by their respective governing bodies.

Even before the boycott letter, the women's national hockey

team provided inspiration for South Koreans to voice their frustrations with the norm. When President Moon's approval ratings reached all-time lows in January, the figures were a direct result of the government's neglect of its women's hockey players, with the largest drops coming from Koreans under forty. One such incensed party was Mia SeungEun Lee. Her Ivy League education at Cornell provided a path to professional success, but it is hockey that shaped her as a woman and motivated her to not be defined by the traditional gender roles her country kept for far too long. Even after retiring, when she returned to Seoul during summer breaks from college, she stayed involved in the sport as a coach and one of the country's first female referees.

"Being the only girl or one of a handful at every practice I went to actually planted confidence in me over time, because I liked showing people that yes, I am a girl, and yes I play ice hockey," Mia said. "I only realized around last year that growing up playing hockey in this community played a huge part in shaping my values, empowering me as a feminist, and learning the importance of visibility and representation."

"The people on our team, they represent something unconventional," Danelle Im added. "They play hockey, first of all, but they also represent a movement and I think young girls look up to that."

Danelle flew back to Toronto without the sorrow that normally accompanied her when she left behind Lee Min-ji and all of her colleagues who made South Korea feel like home. Despite not knowing when she would see her teammates again, Danelle knew they were in a better place, emerging from the storms of the last few months capable of withstanding any obstacle thrown their way.

Danelle herself had grown considerably. At the Olympics, boosted by Choi Yu-jung's note on the eve of the Games, Danelle dressed for every contest and was one of the team's most consistent and dependable players. Off the ice, watching the way in which Minji and others cracked open her shell of timidity, her family no longer fretted about her entering adulthood back in Canada. Danelle also realized that she did not have to be bound by nursing school. Her Olympic experience showed her that life is full of uncertainty and interruptions and she now believed that grace awaited those who welcomed challenges and worked hard to overcome them.

COURTESY OF MARISSA BRANDT

*In March 2018, the Unified team was honored at the Coca-Cola Sports Awards in Seoul. From L to R: Lee Kyou-sun, Danelle Im, Marissa Brandt, Cho Mi-hwan, Park Ye-eun, Park Jong-ah.*

Marissa Brandt arrived back in Minnesota with the same humble, kindhearted soul intact that she always carried, but her family noticed changes in her demeanor aside from the new craving for dishes of kimchi and *tteokbokki*. Robin and Greg Brandt saw Marissa more driven and focused, exuding the qualities of a leader completely comfortable in her own skin and more confident than ever.

"It's unbelievable because she was always so shy," Robin marveled. "To see Marissa blossom like that, I was really happy the girls could give her that experience."

When she moved to South Korea in 2017, Marissa did not embark on a search to find her birth parents. Her priority was her teammates, who became like her adopted sisters. "I told them I'm here for you guys," Marissa said. "I want to play hockey and be the best for you."

Still, American media liked the potential drama in her story, and South Korean audiences were hoping that Marissa was willing to make a spectacle out of a search with a big television reveal like other popular adopted celebrities had done before. Marissa thought that going down that route was unfair—to herself, her parents, her birth parents and especially her teammates.

For the two weeks in Gangneung, camera crews from around the world trailed not only Marissa, but Robin, Greg and her husband, Brett. While Marissa understood the peg that drove interest in her story, she could not help but find rehashing her background overbearing, particularly when hypothetical questions were posed like asking what she would say to her birth mother if she was watching her right now.

"The first time someone asked me that, I was really taken aback and got really emotional," said Marissa, who privately vented to Ko Hye-in when journalists continually asked her questions about being adopted rather than about her teammates. "These people I don't really know are asking a real heavy question that taps a core I never really wanted to tap."

In the end, people did not need to witness a grand reunion to become magnetized by Marissa's story. By being brave enough to represent Korea, she received hundreds of emails and online messages from adoptees, Asian Americans and individuals with no connection whatsoever to South Korea, inspired by her journey. In high school when she was a budding star at Hill-Murray School, Marissa often passed on interviews, shuffling the responsibility to Hannah to speak for her. One decade later, she had grown accustomed to the spotlight and utilizing the platform it created. She had become not only a face for women's hockey

in South Korea, but for tens of thousands of adopted and neglected children who have yearned for a hero, someone whose
story was like theirs.

She also no longer hesitates in calling herself Korean.

"I think if I heard that word growing up, I would immediately get uncomfortable and shy away and divert from that whole
topic," said Marissa of Korea. "I think now when I hear that
word, obviously I think of my experiences there. I think of my
friends. I think of just how I'm proud to be Korean now and
how I want to go back and eat the food. I would never say that
before. Just the three years that I spent there really changed my
life and how I look at myself and how I'm finally comfortable
with who I am and what I look like.

"I want people, younger kids to see, 'She's Asian American
and she's representing her birth country, she's comfortable doing
that,'" Marissa proudly proclaimed. "I want to be that sort of
influence, because I wish I had someone like that when I was
young. I have a story to tell and I'll tell it, and if some people
can relate in any way to it, whether it's adoption or hockey or
anything like that, I want people to find that."

The day after the Olympics ended, Marissa was named an
ambassador for South Korea's Ministry of Health and Welfare,
to further raise adoption awareness in the country. She also decided the time was right to begin a search for her biological
mother. The choice to do so made her relationship to her parents only stronger.

The 2018 Olympics ushered in a groundbreaking new era of
Asian American athletes. Mirai Nagasu helped the United States
win bronze in the team figure skating competition. Teenagers Nathan Chen, Karen Chen and Vincent Zhou gave performances that positioned them as the future of American figure
skating. Maia and Alex Shibutani and Madison Chock made
ice dancing trendy, while Chloe Kim reached superstar levels
of celebrity with a dominating gold medal performance on the

snowboard half-pipe. The imports on the Unified team only fur-
thered that momentum in ways that radiated on and off the ice.

*Han Do-hee (front) and her teammates.*

COURTESY OF LEE JI-YOON

    "The team embodied something that is very rare to see in the
Olympics these days, which is amateurism," Randi Griffin said.
"That concept has been completely lost. Even on Team USA
or Team Canada where maybe the athletes aren't getting paid
that much money, there's just this culture of perfectionism and
the athletes don't matter as individuals. If you get cut, you just
disappear and you're never invited back. It's not like on Team
Korea where if someone got hurt or cut we need to make a job
for them. This is their family. It's kind of completely antitheti-
cal to modern elite sports. This is a group of girls that from the
start played hockey actually because they loved it, when there
was no promise for any kind of glory or any kind of money or
any kind of attention. They're incredibly resilient. The fact that
they were able to go to the Olympics and actually keep it together, it's a pretty cool story."

    During the summer of 2018, the Unified team's valor led the
way for a flurry of inter-Korean exchanges. In July, the two Koreas held basketball friendlies in Pyongyang. Later, they agreed
to field inter-Korean teams in basketball, rowing and canoeing
at the 2018 Asian Summer Games in Indonesia. Sports Minister

Do Jong-hwan also proposed joint teams for the 2020 Summer Olympics in Tokyo, and officials from both countries discussed cohosting the 2021 Asian Winter Games and placing a bid to jointly hold the 2032 Summer Olympics.

The most significant development of this new period of inter-Korean relations was the hundreds of South Koreans that were allowed to reconnect with family members living in the North, some whom they hadn't seen since the Korean War. In late August, at the Diamond Mountain resort in southeast North Korea, scores of elderly Koreans departed off charter buses, some dressed in *hanbok*, carrying bags of watches, medicine and other gifts, as well as photographs of deceased loved ones. Men in their sixties met fathers for the first time. Brothers kneeled and sobbed upon gripping the arms of siblings they had not seen in decades.[1] Some of the attendees had lost their hearing as a result of old age and only communicated by the tears streaming down their faces as they locked eyes with long-lost daughters. More than fifty-six thousand South Koreans applied to a lottery to be selected for the event. Each year, an estimated three thousand South Koreans die unable to reunite with beloved family and friends from the North.[2]

KIHA thought that by suspending the women's hockey team, the players might learn a lesson from their "stupid" actions. It was their version of sending an adolescent to sit in the corner to think about what they've done wrong. Park Jong-ah wondered if KIHA was ever going to evolve out of this inveterate mentality of treating the women's national team like little girls. In reality, though, the players did not care about the suspension. As they proved in Italy, they were a strong enough unit to challenge for one of the qualification spots in the 2022 Olympics. Perhaps also realizing this, KIHA sent Eom Su-yeon, Kim Hee-won and Lee Eun-ji to OHA. KIHA also created their first Under-18 women's squad to start a feeder program into the national team and accommodate the sudden booming interest in hockey among young girls. In January 2019, the U-18 team went undefeated in their first tournament, winning gold at World Championships with Lee Kyou-sun on the coaching staff.

In the weeks after the 2018 Worlds, some players regretted certain aspects of how they approached the strike. But all agreed if they could have gone back, they would not have changed the ultimate decision.

"I think it was a good thing to do in order to change the Korea women's hockey system," said Jongah, who accepted several international awards on behalf of the team and along with Park Ye-eun was celebrated in a ceremony given by the city of Gangneung following the Olympics. "In the process, many people were hurt. But it was necessary."

After World Championships, Sarah Murray returned home to a quiet life and enrolled in graduate school. She was soon hired by a high school in Owatonna, Minnesota, to coach their girls' hockey program and impart the lessons learned from four years abroad to a new class of players.

In South Korea, Han Do-hee and Han Soo-jin joined Minji in coaching youth teams. Back in September 2017, before a practice at the University of Minnesota, Dohee skated onto the ice before everyone else and stared up at a mural of all of the program's past Olympians. Dohee never thought she could be revered in such a manner. "It didn't seem realistic," Dohee said. "It seemed like someone else's story." Now, Dohee was idolized by groups of girls and boys who hung on her every word, admiring her in the same way she looked at the wall of Minnesota's Olympic heroes.

In the sweltering summer months, just like always, the players spent their time at cafés and the beach and movie theaters together. Whenever Park Chae-lin stopped by a rink, swarms of young girls came rushing toward her. Always wishing she could communicate more with the imports, Cho Mi-hwan began attending an English language school in New Zealand, paying for her tuition by using the money she saved from collecting over ten years of stipends from being on the national team.

In her book on transnational sport, Rachael Miyung Joo predicted, "The Korean female athlete exists as a symbol of female empowerment and of the new Korean woman in the twenty-first century. She demonstrates that global recognition can be won without disavowing femininity. She is presented as a middle-class subject who represents the successful development of contemporary South Korea."

Nowhere was that exemplified more than in Shin So-jung.

After World Championships, Sojung retired, saying that it was time to take care of her mother. Shortly after returning from Italy, she initiated the business plans she had been slowly crafting for years and bought a food truck selling *bibimbap*. Within weeks, it became a popular street vendor attraction in Seoul, with hordes of customers recognizing her from her Olympic heroics, even though she often wore a surgical mask behind the grill. Sojung planned to open a full-fledged restaurant by the winter, with goals on expansion into North America in the near future. She also began taking acting lessons, and South Korean media wrote about the imminent arrival of the country's next female action star.

In the US, Marissa and Hannah Brandt embarked on a tour throughout the country, meeting orphaned and adopted children from all backgrounds. Before the end of the year, Marissa further spread her story to international audiences, invited to speak everywhere from South Korea to Estonia. Caroline Park finished her surgery clerkship and was on her way to becoming a doctor; in August, she and Danelle were guests of honor at a Korean festival in Toronto.

Randi earned her PhD and still determined to guide South Korea women's hockey toward a steady landing, signed to play professionally for the Connecticut Whale of the NWHL. Even while she discussed modules on data cleansing and biological anthropology in front of rooms full of scholars, her teammates never left her thoughts, particularly in how they continually influenced her evolution as a Korean American woman.

"There's a big part of me that feels way less Korean than I did before," said Randi, adding that she wished someone like Soojin scored the goal against Japan, because a South Korean player deserved it more. "In the past, because I didn't really have a lot of Korean people in my life that weren't family, being Korean was just a throwaway thing I would say. People always asked me where I'm from, why do you look like this? I'd say I'm Korean. But I can't actually say that with a straight face anymore, because I'm like, I'm not. If a Korean person heard me say I was Korean, they'd laugh, because when I'm in Korea I'm white.

"I guess I'm a little bit more conscious of that now and I guess it's more in the forefront of my mind that I really am something in the middle and I can't claim to be this or that to the other group. I kind of have to accept being something in the middle. I do feel a little bit more protective if I hear someone make a joke or a comment. I think about my friends in Korea. It means something more."

When asked to elucidate the Korean bona fides of Randi and the imports, none of the South Korean players considered them to be any less worthy to claim the status than they were. To Susie Jo, the player who corresponded most with the imports, it was never the Olympics that she saw driving them in practices or games; it was pride in being Korean.

"My wish is they feel this pride as much as I do," Susie said.

Grace Lee went back to Colorado with love for Korea oozing from her pores. When her family went out to eat, using the crayons restaurants store to keep children busy, Grace practiced writing *hangul* on the tablecloth and asked her mother if she was pronouncing the words correctly. She repeatedly relayed that South Korea was her favorite place in the world.

"For me, being Asian was always a joke," Grace reflected. "Not in a bad way. The first real girls' team I was on, we had maybe seven other people that were Asian, too. We thought that was funny, half the team was Asian. We'd laugh at stuff like that. Before going to Korea, I never thought of myself as full Korean. I always thought of myself as American."

Before starting her senior year, Grace visited Seoul, where her days were packed hanging out with Hyein, Jung Si-yun and other members from the team. Lee Yeon-jeong and Susie traveled to Toronto to visit Danelle, and Randi came up from New Haven to reunite with the trio. In August, YeEun accepted an offer to play hockey at Ryerson University in Toronto, where Danelle was beginning graduate classes in the fall. Danelle's father picked YeEun up from the airport and she spent a week with Danelle at her house. On campus, they lived in neighboring buildings and were never far apart. A few months later, Minji moved to Toronto to study English. For Halloween, she, Danelle and YeEun bought matching overalls and yellow shirts and dressed up as the Minion cartoon characters.

"We all gathered with this team due to our love of hockey," YeEun said. "As a result of that we hang out together, we basically live together and we love doing that as a team. Nothing else really matters to us."

After the Olympics, not only did Kim Jong-un meet with President Moon, but he convened in Singapore with US President Donald Trump in the first summit between leaders of those two countries. Relations on the peninsula had never been stronger, although an air of fragility will always remain until there is formal reunification—if that ever happens.

For the time being, Choi Ji-yeon and Dohee had the photo albums on their phones to tide them over, snapshots with the North Koreans entering the Olympic Stadium or on the beaches of Gangneung, which they perused on a daily basis. When Heewon watched the news, seeing such unfathomable developments as

Kim and Trump shaking hands, the only thought she had was the hope that she might see her friends from North Korea again. The members of the Unified team couldn't help but pay attention to what had blossomed from their hockey politics, but did not clamor for credit.

"It was truly an event worth remembering in history and I feel proud to know that I am part of that page in history," Mihwan said. "I hope that forming the Unified team helps progress the inter-Korean relations and that there are in fact advancements as a result of it.

"Many people will remember us as the first ever unified team to participate in the Olympics. But I hope that people will also remember us as a team that worked incredibly hard in the shadows, despite many people's indifference to us and the poor training environments. And that they were small, but strong, and while they had their limitations, they never gave up. Now that I think of it, we did something incredible."

*South Korea's women's national hockey team.*

In the end, South Korea's women's national hockey team was not a puppet, but a family of Olympic-level athletes, diplomats, pioneers, fighters and inspirations. They wore the slogan "Make Korea Proud" on the back of their clothes, for the *ajummas* selling fish-shaped *bungeoppang* pastries in the street markets of Seoul and the female farmers in the Korean countryside, whose lives were predetermined from the moment they were born. Make Korea Proud. They did.

"We bring a new meaning to the word *family*," Marissa said. "We're not a flashy thing in any way. We accepted what was given to us and we've always stuck together. But when push came to shove, we made things happen.

"Family, that's what we are and that's what we've been this whole time."

★ ★ ★ ★ ★

# ACKNOWLEDGMENTS

In early 2017, I helped write a story about South Korea's effort to build its first Olympic hockey teams for the *New York Times*. However, some unexpected wire-crossing led to the piece lacking merited detail on the women's team.

The morning after publication, I received an email from Sarah Murray. Without the use of strong language, she ardently explained her disagreement with the portrayal of her roster. Murray repeatedly emphasized how hard her players had been training and their desire to not only represent South Korea, but further spur girls' and women's hockey in the country.

With any assignment there will be hundreds of words left on the cutting room floor and I agreed that there was more to be told about this inimitable collection of hockey players. When I eventually decided to follow the Korean women's hockey team's yearlong journey to the Olympics, Murray provided unencumbered access, for which I am extremely grateful. Observing her passion was one of the inspirations in writing this book and I am appreciative of her efforts.

Kevin Coyne was the first person I told about my idea for covering what seemed like the most obscure of subjects, and with the same candor and guidance he provided during my graduate school studies, he encouraged me to pursue this story. Euny Hong, Ed Breslin and Jeré Longman also injected me with confidence and helped set a template as I stepped into uncharted territory.

This book would not have been possible without my agent Farley Chase, who never wavered in his belief in the project, and Peter Joseph, Natalie Hallak, Jennifer Stimson, Justine Sha and the team at Hanover Square, whose faith, guidance and support in backing a true underdog story I am blessed to have received.

I am equally thankful to Kathy Yun, my fixer in Seoul, who was an invaluable resource and tireless worker.

A deserved stick tap goes to colleagues Naila-Jean Meyers, Andrew Keh and Jason Stallman for their words of support along the way. There are also individuals who have helped shaped me into the writer I am, so I must thank Do Myung Kang, Jay Schreiber, the late Lillian Ross, Samuel G. Freedman, Larry Cohler-Esses and the late Kevin Houtz for seasoning my reporting chops.

Although we've never met, I'd like to recognize Choe Sang-hun, Robert Carlin and the late Don Oberdorfer for their extensive reporting on Korea throughout their careers. Their work was extremely helpful in teaching me about the innumerable layers of Korean history and culture.

There were many folks I met along this journey whose input made this experience so rich: the Rembeck family, Michelle Yunjung You, Molly McCormick, the Korea Ice Hockey Association, Scott Howe, the Korean Student Association at St. Cloud State University, Carrie Petersen, Lee So-jeong, Kim Sung-soo, Amanda Eunha Lovell, Rob Refsnyder, Jackie Meehyun Lee Kling, Ann Babe, Rachael Miyung Joo, Sunny Pyo, the Japanese women's national team, the Gangwon Provincial Office, and my hosts in Gangneung and Seoul—Woo Sang and family, Seon Ye-eum and family, and Kim Tae-hyun.

I'd also like to acknowledge Will Holloway and Simon Crosse for art and the work of staff, coaches and former players at the following schools who helped with credentials, photos and interviews: Shattuck-St. Mary's, Hill-Murray, St. Francis Xavier, Princeton, Penn State, Harvard, Gustavus Adolphus, Wilfrid Laurier, Minnesota-Duluth, Minnesota, Wisconsin-River Falls, St. Scholastica, St. Cloud State, Minnesota State-Mankato and Quinnipiac. The same goes for the Berthiaumes, Sasha Sherry, Kim Mongrain and the Korean players' teammates at the Ontario Hockey Academy, Dani Rylan, Janine Weber and the Metropolitan/New York Riveters of the NWHL, Jessica Koizumi, Hilary Knight, Meghan Duggan, Jocelyne Lamoureux-Davidson, Monique Lamoureux-Morando, Janine Alder, Shannon Miller, Melody Davidson, Digit Murphy and Brant Feldman.

I will be forever grateful to the members of South Korea's women's national hockey team for welcoming me into their lives and for what they provided in mine. My eternal thanks to Lee Kyou-sun, Genny Knowles, Ko Hye-in, Eom Su-yeon, Choi Yu-jung, Kim Se-lin, Park Jong-ah, Choi Ji-yeon, Park Ye-eun, Kim Hee-won, Lee Eun-ji, Park Chae-lin, Han Soo-jin, Han Do-hee, Lee Yeon-jeong, Jung Si-yun and Cho Mi-hwan. An extra stick tap is in order for Susie Jo and Lee Min-ji, who went out of their way to open the doors to the team. A special thanks is due to Shin So-jung, who was always gracious in finding time to speak with me, as was Rebecca Ruegsegger Baker, whose selflessness is unsurpassed. In addition, I am thankful for the compassion and help of Ruth Murray, Kim Do-yun, Mia SeungEun Lee and the team's managerial and training staff.

Most of all, I will always be indebted to the import players, who were my reporting crutch and helped make me feel like less of a *babo*. Caroline Park was the first member I met and introduced me to the wonderful world of Korean women's hockey. Grace, Eliza and Albert Lee always shared laughter and their generosity was a guiding force during my first days in South

Korea. Danelle Im, her brother Justin, and her parents Hye-jin and Charles extended the utmost kindness and hospitality. Marissa Brandt and her parents Robin and Greg, husband Brett, and sister Hannah welcomed me into their home and always displayed unmatched warmth and cordiality. Marissa's strength serves as an inspiration in my life and those of countless other adoptees. Randi Griffin's trust, openness and sincerity acted as my compass and without that, the telling of this story would have been impossible.

Finally, to my family, whose love and support have always been my backbone and motivation.

# NOTES

## Chapter One

1. Kang Hyun-kyung, "How Hockey Became South Koreans' Dear Sport," *The Korea Times*, January 19, 2018, https://www.koreatimes.co.kr/www/sports/2018/01/702_242756.html.

## Chapter Two

1. Eleana J. Kim, *Adopted Territory: Transnational Korean Adoptees and the Politics of Belonging* (Durham and London: Duke University Press, 2010), 21.

2. Andrew Keh, "I Was Never Jackie Chan, and I'm Not Jeremy Lin," *New York Times*, October 25, 2016, https://www.nytimes.com/2016/10/26/sports/basketball/jeremy-lin-nba-brooklyn-nets.html.

3. "Self-Reported Concussion among NCAA Student-Athletes, Executive Summary, February 2014," National Collegiate Athletic Association, February 12, 2014, https://www.ncaa.org/sites/default/files/Concussion%20%20GOALS%20Exec%20Summary_Feb_12_2014_FINAL-post_0.pdf.

## Chapter Three

1. Don Oberdorfer and Robert Carlin, *The Two Koreas: A Contemporary History Revised, Updated Edition,* (New York: Basic Books, 2013), 50, iBooks.

2. Oberdorfer and Carlin, *The Two Koreas*, 54.

3. Daniel Tudor, *Korea: The Impossible Country,* (Tokyo, Rutland, Singapore: Tuttle Publishing, 2012), 58–59, iBooks.

4. Oberdorfer and Carlin, *The Two Koreas*, 57–58.

5. Oberdorfer and Carlin, *The Two Koreas*, 59–60.

6. Oberdorfer and Carlin, *The Two Koreas*, 66–67.

7. Tudor, *Korea: The Impossible Country*, 64.

8. Oberdorfer and Carlin, *The Two Koreas*, 60–61.

9. Ministry of Foreign Affairs, November 29, 2017, http://www.mofa.go.kr/www/brd/m_3454/list.do.

10. "Koreans in the U.S. Fact Sheet," Pew Research Center, September 8, 2017, http://www.pewsocialtrends.org/fact-sheet/asian-americans-koreans-in-the-u-s/.

11. Jie Zong and Jeanne Batalova, "Korean Immigrants in the United States," Migration Policy Institute, February 8, 2017, https://www.migrationpolicy.org/article/korean-immigrants-united-states.

12. Jeff Z. Klein, "Olympics? First, Small Goals," *New York Times*, August 14, 2014, https://www.nytimes.com/2014/08/15/sports/hockey/jim-paek-is-building-south-korean-hockey-program.html.

13. "Census Profile, 2016 Census," Statistics Canada, accessed November 9, 2018, https://www12.statcan.gc.ca/census-recensement/2016/dp-pd/prof/details/page.cfm?Lang=E&Geo1=CMACA&Code1=535&Geo2=PR&Code2=35&Data=Count&SearchText=Caledon%20East&SearchType=Begins&SearchPR=01&B1=All.

## Chapter Four

1. Choe Sang-hun, "In Changing South Korea, Who Counts as 'Korean'?" *New York Times*, November 29, 2012, https://www.nytimes.com/2012/11/30/world/asia/demographic-shifts-redefine-society-in-south-korea.html.

## Chapter Six

1. Dae Hee Kwak, Yong Jae Ko, Inkyu Kang, Mark Rosentraub, *Sport in Korea: History, Development, Management*, (London and New York: Routledge, 2017), 97, iBooks.

2. Euny Hong, *The Birth of Korean Cool: How One Nation is Conquering the World Through Pop Culture*, (New York: Picador, 2014), 59.

3. Ha Nam-gil and J.A. Mangan, "Ideology, Politics, Power: Korean Sport-Transformation, 1945–1992," *The International Journal of the History of Sport* 19, no. 2 (2002): 231.

4. Kwak, Ko, Kang, Rosentraub, *Sport in Korea*, 83.

5. Carlos Tejada, "Money, Power, Family: Inside South Korea's Chaebol," *New York Times*, February 17, 2017, https://www.nytimes.com/2017/02/17/business/south-korea-chaebol-samsung.html.

6. Hong, *The Birth of Korean Cool*, 240.

7. Eunah Hong. "Elite Sport and Nation-Building in South Korea: South Korea as the Dark Horse in Global Elite Sport," *The International Journal of the History of Sport* 28, no. 7, (2011): 977–989.

8. Tracy Dahl, "Award of 1988 Olympics Boosts S. Korea's Effort For Political Security," *Washington Post*, October 4, 1981, https://www.washingtonpost.com/archive/politics/1981/10/04/award-of-1988-olympics-boosts-s-koreas-effort-for-political-security/2db0f29f-29cd-4581-8771-2f08c225181f/?utm_term=.9e81024c0334.

9. Kwak, Ko, Kang, Rosentraub, *Sport in Korea*, 122.

10. Tudor, *Korea: The Impossible Country*, 65.

11. Hong, *The Birth of Korean Cool*, 53–54.

12. Juliet Macur, "Kim Yu-na Wins Gold in Figure Skating," *New York Times*, February 26, 2010, https://www.nytimes.com/2010/02/26/sports/olympics/26skate.html.

13. Raymond Zhong and Park Jeong-Eun, "For Korea Inc., Money and Politics Make an Awkward Olympics," *New York Times*, February 7, 2018, https://www.nytimes.com/2018/02/07/business/olympics-samsung-south-korea.html.

14. Oberdorfer and Carlin, *The Two Koreas*, 180–181, hardcover.

15. John Branch, "In Speedskating, South Korea Sees a Fast Track to Olympic Glory," *New York Times*, February 23, 2018, https://www.nytimes.com/2018/02/23/sports/south-korea-speedskating.html.

16. Eun-Young Jeong, "South Korea Has a Strong Economy, Fast Internet—and a Big Gender Gap," *Wall Street Journal*, February 9, 2018, https://www.wsj.com/articles/south-korean-women-declare-us-too-1518172206.

17. Choe Sang-hun, "Gender Colors Outrage Over Scandal Involving South Korea's President," *New York Times*, November 21, 2016, https://www.nytimes.com/2016/11/22/world/asia/south-korea-park-geun-hye-women.html.

18. Choe Sang-hun, "Ex-Dictator's Daughter Elected President as South Korea Rejects Sharp Change," *New York Times*, December 19, 2012, https://www.nytimes.com/2012/12/20/world/asia/south-koreans-vote-in-closely-fought-presidential-race.html.

19. Oberdorfer and Carlin, *The Two Koreas*, 128.

20. Choe Sang-hun, "South Koreans 'Ashamed' Over Leader's Secretive Adviser," *New York Times*, November 5, 2016, https://www.nytimes.com/2016/11/06/world/asia/south-koreans-ashamed-over-les-secretive-adviser.html.

21. Choe Sang-hun, "South Korean President's Leadership Style Is Seen as Factor in Scandal," *New York Times*, November 11, 2016, https://www.nytimes.com/2016/11/12/world/asia/south-korea-park-geun-hye.html.

22. Choe Sang-hun, "South Koreans Rally in Largest Protest in Decades to Demand President's Ouster," *New York Times*, November 12, 2016, https://www.nytimes.com/2016/11/13/world/asia/korea-park-geun-hye-protests.html.

23. Choe Sang-hun, "South Korea Removes President Park Geun-hye," *New York Times*, March 9, 2017, https://www.nytimes.com/2017/03/09/world/asia/park-geun-hye-impeached-south-korea.html.

24. James Mirtle, "How South Korea Added Nine Hockey Ringers for the 2018 Olympics," *Globe and Mail*, May 16, 2016, https://www.theglobeandmail.com/sports/hockey/how-south-korea-added-nine-hockey-ringers-for-the-2018-olympics/article30055116/.

## Chapter Seven

1. Hong, *The Birth of Korean Cool*, 251.

## Chapter Nine

1. Arirang K-Pop, "Showbiz Korea_Run Off (국가대표 2)_Interview," July 28, 2016, video, 5:15, https://www.youtube.com/watch?v=AWb5q5gBkFE.

2. Wolf Blitzer, "North Korean Leader Loves Hennessey, Bond Movies," *CNN*, January 8, 2003, http://www.cnn.com/2003/US/01/08/wbr.kim.jong.il.

3. Nathan Vanderklippe, "How a North Korean Defector Became the Mother of Women's Hockey in the South," *Globe and Mail*, February 12, 2018, https://www.theglobeandmail.com/sports/olympics/how-a-north-korean-defector-became-the-mother-of-womens-hockey-in-thesouth/article37949363.

4. Yoo Jee-ho, "S. Koreans Come Out in Droves to Cheer on N. Korean Hockey Players," *Yonhap*, April 2, 2017, http://english.yonhapnews.co.kr/news/2017/04/02/0200000000AEN20170402002800315.html.

5. Yoo, "S. Koreans Come Out in Droves to Cheer on N. Korean Hockey Players."

6.  Yoo Jee-ho, "S. Korean Hockey Players Enjoy 'Cool' Experience after Beating N. Korea," *Yonhap*, April 7, 2017, http://english.yonhapnews.co.kr/ northkorea/2017/04/07/0401000000AEN20170407000600315.html.

7.  Yonhap Staff, "Truth Committee: More Than 9,000 Politically Active Artists Blacklisted Under Ex-President Park," *Yonhap*, April 10, 2018, https://en.yna.co.kr/view/AEN20180410008100315.

8.  Choe Sang-hun, "South Korea Leader Hopes for Unified Olympic Team With the North," *New York Times*, June 24, 2017, https://www. nytimes.com/2017/06/24/world/asia/korea-joint-winter-olympics. html.

9.  Oberdorfer and Carlin, *The Two Koreas*, 62–63.

10. Alex Park, "Stumbling Blocks Ahead for Koreas to Assemble Joint Women's Hockey Team at PyeongChang 2018," *Korea Herald*, June 30, 2017, http://www.koreaherald.com/view.php?ud=20170630000554.

11. Oberdorfer and Carlin, *The Two Koreas*, 89–90.

12. Reuters staff, "Most South Koreans Doubt the North Will Start a War: Poll," Reuters, September 8, 2017, https://www.reuters.com/article/ us-northkorea-missiles-southkorea-poll/most-south-koreans-doubt- the-north-will-start-a-war-poll-idUSKCN1BJ0HF.

13. JoongAng Ilbo, Accessed on June 3, 2017, http://news.joins.com/ pyeongchang2018/Daily/Article/21724217.

14. JoongAng Ilbo, Accessed on June 3, 2017, http://news.joins.com/ pyeongchang2018/Daily/Article/21724217.

15. Associated Press report, "Pyeongchang Olympics Are Icy Path to Warmer Korean relations," *USA Today*, July 3, 2017, https://www. usatoday.com/story/sports/olympics/2017/07/03/unlikely-for-winter- olympics-to-be-icebreaker-between-koreas/103404600.

16. Yoo Jee-ho, "S. Korean Hockey Chief, Coach Tiptoe around Joint Korean Team Controversy," *Yonhap*, July 19, 2017, http://english.yonhapnews. co.kr/news/2017/07/19/0200000000AEN20170719007400315.html.

## Chapter Twelve

1. "Far From Home," Olympic Channel video, 7:49, 2018, https://www.olympicchannel.com/en/playback/far-from-home/core-branded-far-from-home/fearless-goaltender-chooses-ice-hockey-despite-familys-worries/.

## Chapter Fourteen

1. Choe Sang-hun, "Kim Jong-un Offers North Korea's Hand to South, While Chiding U.S.," *New York Times*, December 31, 2017, https://www.nytimes.com/2017/12/31/world/asia/north-korea-kim-jong-un-olympics.html.

2. Hong, *The Birth of Korean Cool*, 143.

3. Kang, "How Hockey Became South Koreans' Dear Sport."

4. Pak Soo-chan, "Most Young S. Koreans Don't Believe in Reunification," *Chosun Ilbo*, January 27, 2018, http://english.chosun.com/site/data/html_dir/2018/01/27/2018012700289.html.

5. Seong Yeon-cheol and Hong So-jin, "President Moon's Approval Rating Drops below 60% for First Time Since Inauguration," *Hankyoreh*, January 27, 2018, http://english.hani.co.kr/arti/english_edition/e_national/829656.html.

6. Lee Chi-dong and Kim Soo-yeon, "Koreas to Field Joint Women's Hockey Team for Olympics, March Together at Opening Ceremony," *Yonhap*, January 17, 2018, http://english.yonhapnews.co.kr/northkorea/2018/01/16/0401000000AEN20180116009957315.html.

7. Heekyong Yang and Josh Smith, "'Pyongyang Olympics?' Backlash Reveals Changing Attitudes in South Korea," Reuters, January 18, 2018, https://www.reuters.com/article/us-olympics-2018-northkorea/pyongyang-olympics-backlash-reveals-changing-attitudes-in-south-korea-idUSKBN1F716G.

8. Choe Sang-Hun and Mark Landler, "Olympic Détente Upends U.S. Strategy on North Korea," *New York Times*, January 17, 2018, https://www.nytimes.com/2018/01/17/us/politics/trump-north-south-korea-olympics.html.

## Chapter Fifteen

1. JoongAng Ilbo, Accessed on February 1, 2018, https://news.joins.com/pyeongchang2018/Daily/Article/22338821.

2. Karolos Grohmann, "North Korean Athletes, a Diplomatic Bargain at $2,300 Each," Reuters, February 15, 2018, https://www.reuters.com/article/us-olympics-2018-northkorea-subsidies/north-korean-athletes-a-diplomatic-bargain-at-2300-each-idUSKCN1FZ1JE.

3. Jun Hyun-suk, "How Did N.Korean Cheerleaders Get Tickets to Olympics Matches?," *Chosun Ilbo*, February 19, 2018, http://english.chosun.com/site/data/html_dir/2018/02/19/2018021901447.html.

4. Kang Hyun-kyung, "Decoding Politicians' Obsession with Sports Diplomacy," *Korea Times*, January 14, 2018, https://www.koreatimes.co.kr/www/nation/2018/01/356_242417.html.

5. Kim Chang-keum, "North Korean Women's Hockey Players May Train with South Korean Counterparts," *Hankyoreh*, January 15, 2018, http://www.hani.co.kr/arti/english_edition/e_northkorea/827814.html.

6. Yoo Jee-ho, "IOC President Thomas Bach Hoping to Watch Joint Korean Hockey Team—as Neutral," *Yonhap*, January 31, 2018, http://english.yonhapnews.co.kr/interview/2018/01/31/39/0800000000AEN20180131010300315F.html.


## Chapter Sixteen

1. Joo Hyung-sik, "Women's Ice Hockey Goalie Speaks Out," *Chosun Ilbo*, January 19, 2018, http://english.chosun.com/site/data/html_dir/2018/01/19/2018011901422.html.

2. Paul Fischer, *A Kim Jong-il Production: The Extraordinary True Story of a Kidnapped Filmmaker, His Star Actress, and a Young Dictator's Rise to Power,* (New York: Flatiron Books, 2015), 59–61, iBooks.

3. Paul Fischer, *A Kim Jong-il Production*, 173.

4. Paul Fischer, *A Kim Jong-il Production*, 122.

5. Rachael Miyung Joo, *Transnational Sport: Gender, Media, and Global*

*Korea*, (Durham and London: Duke University Press, 2012), 56–57, 60–61, iBooks.

6. Hong, *The Birth of Korean Cool*, 137–139.

## Chapter Eighteen

1. Andrew Keh, "A Tune Heard Often at These Olympics Gets to the Heart of Being Korean," *New York Times*, February 22, 2018, https://www.nytimes.com/2018/02/22/sports/olympics/arirang-korean-song-olympics-.html.

2. Choe Sang-hun, "Fight Over Rocky Islets Opens Old Wounds Between South Korea and Japan," *New York Times*, October 4, 2012, http://www.nytimes.com/2012/10/05/world/asia/south-korea-and-japan-fight-over-rocky-islets.html.

3. "Japan Protests Unified Korea Olympic flag with Disputed Isles," Agence France-Presse, February 5, 2018, https://sg.news.yahoo.com/japan-protests-unified-korea-olympic-flag-disputed-isles-053025909.html.

4. Corey Baird, "Japan Opens Permanent Exhibition on Territorial Disputes over Senkakus and Takeshima," *Japan Times*, January 25, 2018, https://www.japantimes.co.jp/news/2018/01/25/national/japan-open-permanent-exhibit-territorial-disputes-senkakus-takeshima/#.WrVEL-ZMbNAY.

5. "Moon Says Olympics a Chance to Mend Ties, Promote Peace with N. Korea," *Yonhap*, February 9, 2018, http://english.yonhapnews.co.kr/national/2018/02/09/0301000000AEN20180209010300315.html.

## Chapter Nineteen

1. Hong, *The Birth of Korean Cool*, 145.

2. Andrew Keh, "A Night Out With North Korea's Cheerleaders: Matching Snowsuits, Military Discipline and Chaperoned Bathroom Trips," *New York Times*, February 12, 2018, https://www.nytimes.com/2018/02/12/sports/olympics/north-korean-cheerleaders.html.

## Chapter Twenty

1. Joo Kyung-don, "IOC Chief Told Korean Hockey Players to Be Proud of Their Work: Spokesman," *Yonhap*, February 11, 2018, http://english.yonhapnews.co.kr/culturesports/2018/02/11/0702000000AEN20180211002900315.html.

2. Karolos Grohmann, "Exclusive: U.S. IOC Member Suggests Joint Korean Team for Nobel Peace Prize," Reuters, February 11, 2018, https://www.reuters.com/article/us-olympics-2108-koreas-nobel-exclusive/exclusive-u-s-ioc-member-suggests-joint-korean-team-for-nobel-peace-prize-idUSKBN1FV0A8.

3. Andrew Keh, "A Night Out With North Korea's Cheerleaders."

## Chapter Twenty-Three

1. Steve Wulf, "Can Sarah Murray, Daughter of Former NHL Coach Andy Murray, Lead Korean Team to Hockey Glory?" *ESPN*, February 10, 2018, http://www.espn.com/olympics/story/_/id/22367300/olympics-sarah-murray-daughter-former-nhl-coach-andy-murray-leads-unified-korean-women-hockey-team.

2. Yoo Jee-ho, "Joint Korean Hockey Team Coach 'Proud' of Players for Making It All Work," *Yonhap*, February 20, 2018, http://english.yonhapnews.co.kr/pyeongchang2018/2018/02/20/7201000000AEN20180220006600315.html.

## Chapter Twenty-Four

1. Jerry Brewer, "There's Peace in the Air at PyeongChang Olympics, but Something Doesn't Smell Right," *Washington Post*, February 10, 2018, https://www.washingtonpost.com/sports/olympics/theres-peace-in-the-air-at-pyeongchang-olympics-but-something-doesnt-smell-right/2018/02/10/2ef3ac16-0e19-11e8-8890-372e2047c935_story.html?noredirect=on&utm_term=.cd9848c5396a.

2. Jerry Brewer, "For 16 Days, PyeongChang Games Turned All of Us into One Unified Team," *Washington Post*, February 25, 2018, https://www.washingtonpost.com/sports/olympics/for-16-days-pyeongchang-

games-turned-all-of-us-into-one-unified-team/2018/02/25/9011c378-1956-11e8-92c9-376b4fe57ff7_story.html?utm_term=.44181b900472.

3. Juliet Macur, "Two Koreas, One Flag and All Those Memories of Unification," *New York Times*, February 9, 2018, https://www.nytimes.com/2018/02/09/sports/olympics-korea-unification.html.

## Chapter Twenty-Five

1. Liam Morgan, "Bach Admits Pyeongchang 2018 'Very close' to Being Cancelled Amid Security Fears," *Inside the Games*, August 22, 2018, https://www.insidethegames.biz/articles/1069089/bach-admits-pyeongchang-2018-very-close-to-being-cancelled-amid-security-fears.

## Chapter Twenty-Six

1. "Suwon City Holds Celebratory Dinner for Korean Women's Ice Hockey Team," *Hankyoreh*, March 27, 2018, http://english.hani.co.kr/arti/english_edition/e_entertainment/837907.html.

2. "The National Anthem—Aegukga," Korean Ministry of the Interior and Safety, accessed August 29, 2018, http://www.mois.go.kr/eng/sub/a03/nationalSymbol_2/screen.do.

## Chapter Twenty-Seven

1. Joint Press Corps, "Second Round of Inter-Korean Family Reunions Begins at Mount Kumgang," *Yonhap*, August 24, 2018, http://english.yonhapnews.co.kr/news/2018/08/24/0200000000AEN20180824011051315.html.

2. Choe Sang-hun, "Korean Families, Separated for 6 Decades, Are Briefly Reunited," *New York Times*, August 20, 2018, https://www.nytimes.com/2018/08/20/world/asia/north-south-korea-family-reunions.html.

# INDEX

Page numbers in *italics* indicate photographs.

A

Adachi, Yurie, 270
adoption, history in South Korea, 29, 41–42, 142, 300–301
Ahn Kun-young, 160
*ajummas*, 156, 284, 302
Alder, Janine, 256, 284–85
AMSOIL Arena, 15, 163, 165
Anyang Halla, 23, 43, 62, 204
"Arirang," 240
*On the Art of Cinema*, 214
Asia League, 23, 43, 79
Asian Summer Games, 314, 342
  2002, 252
Asian Winter Games
  1999, 21
  2003, 112
  2007, 21, 117
  2011, 25–26, *27*, *119*
  2017, 320
  2017, Japanese victory in, 268
  2017 Sapporo, Japan, 151–54
  discussion of hosting future games, 343
  Japan's record at, 267–68
  Marissa and, 334
  and movie *Run-Off*, 112
  North Korea vs. South Korea, 2007, 2011, 113
  and South Korean national team, 96
Athletes Village, 243

B

*babo* (fool), 109–10, 155
Bach, Thomas, 125, 211, 260–61, 307, 314

Baker, Mitch, 100
Baker, Rebecca Ruegsegger
  as assistant coach, 165, 168, 319, 353
  congratulates Marissa, 100
  life of, injuries and hockey, 285–290
  photos of, *289*, *308*
  pride in team, 301
  returns to US after World Championships, 333
  sends team back to South Korea from training, 185–86
  works with Sojung and Dohee in goal, 151
  World Championships, Asiago Italy, 331
banana, person as, 16
beauty culture in Korea, 225–26
Benz, Sara, 258
Berthiaume, Ben, 63–64
Berthiaume, Brenda, 68–69, 279, *292*
*bibimbap* (Korean dish), 213
*The Birth of Korean Cool: How One Nation is Conquering the World Through Pop Culture* (Hong), 72
Boucher, Courtney, 34, 37, 292
boycott letter to KIHA, 323, 325–27
Brandt, Greg
  adopts Marissa, 28–29
  game against Japan at Kwandong, 271, 273
  greets team at home in MN, 141
  on Marissa traveling to North Korea, 309
  on Marissa's concussions, 35

on Marissa's personal growth, 339
on Marissa's pride in her team, 189
party for players, 127–28
at PyeongChang Games, 297
and raising two players, 37
reaction to Unified team, 194
Brandt, Hannah
and 2018 Olympics, 100
captures gold with US national team, 154–55
goes on tour with Marissa, 345
growing up with Marissa, 29–38
Hannah and Marissa Brandt Day, 141
and Marissa's heritage, 128
meets up with Marissa in Athletes Village, 243
photos of, 30, 33, 301
US national team at Olympics, 298–99
Whitecaps cheered on by South Korean team, 130
Whitecaps stars, 164
as Yoon-jung Park's sister, 301
Brandt, Marissa. see also Korean Women's Ice Hockey National Team; Unified Korean team
on arrival of North Korean teammates, 209–10
at the beach with team, 245
closing ceremonies, 309
communication issues with Unified team, 233
dislike of Korean food, 105
on Doyun, 165–66
early life of, 28–38
fan appreciation of, 292
final days together, 309
game against Japan at Kwandong, 270–71
on Hannah and fan appreciation, 301
hockey team and Korean identity of, 127–130

at home in MN with Grace Lee, 140
joins Korean women's hockey team, 100–103
on Kim Un-jong, 245
Korean heritage and, 215–16
and Korean perceptions on marriage, 143
language and cultural barriers, 108–10
life after leaving Korea, 339–341
meets up with Hannah in Athletes Village, 243
as member of South Korean women's hockey team, 13–15
on North Korean cheerleaders, 255–56
photos of, 30, 33, 101, 131, 146, 176, 211, 273, 301, 333, 339
on politicization of PyeongChang Games, 195
and postseason blues, 144
relationships with Korean teammates, 138–39
returns to Korea after training camp, 201
returns to US after World Championships, 333–34
on Ruggiero's speech in locker room, 262–63
Shattuck-St.Mary's game, 175–76
on team as family, 349
tours with Hannah, 345
and Un Jong, 235
World Championships, 154–55
worried about war between two Koreas, 122
Brandt, Robin, 28–29, 36–37, 127, 133, 194–95, 301, 339
Brewer, Jerry, 304–5
Bujold, Sarah, 213
bullying, North Korea of South Korea team, 112

C

Canadian International Hockey

Academy (CIH), 66, 106,
    145–46, 149. *see also* Canadian
    International Hockey Academy
    (CIH)
Canadian Olympic Committee, 94
Canadian Women's Hockey League,
    89
Carlin, Robert, 41, 77, 121, 123
Carroll, Mike, 34, 36
Catholic Kwandong University, 251
Cha Bong-hwa, 53
*chaebols*, 72, 75, 226–27
Cheaung Bin-yu, 252
Cheaung Ha-yoon, 252
Chen, Karen, 341
Chen, Nathan, 341
Cho Mi-hwan
    at 2007 Asian Games, 117–18
    at 2017 Asian Games, 153
    attends English language school
        in New Zealand, 344–45
    final days together, 310
    and imports, 110, 129–130
    life changed by hockey, 228–29
    meets and studies with
        teammates, 138
    on memories of Unified team,
        348
    on North Korean players, 113
    and North/South merger, 190,
        197
    and Park Geun-hye's
        impeachment, 78
    party at Murray's home, 172
    photos of, *339*
    team as a place to belong, 228–29
    views of adoption, 142
Cho Yang-ho, 75
Chock, Madison, 341
Choe Jong-hui, 247
Choe Un-gyong, 210
Choi Eun-hee, 213
Choi Eun-young, 220
Choi Ji-yeon
    at 2016 World Championships,
        115–16

    at 2017 Asian Games, 153–54
    on adoption, 142
    chosen for national team, 53–54
    on coach Murray, 169
    death of father, 222–25
    description of men's team
        imports, 137
    game against Japan at Kwandong,
        275
    life and hockey, 79–82
    meets Hilary Knight, 298–99
    on North Korea, 122
    and North Korean teammates,
        118, 308
    and opening ceremony at
        PyeongChang, 247
    photo albums of Unified team,
        347
    photos of, *298–99, 312*
    pictures with Ilya Kovalchuk, 300
    pictures with teammates, 244
    problems with flat feet and skates,
        58
    in Unified tune-up match against
        Sweden, 242
    use of American slang, 138
    at World Championships, Italy,
        331
Choi Moon-soon, 205
Choi Soon-sil, 77
Choi Tae-min, 77
Choi Yu-jung
    after first two Olympic losses,
        265
    on communication with Murray,
        321
    described as good natured
        (*chakhae*), 199
    final days together, 311
    game against Japan at Kwandong,
        274
    on Kim Jong-un, 124
    letter to Danelle, 246
    life and hockey, 79, 82
    on objectification of North
        Korean players, 236

and opening ceremony at
    PyeongChang, 247–48
photos of, *176*
rejoins team for World
    Championships, Italy, 330
resumed studies after Olympics,
    324
Unified team and identity loss,
    215
Chongshin University, 224
Chosun Hockey Federation, 267
*The Chosun Ilbo,* 212, 214
Chun Se-hee, 252
Chung Ju-yung, 72, 75
Chung Mong-won (KIHA president),
    43, 75, 126, 158, 190, 228, 337
CIH (Canadian International
    Hockey Academy). *See* Canadian
    International Hockey Academy
    (CIH)
Coyne, Kendall, 130
Crosby, Sidney, 106
Culture, Sports and Tourism,
    Ministry of, 77

D
Datsyuk, Pavel, 300
Davidson, Melody, 94–95
Dawson, Toby, 142
Decker, Brianna, 85
Democratic People's Republic of
    Korea, 41
denuclearization talks, 314
Department for Movies and Arts
    (North Korea), 214
Do Jong-hwan, 119, 194, 198, 228,
    343
Dokdo islets controversy, 243
Doosan Group, 75
Dosdall, Kiira, 159
Downey, Jenna, 63–64, 70
Duluth, Minnesota, 13

E
Edge School, Calgary, Alberta, 24
Eom Su-yeon

on arrival of North Korean
    teammates, 207–8
at Connecticut Whale game, 157
first game, Olympics, 257
game against Japan at Kwandong,
    274
life after hockey, 216–17
meets Murray during training,
    95, 297
and opening ceremony at
    PyeongChang, 246–47
photos of, *80*
on politicization of PyeongChang
    Games, 260
relationship with Murray, 319–
    320
sent to OHA, 343
training schedule, 80
in Unified tune-up match against
    Sweden, 242
*eonni* (older sister), 150

F
fan appreciation, 277–280, 291–92,
    294, 300, 302
Fasel, René, 42, 117, 196, 307, 314
Fialova, Drahomira, 273
FIFA World Youth Championship,
    1991, 125
final Olympic game, 294–97
Finchum-Sung, Hilary, 240
Fletcher, Bob, 141
"A Foggy Road," 307
Frost, Brad, 100
Fujimoto, Nana, 280

G
*galmaegi,* 245
Gangneung Hockey Center, South
    Korea, 117
gender inequality in hockey, 316–17
gender inequality in Korea, 327–28,
    337–38
goalie helmets, 281–82
"golri," 69, 109

Goyang Twins roller hockey team, 277

Grahn, Sara, 294

Griffin, Elizabeth Heesoo Kang, 271–72

Griffin, Randi
  on arrival of North Korean teammates, 207
  on being American in Korea, 109
  on communication issues with Unified team, 233–36
  communication with team, 173–74
  and crowds at Seonhak International Ice Rink, 239
  dealing with mixed heritage, 103–5
  earns PhD, signs with Connecticut Whale, 345–46
  fan appreciation of, 292
  first game, Olympics, 257
  on gaining an Olympic spot, 170–71
  game against Japan at Kwandong, 270–71, 274–75
  on her grandparents and Koreanness, 272
  ice cream and North Korean players, 232
  IIHF camp, joining Korean team, 107–9
  interview after first PyeongChang game, 259
  invited by KIHA, 105–6
  on joining Korean team, 135–37
  on joint-Korea women's hockey team proposal, 122
  life and hockey, 15–16
  meeting to discuss team's future, 324
  on One Body nickname, 325
  and opening ceremony at PyeongChang, 247
  photos of, 108, 273, 333
  on politicization of PyeongChang Games, 261
  and postseason blues, 144–45
  reaction to Unified team, 190
  returns to Korea after training camp, 201
  returns to US after World Championships, 333–34
  Shattuck-St.Mary's game, 174–75
  on Sojung's hand injury, 160
  on strike and team frustrations, 328
  on team after the death of Jiyeon's father, 224
  team as a place to belong, 226–27
  team as family, 342
  team emotions after strike meeting, 326–27
  and teammates curiosity on gayness, 143–44
  time with families after game, 279
  at World Championships, Italy, 331

Griffin, Thomas, 104, 271

Gustavus Adolphus College, 34, 36–37

Gyeongpo Beach, 244

H

Halla Corporation, 43

Han, 74

Han Do-hee
  after Division II Group A World Championships, 154
  arranges video calls with Grace, 150
  on arrival of North Korean teammates, 206, 209
  attitudes toward North Korea, 126
  coaches youth teams, 344
  at Duluth, Jan 2017, 166
  and fan appreciation, 276–77
  final days together, 312–13
  final Olympic game, 296
  game at Gangneung with North Korea, 117

at Gyeongpo Beach before
    opening game, 244
and Korean gender culture, 226
North Korean members arrive,
    206
personality of, 121–22
photo albums of Unified team,
    347
photographs with Moon after
    game, 197
photos of, *228, 312, 342*
plays North Korea songs in locker
    room, 235
saying goodbye, 312–13
state of gear at Taereung, 24
teaches teammates Korean curse
    words, 138
team as a place to belong, 227–28
time with families after game, 279
trained by "Becca," 287–89
Han Seo-hee, 264
Han Soo-jin
    on boycott letter, 317
    boycott letter to KIHA, 326
    as captain, 98
    coaches youth teams, 344
    communication issues with
        Murray, 171–72
    communication issues with the
        imports, 110
    describes hockey as addiction,
        190–91
    on disrespect of hockey, 111
    at Duluth, Jan 2017, 166
    final days together, 310
    game against Japan at Kwandong,
        276
    as hockey lifer, 216
    on Korean ice hockey, 79
    life and hockey, 14–15, 55–56, 59
    and opening ceremony at
        PyeongChang, 246–47
    opening face-off, first game,
        Olympics, 256–57
    photos of, *57*
    pictures with Moon, 117–18

power play of, 295
reaction to Minister Do's
    meeting, 200
reaction to Unified team, 189–
    190
relationship with Murray, 320–21
team emotions after strike
    meeting, 326–27
use of Japanese strategy, 267
at World Championships, Italy,
    330–31
Hanae Kubo, 151, 269
*hanbok* dresses, 252
Hannah and Marissa Brandt Day, 141
HC Lugano, Switzerland, 89
Henderson, Gregory, 41
Herb Brooks National Hockey
    Center exhibition game, 220
Hockey Canada, 88, 94
Hockey Hall of Fame, Toronto, 273
Hodge, John R., 41
Hong, Euny, 72, 74, 92–93, 186, 225,
    252–53
Hospital for Special Surgery, 50
Howe, Scott, 114
Howe International Friendship
    League, 114
Hurrell, Jessie, 47
Hyundai, 75
Hwangbo Young, 111, 114
Hwang Chung-gum, *312,* 247, 263,
    308
Hwang Sol-gyong, 235

I

IIHF (International Ice Hockey
    Federation). *See* International Ice
    Hockey Federation (IIHF)
IIHF Division II Group A World
    Championship, 2016, 115
Im, Charles, 48
Im, Danelle
    birthday party, 192
    boycott letter to KIHA, 326
    and brother Justin, 135

buys friendship bracelets for team, 129

on Choi Yu-jung, 199

on communication with Murray, 322

final days together, 308

game against Japan at Kwandong, 271

and gender inequality, 338

"I am babo.", 110

joins Korean women's hockey team, 50

Korean identity of, 137–38

life and hockey, 44–48

love of hockey, 222

Marissa on, 102

meets Molly McCormick, 218

on objectification of North Korean players, 236

photos of, *46, 131, 136, 211, 298, 333, 339*

reaction to Unified team, 189–190

regrets on Murray's treatment, 329–330

relationships with Korean teammates, 139

stress and role on Unified team, 245–46

at Taereung, 60–62

on unification move, 193

at World Championships, Italy, 331

YeEun and Jongah stay at Danelle's house, 150

Im, Justin, 135, *136*

Im Hye-jin, 62

Immigration and Naturalization Act, 1965, 42

imports and gender equality, 328–29

imports return to US, 333–34

"imports"/team roster, 14

inter-Korean exchanges, 342–43

International Day of Sport for Development and Peace, 116

International Ice Hockey Federation (IIHF), 24, 26, 39, 42–43, 91, 97, 107, 117, 120, 194, 196, 224, 300, 315, 330

International Olympic Committee (IOC)

approves, sets rules for Unified team, 194

approves Sojung interview, 212

backs idea of joint Korean women's hockey team, 120–22

*chaebol* members of, 75

cost of adding North Korean players, 203

endorses idea of Unified team, 125

notices skepticism by players toward Unified team, 211

PyeongChang Games and North Korean aggression, 314

rules and Unified team, 281–82

South Korea awarded 2018 Games, 26, 73

suggests Nobel Peace Prize for Unified team, 262

takes credit for Unified team, 307

International Vaccine Institute, 135

IOC (International Olympic Committee). *See* International Olympic Committee (IOC)

J

Jagr, Jaromir, 44

Jeon Si-huck, 252

Jin OK, 210, 311

Jo, Susie

at 2007 Asian Games, 117

boycott letter to KIHA, 326

on ex-coaches, 98

and fan appreciation, 279

first game, Olympics, 257

on Kyousun, 162

on Marissa, 143

on Murray's advice to team, 193

at Murray's party, 172–73

on North Korean players, 311

on North Koreans, 122, 124–25

photos of, *123*, *228*, *298*
player injuries, 228
on politicians and the Unified
    team, 307
on politicization of PyeongChang
    Games, 260
on pride in being Korean, 346
at PyeongChang, 241
rematch against Switzerland, 283
on Sojung, Soojin and Kyousun,
    57–58
studies English and hockey in
    Canada, 61
team as family, 224–25
as translator, 208
as translator for Murray, 168
worried about conflict between
    teammates, 206
Johansson, Erica Uden, 263
Johansson, Lisa, 263
joint-Korea table tennis team, 125
joint-Korea women's hockey team
    proposal, 120–25
Jong Su-hyon
    first game, Olympics, 241–43,
        257
    loss of second Olympic game, 266
    and opening ceremony at
        PyeongChang, 248–49, 305
    photos of, *312*
Joo, Rachael Miyung, 78, 345
*JoongAng Ilbo*, 125, 195
Jordan, Michael, 123
Jubilee Ducks club team (Seoul), 252
Jung Si-yun, 117, 139, 218, 277,
    306–7
Jung Soo-yoon, 242
"Junger" (Sojung as), 69

K
Kaminski, Nicole, 148, 226
Kampersal, Jeff, 48
Kang, Elizabeth Heesoo, 103–4
Kang, Margaret Hyosook, 271
Kang, Peter Taidoo, 271

Keh, Andrew, 240
Kessel, Amanda, 158–59
Kessler, Christine, 106–7, 292
KIHA (Korea Ice Hockey
    Association). *See* Korea Ice
    Hockey Association (KIHA)
Kim, Chloe, 341
Kim, Christine Soojung, *99*, 218
Kim, Ryan Minjae, *99*
Kim Do-yun
    appointed interim head coach,
        326–27
    as assistant coach, 165–66, 296
    at beach with team, 244
    comforts Jiyeon after father's
        death, 223
    final Olympic game, 296
    on news of unified team, 192
    North Korea invited to join
        South Korea's hockey team,
        185
    photos of, *99*
    reaction to North Korea invited
        to join South Korea's hockey
        team, 188
    Shattuck game, 180
    as translator for Murray, 168
Kim Eun-jin, *119*
Kim Hee-won
    on communication with Murray,
        168
    first game, Olympics, 256
    game against Japan at Kwandong,
        270–71
    happiness and hockey, 82
    life after hockey, 216
    at Murray's party, 172
    sent to OHA, 343
    time with families after game,
        279
    victory at 2017 Asian Games,
        153–54
Kim Hyang-mi, 308, *312*
Kim Il-sung, 214, 254
Kim Jong-il, 113, 115, 122–23, 214
Kim Jong-un, 16, 19, 112, 121, 123–

24, 186–87, 231, 238, 248, 254,
  314, 335–36, 347
Kim Jung-min, 44, *46*, 50–51, 103
Kim Ki-hoon, 75
Kim Kum-bok, 117
Kim Kwok-chul, 305–6
Kim Nong-gum, 208
Kim Se-lin
  and beauty culture in Korea, 226
  at Bulldogs game, 165
  communication issues with
    Unified team, 235
  fan appreciation of, 292
  game against Japan at Kwandong,
    270–71
  at OHA, 146–48
  photos of, *149*
  relationships with imports, 138–
    39
  and social situations, 145
  on Soojin, 110
  views of Japan and its people, 268
Kim Sung-ye, 156
Kim Taek-soo, 305–6
Kim Un-hyang, 235, 240, 244
Kim Un-jong, 209–10, 233, 244–45,
  308–11
Kim Yo-jong, 19, 248, 252, 260, 262
Kim Yong-chol, 310
Kim Yong-nam, 248
Kim Yu-na, 74, 78–79, 162, 249, 305
Knight, Hilary, 298–300
Knowles, Genevieve, 135, 293, 324
Ko Hye-in
  on arrival of North Korean
    teammates, 209–10
  on communication issues with
    Unified team, 234–35
  on communication with Murray,
    321
  on defense without Mihwan, 315
  Dohee on, 227
  early life and hockey, 221–22
  on first game on national team,
    154

friendship with imports, 110
on gender roles, 76
humor of, 233
life and hockey, 221–22
on marriage, 142–43
on North Korean players, 113
photos of, *234*
player injuries, 228
resumed studies after Olympics,
  324
spies and communication with
  North Korean players, 231–32
visit from Grace, 347
Koike, Shiori, 269
Koizumi, Jessica, 87–88, 293
Kong Minghui, 152
Konishi, Akane, 270
Korea
  female gender roles, 76
  history of, 40–42
  ice hockey association. *see* Korea
    Ice Hockey Association
    (KIHA)
  sports and patriotic identity,
    71–76
Korea Ice Hockey Association
  (KIHA)
  begins contacting Korean
    Americans, 39–40
  boycott letter, 316–17, 323
  camp for women hockey players,
    61–62
  Chung Mong-won and *chaebols*,
    75
  decides to send women overseas
    for training, 66
  forms first women's hockey team
    in 1998, 267
  hires Canadian coaches for men's
    and women's teams, 45
  hires Paek to revitalize hockey,
    90–91
  learns of Unified team, 190
  organized under Ministry of
    Culture, Sports and Tourism,
    77

and pressure for hockey to
    succeed in South Korea, 158
pressure to rapidly upgrade teams,
    42–44
punishes team for boycott letter,
    327
Randi contacted by, 272
responds to boycott letter with
    sanctions, 336–37
search for imported hockey
    players, 79
sends women to Canada for
    training, 66
at Seonhak International Ice
    Rink, 242
and unified North/South Korean
    team, 188
veterans treatment of new players,
    57–58
*Korea: The Impossible Country* (Tudor),
    74
Korean Air, 75
Korean Demilitarized Zone, 250
Korean Football Association, 75
Korean Olympic Committee, 43, 75,
    158
Korean War, 41, 239, 267
Korean Women's Ice Hockey
    National Team. *see also* Kwandong
    Hockey Center; players by name;
    Unified Korean team
    2017 Asian Winter Games, 154
    Canadian players meet Korean
        players, 60–61
    comparison to men's hockey team
        conditions, 191
    creation of, 39–50
    cultural differences of, 170
    disrespect of, 216–17
    Division II Group A World
        Championship, 154
    at Duluth, Jan 2017, 163–64
    as a family at exhibition game,
        Miskolc, 223
    going away party, 332–33

hardships of, 23–24
interest in US culture of imports,
    137–38
life after PyeongChang, 216
meets students of St. Cloud State
    University, 219–221, *219, 221*
photos of, *83, 149, 181, 192, 319,
    322, 342, 348*
players' injuries, 228
players visit each other in states,
    347
pools money for housing for
    Randi and Marissa, 327
practice, poor conditions, and
    social life, 58–59, *59*
preparing for PyeongChang, 158,
    164, 167, 179, 185
reaction to Unified team, 190
relationships between imports
    and Korean teammates, 138–
    140
Shattuck-St.Mary's game, 174–75
social life and team ties, 81–83
social media pages/message of
    solidarity, *328*
team chemistry and
    communication, 167–170
team party at Ruth Murray's
    home, 172–73
US fans of, 218–19
visits to US, 127–131
Korean Women's National Team, 158
Kovalchuk, Ilya, 300
Krause, Mickie, 263
Kubo, Hanae, 269
Kwandong Hockey Center, 19, 243,
    251–53, *254,* 269, 282, 294, 306

L

Lamoureux-Davidson, Jocelyne, 85,
    285, 299–300
Lamoureux-Morando, Monique, 85,
    164
Lee, Albert, 133, 176, 178, 297
Lee, Eliza, 132–34, 176–178, *265*

Lee, Grace
    on arrival of North Korean
        teammates, 207
    and beauty culture in Korea, 226
    at Brandt's, 140
    closing ceremonies, 309
    early life and hockey, 176–78
    and fan appreciation, 295–96
    first game, Olympics, 259
    game against Japan at Kwandong,
        274–76
    joins Korean women's hockey
        team, 131–34
    on Kim Un-jong, 210
    on love of Korea, 346–47
    on Murray's attachment to team,
        329
    on Murray's coaching style, 170
    and opening ceremony at
        PyeongChang, 248
    opening face-off, first game,
        Olympics, 256
    photos of, 134, 176, 211, 265, 333
    relationship with teammates, 139
    returns to Korea after training
        camp, 201
    returns to US after World
        Championships, 333–34
    Shattuck-St.Mary's game, 180
    team as a place to belong, 229
    Unified team and identity loss,
        215
    video calls with Dohee, 150
Lee, Mia SeungEun, 81, 138, 338
Lee Chang-bok, 116
Lee Charm, 186
Lee Eun-ji
    and fan appreciation, 279
    impeachment of Park Geun-hye,
        78
    misses Olympic game due to
        injury, 247
    photos of, 310
    Rembecks' support of team, 218
    sent to OHA, 343

as smallest player, 117
    at World Championships, Asiago,
        Italy, 330
Lee Hee-beom, 117
Lee Ji-yoon, 101–2, 208
Lee Jung-hyeok, 221
Lee Kun-hee, 75
Lee Kyou-sun
    coach at World Championships
        2019, 344
    concern for Sojung, 160–61
    at Gangneung, 117
    and imports, 60
    and lack of professional
        opponents, 199
    love for hockey, 79
    misses opening ceremony, 247
    and North Korean players, 112–
        13
    photos of, 164, 339
    relationship with Murray, 320
    as veteran player on team, 57
Lee Min-ji
    asked to provide color
        commentary on Olympic
        games, 274
    on Brandt family, 141–42
    coaches youth teams, 344
    on gender roles, 226
    missed at opening ceremonies,
        247
    moves to Toronto to study
        English, 347
    at Murray's party, 172–73
    photos of, 146, 298
    relationship with Murray, 143
    on rumor of North/South team,
        113–14
    says goodbye to imports, 333
    voices opinion on merger, 203–5
Lee Nak-yeon, 195, 204
Lee Yeon-jeong
    friendship with imports, 138–39
    on imports, 51–52, 109

injuries and future as hockey
     player, 324
on nicknames, 152–53
on North Korean players, 306–7
and opening ceremony at
     PyeongChang, 247–48
player injuries, 228
promise to Jiyeon's father, 224
records Whitecaps game, 164
on Soojin and Sarah, 98
teammates as sisters, 59
Lemieux, Mario, 44
Livingston, Carole, 29

M

Macur, Juliet, 306
marriage, Korean perceptions of,
     142–43
McCormick, Molly, 218
Metropolitan Riveters, New Jersey,
     159
Minister of Culture, Sports and
     Tourism, 119, 190
Minnesota State-Mankato game, 218
Minnesota-Duluth Bulldogs, 15,
     87–88
Mongrain, Kim, 146–47, *149*
Moon Jae-in, 19, 120–21, 125, 186–
     87, 196, 198–99, 204, 228, 248,
     250, 252, 256, 260–61, 280, 307,
     310, 314, 336, 338, 347
Muller, Alina, 257
Murase, Minatsu, 241, 295
Murray, Andy, 84, 86–87, 90–91, 97,
     293
Murray, Brady, 90
Murray, Jordy, 85, 90
Murray, Ruth, 84–86, 88, 97, 172,
     279
Murray, Sarah
     attends World Championships as
          team manager, 326–27
     childhood and high school
          hockey, 84–86
     college hockey, Minnesota-
          Duluth Bulldogs, 86–87

on competing and performance,
     265
at Duluth, Jan 2017, 164–65
as English teacher in Beijing,
     89–90
final days together, 311
final Olympic game and
     memories, 294–97
game against Japan at Kwandong,
     270–71
HC Lugano, Switzerland, 89
impressed by North Korean
     players, 116
institutes overseas training camps,
     151
interest in Grace Lee, 131
and joint-Korea women's hockey
     team proposal, 120, 125–26
as KIHA coach, 91–99
and lack of respect for team, 216–
     17
and Lee Kyou-sun's injuries, 162–
     63
mother visits Gangneung, 293
NWHL game at Connecticut,
     156–57
and opening ceremony at
     PyeongChang, 247
organizes beach outing before
     Olympics opening game, 244
photos of, *89, 92, 99*
reaction to North Korea invited
     to join South Korea's hockey
     team, 185–89, 192–94
relationship with team after
     Olympics, 317–323
returns to US after Olympics, 344
at Seonhak International Ice
     Rink, 242–43
sizes up new additions from
     North Korea, 208
speech at Shattuck-St.Mary's
     game, 175
team chemistry and
     communication, 167–172
team final meeting before
     Olympics, 172–74

**N**

*naengmyeon*, 309

Nagasu, Mirai, 341

National Collegiate Athletic Association (NCAA), 15

National Hockey League (NHL), 22, 44

National Women's Hockey League (NWHL), 89, 156, 158–59, 214, 289, 345, 353

*New York Times*, 240, 306

No Gun Ri, 41

North Korea cheerleading squad "beauty squads," 125, 252, *254*, 263–64, 271

North Korea versus South Korea game, 2017, 116–18

NWHL (National Women's Hockey League). *See* National Women's Hockey League (NWHL)

**O**

Oberdorfer, Don, 41, 77, 121, 123

Oh Yeon-seo, *123*

OHA (Ontario Hockey Academy). *See* Ontario Hockey Academy (OHA)

Olympics. *see also* Korean Women's Ice Hockey National Team; Kwandong Hockey Center; Peace Olympics/Political Games; PyeongChang Games, 2018; Unified Korean team

1988, Korean bid for, 73

1988 Seoul, 297, 300

1998 US hockey team, 262

2010, Vancouver, 74

2014, Sochi, 256

2018 Winter, 164

Korean speed skate winners, 75–76

Summer 1964, 73

Summer 2000, Sydney, Australia, 125

Summer 2004, Athens, Greece, 125

Winter 2006, Torino, Italy, 125

Winter 2018, PyeongChang Games, 281–82

Olympics women's hockey tournament groups, 264–65

"One Body" Kakao account, 325

Ono, Shoko, 269

Ontario Hockey Academy (OHA), 145–150, 165, 224, 226, 292, 343

Osborne, Rick, 46–47

**P**

Paek, Jim, 44, 90–91, 103

Pak Chol-ho, 206, 231, 242, 247–49, 268–69, 311

Park, Byung-ho, 217

Park, Caroline

2017 Asian Winter Games, 153–54

finishes surgery clerkship, 345

friendships with team, 110, 139

game against Japan at Kwandong, 270–71

intensity of, 282–83

life and hockey, 48–50

and opening ceremony at PyeongChang, 247

photos of, *49*

returns to US after Olympics, 324

at Taereung, 60–62

Park, Chan-ho, 63

Park, Diana, 48

Park Chae-lin

at 2017 Asian Games, 154

emotion at hearing "Arirang," 240–41

fan appreciation, 279, 344

on hearing national anthem, 199–200

Marissa and, 108–9

mother of, after game, 278

and Murray's remarks to press, 193

and North Korea, 122

photos of, *228*

on Randi, 173

reaction to Lee Nak-yeon's
    remarks, 195
reaction to Unified team, 190
school and training schedule,
    80–81
Shattuck-St.Mary's game, 179–
    180
told not to say North Korea, 231
Unified team and identity loss,
    215
Park Chung-hee, 45, 71–74, 76–78,
    271
Park Geun-hye, 76–78, 119, 201
Park Jong-ah
    and beauty culture in Korea, 226
    boycott letter to KIHA, 326
    on changing women's hockey
        system, 344
    on Coach Pak's speech, 269
    communication issues with
        imports, 66–67
    fan appreciation of, 292
    first game, Olympics, 258–59
    friendships with team, 150
    and gender inequality, 317
    joins Korean women's hockey
        team, 53–57
    on KIHA, 343
    loss of second Olympic game, 266
    love of hockey, 59
    Murray and team structure, 94
    on North Korean players, 118
    at OHA, 146–47
    and opening ceremony at
        PyeongChang, 248, 305
    photos of, 149, 202, 228, 339
    on politicization of PyeongChang
        Games, 261
    reaction to politicians' remarks
        about women's hockey, 198–
        99
    reaction to Unified team, 189–
        190
    at Seonhak International Ice
        Rink, 242–43
    successes in Canada, 148–49

on Unified team, 121
use of Japanese strategy, 267
Park Ye-eun
    at 2017 Asian Games, 116–17
    and the *babos*, 109–10
    and beauty culture in Korea, 226
    at CIH, 66–67
    on communication with Murray,
        322
    fan appreciation of, 292
    hockey and emotions, "postseason
        blues," 144–46
    on impeachment of Park Geun-
        hye, 78
    interests outside hockey, 222
    life and hockey, 52–55, 59
    at OHA, 146–47
    on Park Jong-ah, 201
    photos of, 146, 149, 228, 339
    plays hockey for Ryerson
        University, Toronto, 347
    relationships with imports, 150
    on team as family, 237
Park Yong-sung, 75
Park Yoon-jung. *See* Brandt, Marissa
Peace House, meeting between
    North and South, 335–36
Peace Olympics/Peace Games,
    250, 252, 304, 325. *see also*
    PyeongChang Games, 2018
Phillips Academy Andover, MA, 24
politicization of PyeongChang
    Games, 252–53, 260–62, 314–15
postseason blues, 144–45
Pound, Richard W., 73
protestors at Kwandong Hockey
    Center, 251–52
public backlash, Unified team, Korea,
    195–97
public response to Unified team,
    worldwide, 202–3
PyeongChang Games, 2018. *see also*
    Korean Women's Ice Hockey
    National Team; Kwandong
    Hockey Center; Olympics; Peace

Olympics/Political Games; players by name; Unified Korean team
  both South Korean hockey teams qualify, 43
  fears of North Korea aggression, 314
  first women's hockey game, 251–59
  and future of South Korean women's hockey, 158
  IOC and IIHF back a joint women's hockey team, 120–21
  Lee Hee-beom as president of Organizing Committee, 117
  North Korean cheerleaders at, 255
  opening ceremony at PyeongChang, 246–250
  photos of, 246
  politicization of, 187–88, 196, 281
  as symbol of peace, 242
  Unified Korean team and Peace Olympics, 325
  Unified team against Japan, 267–280
  as Winter Olympics, 26
  women's hockey squad debut at, 13–16
PyeongChang Organizing Committee, 117
Pyongyang rinks, North Korea, 114–15

R

Rembeck, Archer Jaewon, 217–18
Rembeck, Desirae, 217–18
Rembeck, Simon MinHawn, 217–18
Rembeck, Steve, 217–18
Republic of Korea, 41
Rhee, Syngman, 121
Ri Pom, 308
Rigsby, Alex, 285
Rodgers, Allie, 148, 165
Roh Moo-hyun, 120
Rose, Hanna, 147–48

Ruggiero, Angela, 262
Run-Off, 111–12, 122
Rylan, Dani, 158
Ryo Song-hui, 235, 241, 312

S

Samsung, 75
Schafhauser, Bill, 34–35
Schelling, Florence, 256
Se Ri Pak, 22
Sejong Academy, 218
Seol Kyoungrang, 21, 277–78, 302–3
Seonhak International Ice Rink, Incheon, 238, 241
Shattuck-St.Mary's, 172
Sherry, Sasha, 49, 49, 86
Shibutani, Alex, 341
Shibutani, Maia, 341
Shin Kwangsik, 21
Shin Sang-ok, 213–14
Shin So-jung
  at 2016 World Championships, 115
  2017 Asian Winter Games, 151–53
  after final game, fan appreciation, 301–2
  athletic scholarship to St. Francis Xavier University, 63–70
  babo as term of endearment, 110
  and beauty culture in Korea, 226
  as dedicated lifelong player, 39
  defies gag order on team, dreams of being an actress, 212–14
  at Duluth, Jan 2017, 166
  emotional Lee's goodbyes, 133
  emotions; first game against Switzerland vs. last, 302–3
  and fan appreciation, 277–78
  first game, Olympics, 263
  game against Japan at Kwandong, 269–270, 274–75
  give Christine Soojung Kim, 218
  greets North Korean teammates, 206–7
  and hockey, 214–15

and imports, 61–62
life and hockey, 19–28
meeting to discuss team's future,
    324
molded as goalie by "Becca,"
    287–290
and new players, 57
on North/South division, 124
NWHL game at Connecticut,
    157
and opening ceremony at
    PyeongChang, 247
party at Murray's home, 172–73
photos of, *20, 27, 65, 68, 80, 161,
    280, 292*
physical and emotional stress from
    hockey, 159–161
power play of, 296
reaction to Minister Do's
    meeting, 199–201
rematch against Switzerland,
    281–85
response to Japanese taunts, 268
retires, 345
Shattuck-St.Mary's game, 174
signs with NWHL, 158–59
sits out at Gangneung North/
    South game due to injuries,
    117
time with families after game,
    279
*sogo* drums, 220
Sohn Kee-chung, 71, 74
Sol Gyong, 235
Song Hui, 235
Soo Ae, 111–12
Sookmyung Women's University,
    Seoul, 25
South Korean National Assembly,
    119–120
South Korean women's national
    hockey team, *16*
spies, 230–31
St. Francis Xavier University, Nova
    Scotia, 62
Stafford, Gordie, 285

Stalder, Lara, 256
Stanley Cup, 44
Stone, Katey, 105, 107, 173
"Sunshine Policy," 120–21, 125–26
Synishin, David, 62–63

T
table tennis unified team, 305–6
Taereung national training center, 54,
    58, 60–62, 72, 80, 95, 102, 109,
    134, 150, 155, 169, 171, *181*, 191,
    196, 247, 250
Taft, William Howard, 40
team dance party, Brandt's house, 127
"Team Kim" curling team fights
    discrimination, 337
Team Manitoba, 86
Team USA, 35, 106, 130, 159, 285,
    298, 342
Test of English as a Foreign Language
    (TOEFL), 25
Toko, Ayaka, 294
Toko, Haruka, 269
torch lighting at PyeongChang, 248–
    250, 305
*Transnational Sport: Gender, Media, and
    Global Korea* (Joo, 2012), 78
Trump, Donald J., 124, 314
*tteokbokki*, 155, 230
*tteokguk*, 156
Tudor, Daniel, 74
*The Two Koreas* (Oberdorfer and
    Carlin, 2013), 41, 121

U
Ukita, Rui, 275
Un Gyong, 234–35
Under-18 World Championships, 35,
    285, 343
Unified Korean team. *see also*
    Kwandong Hockey Center; players
    by name; PyeongChang Games,
    2018
    celebrating birthdays, 210–11
    cost of adding North Korean
        players, 203

fan appreciation of, 291–92, 295–96, 301–2

feelings after first game defeat, 262–63

final days together, 304–13

final Olympic game, 294–97

IOC officially approves Unified team, 194

against Japan, Olympic game, 266–280

loss of first Olympic game, 251–59

loss of second Olympic game, not Unified, 265

media attention, 243–44

media rumors, spies and communication issues, 230–34

North Korean members arrive, 205–7

and objectification of North Korean players, 236

and opening ceremony at PyeongChang, 246–250

and Peace Olympics, 325

photos of, *232*

players response to, 185–89, 192–202

public backlash to, 195–97

rematch against Switzerland, 282–84

share McDonald's after last game, 305

time with families after game, 276–77

tune-up match against Sweden, 238–242

wins Coca-Cola sports award, 339

worldwide public response to, 202–3

University of Minnesota, 35

US culture, hockey team interest in, 137–38

US Women's Olympic Team, 2014, 107

US Women's Open, 22

USA Hockey, 34, 36, 105, 317

USA Hockey camps, 285

USA Hockey, recognition of women's teams, 298

Utecht, Theresa, 218

V

Valentine, Bobby, 93

Vicious, Sid, 106

W

Wang Yuqing, 153

*Washington Post*, 304

Wayne State University, 46

*Why Was I Adopted?* (Livingston, 1960), 29

Wilfrid Laurier University, Ontario, 44

Wiseman, Chad, 158

Women's World Championship, 42

Won Chol-sun, 208

World Championships
  2007 North/South Korea game, 116–17
  2014, 43
  2015, 97
  2016, 151
  2016, success at, 154, 157
  2017, 161–62, 200, 208, 282–83, 309
  2017 and losses, 275
  2017 Asian Winter Games, 309
  Asiago, Italy, 330–31
  and boycott letter to KIHA, 316, 326
  division break down of, 24
  gender inequality and USA hockey, 298
  and possible team unification, 120
  team after end of Championships, 331, 337
  YeEun and Jongah left OHA to play in, 149

World Shooting Championships, 1978, 73

X

X-Women (St. Francis Xavier
    women's hockey team), 64–66,
    69–70

Y

Yamaguchi, Kristi, 217
Yamanaka, Takeshi, 268
Yang Seung-jun, 324, 336–37
Yeom Tae-young, 325

Yonhap, 116
Yonsei University, Seoul, 55
Yoshihide Suga, 244
You, Michelle Yunjung, 218
Young Generation (cheering squad),
    242

Z

Zhou, Vincent, 341
Zollinger, Sabrina, 283